TABLE OF CONTENTS

Appendix – Documents of Historical Interest

By the same author:

L'Information en Israël (How the news works in Israel), Paris, 1972.

La Presse française pendant la guerre du Kippour
(The French media during the Yom Kippur War), Paris, 1974.

David et Marianne, Alain Moreau, Paris, 1986.

Le conflit israélo-arabe de Balfour à nos jours
(The Arab-Israeli conflict from the Balfour Declaration until today),
Akademon, Jerusalem 1988.

La Poudrière. Guerre et Paix au Proche-Orient
(The Powder-keg. War and Peace in the Middle East),
Biblieurope, Paris 1990.

Shimon Pérès au carrefour du destin (Shimon Peres at the cross-roads of destiny), Editions du Rocher, Paris 1996.

Keren Or, Yediot Aharonot, Tel Aviv 2004.

Les secrets d'un diplomate (A diplomat's secrets), with Avi Pazner,
Editions du Rocher, Paris 2005.

La France, Israël et les Arabes: le double jeu
(France, Israel and the Arabs: the double game),
Jean Picollec, Paris 2005.

Sharon, le bras de fer, Jean Picollec, Paris 2006

L'Autre Visage d'Israël (Israel's Other Face),
Éditions du Rocher, Paris, 2006.

Foreword

For more than fifty years now, Ariel Sharon – Arik, as we Israelis call him – has been a significant player on the stage of Israeli history. The former General, a blustering hero of the Six Day War, is a man who won spectacular military victories, but also a man who suffered humiliating failures such as his adventure into Lebanon. Ariel Sharon is a man of legend, a figure of high controversy, a man now lying at the edge of death but whose strength as Prime Minister of the Jewish state placed him at the crossroads of his people's destiny.

At age seventy-eight, he waged his ultimate combat on many fronts, simultaneously fighting against enemies on all sides of the Israeli-Palestinian conflict including recalcitrant settlers and political adversaries within and without the Likud Party. In the end, he sacrificed his own health to achieve a peace settlement with the Palestinians – with or without their active participation!

I first met Ariel Sharon in 1965, when I was a young soldier in Tsahal – the Israeli Defense Forces (IDF). He was then a paratrooper colonel and his very presence in the military bases gave everyone the jitters. He had just lost the command of the Northern Sector was now supervising training; it was a task he took up with an iron discipline.

Later in that same decade, when I was privileged to serve at Army Headquarters under the command of General David Elazar, I witnessed the ebb and flow of discussions between senior military men, and Ariel Sharon was always in their line of fire. Since then I have made it my business to closely follow the spellbinding career of the *enfant terrible* of Tsahal, the man known as Israel's most politicized soldier, and a man who David Ben-Gurion, Israel's founder, held in high esteem and affection.

Like many other observers, I needed to know more about this extraordinary human being, a man with roots in the soil of the land, whose outlook on life – perhaps hardened by the force of the Israeli sun – first made him a controversial soldier and in later years a statesman whose multifaceted personality seemed to hold the key to peace in the Middle East and perhaps in much of the international arena.

This book does not seek to be an exhaustive biography of Ariel Sharon. I'm not that ambitious! My goal can be better described as a deeper than usual piece of investigative journalism. The pages that follow trace Arik's long and event-filled career from its beginning, when he first joined the Israeli army, until today. I have tried to faithfully recount this man's tumultuous life, led by a steady lust for victory in the sharp edge of combat.

Before suffering the stroke that felled him, Ariel Sharon had been in power for five years, long enough to permit a balanced evaluation of his politics, and his policies. I have tried to understand and bring out why and how Sharon developed such an independent spirit. Why did he suddenly change gears and decide to disengage from Gaza and the very territories – the West Bank and the Golan Heights – that he had himself conquered? How did he succeed in doing an about-face in what had been an unshakeable position, and how could he make people forget his former, extremist stance? Was this just a tactical maneuver on the part of a master strategist, or a sincere and well thought out fundamental change? How did he maintain the confidence of the Israeli people throughout all of this? Why did the majority of Arab and Western leaders respect him and support his policies? How did his political adversaries and the fanatical settlers attempt to block his moves? Would they in the end sacrifice their dream of Eretz Israel, or try to overthrow Prime Minister Sharon? And what role did Washington and Europe play in these crucial changes? How had Sharon succeeded in amassing enough political power to steer the Ship of State in a new direction? Finally, how did his own family crises and the financial and legal problems of his sons – one of whom has now been sentenced for influence peddling and corruption – play into the changes in government and policy that Arik was attempting to make?

I have tried to answer these and many other questions objectively and honestly, analyzing Sharon's major decisions and attempting to make the career of a military man become peacemaker out of his confronting the harsh reality of the occupation an understandable evolution. In a way not foreign to the experience of the rest of his life, sudden and unpredictably dramatic events brutally pushed Arik from power. Throughout his life, he often surprised us, rebounding from great difficulties and exhibiting the qualities of a providential leader. But this time, his work has been left for others to finish, with Ehud Olmert and Kadima now in charge of the destiny of Israel. Ariel Sharon wanted so much to be the one to sign a comprehensive peace accord with the Palestinians, but the curtain fell and he left the political stage before the final act could play out.

This book follows the vicissitudes of Israeli history, zigging and zagging with the unpredictable and sometimes incredible events that we have survived, and it is replete with anecdotes and incidents I personally witnessed.

I would like to warmly thank all those who kindly lent their hands, and their memories, and who made this delicate work easier. Needless to say, any errors of fact or interpretation are mine alone.

Jerusalem, May 2006.

Part One

Chapter 1

The Land

The hope of returning to The Holy Land is the permanent source of Judaism's unique nature.
Rabbi Kook

It was a chilly night, the nineteenth of December 1999, and eight o'clock. A few kilometers from the town of Sderot, in the north of the Negev Desert, a squadron of firemen was fighting a blaze raging through the Sycamores Farm on the crest of a hill. The men made slow but steady progress with their hoses, attempting to stop the flames from razing the main ranch buildings. The livestock, panic-stricken by the heat and the noise, were bleating wildly.

The farm's owner arrived, out of breath, looking somewhat haggard, but in control of his emotions, exuding calm in the face of disaster. He could see at once – it was bitterly clear – that a significant part of his property had gone up in smoke, the fire taking with it the rustic furniture, the rare carpets and paintings, the books, records and photo albums. The mementos of a lifetime were no more, his own residence reduced to rubble and ashes.

It was as if the fire had deliberately set out to erase from the history of Israel the glorious exploits of this family that had such deep roots in the soil of the land. Moments like these make a man look back to the memories of his youth to counter the despair, remembering the agitated times lived in the maelstrom of harsh events, but also the love for the bounty of the land and the devotion to family.

Ariel Sharon was born in the village of Kfar Malal, in what was then known as Palestine. On his identity card that bore the number 236248, he was described as the son of Shmuel and Vera Scheinermann of Brest-Litovsk, Russia. This was 1928, the year when the Bolshevik Joseph Stalin had pushed his rival Leon Trotsky – a rabbi's son from Odessa – from Soviet power, and exiled him to Alma-Ata in Central Asia. The Chinese nationalist Chiang Kai-shek had taken Peking, and Herbert Hoover was in the White House. Henri Bergson was given the Nobel Prize for literature, and in France, the crooner Maurice Chevalier wowed enthusiastic crowds at the Casino de Paris.

Life was somewhat different in Kfar Malal. The Scheinermanns lived in a tent, with no running water and certainly no electricity. The father tilled the arid soil in difficult conditions. He had to get irrigation water by the barrel from the river, kilometers away, and cart it to his plot of land. Little Arik followed his parents with admiration, watching their every move, observing how they labored the soil, planted their crops, watered, and finally, harvested. He watched as the farm grew and prospered, as they were able to add a chicken coop, then a barn, and finally a stable. He imagined himself a hero in a Hollywood Western, mounting a venerable steed and galloping across the prairie, working at rodeos and lassoing recalcitrant calves. He dreamed of one day running the farm and becoming a famous rancher.

One day, as night was falling, little Arik climbed on the back of a donkey, hit against a rock, and fell off, opening a gash on his face. He ran to his mother, Vera, covered in blood, but because of a simmering quarrel with the village neighbors, she did not want to have him treated at the local clinic, preferring instead to take her injured son miles away, to the home of a friend, Doctor Fogiel of Kfar Saba.

Years later, Arik would still remember the trauma of the incident, the donkey, the injury, and his mother's behavior.

At his graduation ceremony from elementary school, where he was to recite a fairy tale before the gathered students and parents, Arik froze on stage and the words, so carefully memorized during the days before the event, would not come out. He stood stock-still for what seemed to him an endless time before the curtain was mercifully lowered, and afterwards kept a composed face until he arrived back home, when the tears, not the words, finally came.

He was a solitary child, preferring the company of farm animals to the village children. Shiptz, the faithful family dog, was his best friend.

Each evening, Arik would climb to the attic to watch the fascinating play between the cat and the mice. He would never go to bed without having studied "the theatre of operations," appreciative of the offensive strategy of the cat and the tactics of the scattering mice. After watching the series of attacks which inevitably led to the overwhelming victory of the cat, he would go to his room satisfied at the outcome of the combat, and fall asleep listening to the popular Russian songs echoing from the living room, where his father's admirable talent on the violin was such a pleasure to hear. In his parents' home, not just the land was cultivated. Art and music were a vital part of life for the secular Scheinermanns – the name signifies "handsome man" in Yiddish – who were liberal, open-minded and cultured. The hard physical labor during the day would be reconciled in the evening with the needs of the soul. While little Arik quickly learned to love and appreciate music, he never became a virtuoso like his father. In fact, he was completely incapable of even tuning his violin!

Shmuel Scheinermann was typical of the Jewish pioneers from Russia, solidly entrenched in the redemptive culture of the soil. This was a man endowed with an iron will, determined to seize hold of life, whatever the cost. He affected a pencil moustache that he always kept neatly trimmed. A dry man with a hardened face and heavy eyebrows, he had a profound look in his big, dark eyes, hollow cheeks, and a thick head of hair. He exuded righteousness, and boundless energy, and was uncompromising, rejecting concessions or "arrangements," and was ready to go to the ends of the earth to prove himself right. And he always thought he was right, which was in itself a great character flaw.

In his view, physical labor sanctified life, but he was opposed to the collective spirit of the kibbutz. An agronomist by profession, he worshipped the cult of working the land, and the ethic of individual acts. Scheinermann was a puritan, living modestly, despising luxury, and acting on his own decisions. He found through art – his hobby – another avenue for the expression of his deepest emotions.

Arik would inherit many of his father's character traits. Proud to follow in Shmuel's footsteps, he helped his dad with the work on the farm. He would rise at dawn to plow the fields with a cart drawn by a mule, and as he progressed, enjoyed contemplating the perfectly straight rows he had made in the soil, and watched as the swallows flew around him then dived to feast on the insects and the worms exposed by his labor. In the afternoons he would work the orange groves, tearing out the weeds that grew around the saplings, hollowing out a space around each and patiently watering with a rubber hose pulled from tree to tree. The evenings were a time to help his mother – a nurse by profession – milk the cows; also a time to wolf down a bowl of warm, unpasteurized milk when she wasn't looking, and to observe with fascination the birth of new calves.

In the little village of Kfar Malal, inter-family friction was common, and pastoral life not always idyllic. On the family farm, Vera Scheinermann was ambitious and domineering. Small in stature but strong in spirit and character, she could work an eighteen hour day without speaking a word to her neighbors. Shmuel, with his own personality problems, was also a marginal individual in community life. He refused to obey collective decisions he thought ill advised, even when they were taken by a large majority. The give and take required for the smooth running of the village were foreign concepts to him.

He could simply not stand losing a bet, or a challenge, or a more serious struggle. He was of the opinion that his knowledge of agronomy should be sufficient reason for his theses and conclusions to carry the day. For example, he tried to impose changes in the kinds of fruits to be grown, demanding that everyone follow his own choices at all cost. The village families did not take kindly to his dictatorial style and refused to follow his advice. But the stubborn and secretive Scheinermann carried on with his research, and in fact became the first in Palestine to grow avocados. Barbed wire surrounded his farm and his fields, and with Arik and Shiptz, the German Shepherd guard dog at the watch, no one was allowed in, and that included strangers, curious locals, and of course roving bands of Arab thieves.

At age thirteen, Arik was allowed to stand guard on the graveyard shift. Armed with a night stick and a dagger – a Bar-Mitzvah present – he paced back and forth in the obscurity, always alert, scanning the darkness for anything moving, always ready to attack his prey.

The solitary nature of this work made Arik more independent, able to think on his own and reach decisions without consulting others. He preferred working with his father to the requirements of school education, and was a very average student, unlike his older sister Dita, who was a brilliant scholar. His parents sent him to Tel-Aviv ("spring hill" in Hebrew) to study at the Geula Lyceum. He had to rise very early each morning to catch a run-down bus for the dusty, daily, commute. The round trip was nearly thirty miles. After class, he would usually stroll the newly-built boulevards of the city, visit the local market, watch the merchants and gaze at the goods they sold, and smell the aromas of the spices and the odors emanating from the roasted lamb, hot oil and the bread fresh from the bakers' ovens. He always found time for a soda and a falafel sandwich on pita and a visit with his grandmother Myriam, listening patiently to her stories and tales in recounted Russian, eating her cookies and cakes. Later on, he and his classmates would chase the girls, or sometimes, alone and daring, he would watch in fascination as the slim-waisted and streetwalkers showed off their well-formed wares on the quarter's sidewalks.

What a contrast to the austere and monotonous life in his village, or to the harsh labor on the farm! Tel-Aviv was a wonderful place to have fun, let your emotions run wild. Arik could not but be amazed at this brand-spanking new city, modern, full of life and *joie de vivre,* with its cafes, movie theatres, amusement parks and magnificent beaches.

Unhappy news from Europe of the proclamation in Nazi Germany of the anti-Semitic Nuremberg Laws soon brought an end to the insouciance of Ariel's youth. The Jewish communities of Europe and the Diaspora seemed completely powerless to defend themselves against the growing evil. Great Britain was clearly indifferent to the fate of European Jews. It severely curtailed immigration to Palestine, then under its mandate. For their part, Jews joined every movement in the struggle against the Nazis, even forming a Jewish Brigade in the British Army.

The Jews of Palestine were confronted with an enormous dilemma in the face of the Nazi extermination plan, British occupation of Palestine, and threats by Arabs with links to Hitler. The existence of three fronts in the struggle provoked major conflicts within the Zionist movement itself, especially between the two main Defense organizations, the Haganah – founded in 1920, and Etsel – the Irgun Tsavai Leumi founded in April 1937 by Jabotinsky, Begin and the Betar movement – which took up arms against the British authorities in Palestine.

The members of the Kfar Malal kibbutz, including the Scheinermanns, belonged to Ben-Gurion's Mapai Labor Party, and were active in the Haganah. They believed that the conflict with the British was essentially political and that it was more important to respond in kind to the threats of the surrounding Arab countries. These people were strongly opposed to Etsel, which promoted struggle against the British on all fronts, and in all ways, including spectacular, armed attacks. A collision between these two diametrically opposed and strongly held views was inevitable, and led to bloody, fratricidal incidents between Jews. Kfar Malal was not immune to this confrontation and village Etsel combatants were denounced and handed over to the British.

Shmuel Scheinermann was opposed to those in the Haganah who wanted to fight Etsel and its methods. He called for reconciliation among Jews and warned against the spark that could light a civil war. The spectacle of Jew fighting Jew before there even was a State of Israel was unthinkable to him, especially when at the same time, the Nazis were rounding up European Jews and sending them by the trainload to concentration camps.

But Scheinermann's stance brought him no succor. For his courageous political and nationalist positions, he was quarantined and cast out of the Mapai. Ariel Sharon's formative adolescent years were lived in this climate of tension, intense discussion, and raucous, often hateful, public quarrelling.

He was now seventeen. World War Two had just ended with the defeat of the Germans. All young people of his age were mobilized, and against the counsel of his father, Arik decided to join the Palmah, a combat unit known as the Haganah's spear. Before he left Kfar Malal to take part in armed combat, his father took him aside and said, "My son, you are now old enough to choose your own path in life. This is your right. You are an independent man, able to take decisions by yourself. But promise me this, never raise your hand to another Jew, and never deliver a Jew to the British."

Arik swore this to his father, then put on the uniform of combat and joined the Defense forces under a new name, Ariel Sharon. A brilliant military career was about to begin for this sabra, a career that would put its print on the history of the young State now on the road to independence.

The countdown began with a series of daily incidents as a wave of violence spread across the land. On the diplomatic front, events moved forward quickly until the day when the United Nations voted on the question of Palestine. This historic vote set off a veritable explosion of joy and celebration. In the streets of Tel-Aviv and throughout the land, people were singing and dancing. The right of Jews to establish their own independent and sovereign State in Palestine had been recognized by the international authorities.

The British departed, leaving the Jews and the Arabs to fight it out for control over the Holy Land. Combat was harsh. The Yeshuv – as the minority Jewish community in Palestine was known before the birth of Israel – short of weapons and munitions, had to fight on many fronts and against many Arab armies. Guerilla warfare became its tactic of choice: ambushes, hit-and-run raids, attacks on vital strategic targets like bridges, military bases, convoys and enemy leaders were all planned and executed.

The young soldier Arik participated in many operations against armed Arab groups, and was responsible for dynamiting the Qualqulia bridge, not far from his village, an attack which cut off a convoy of Iraqi troop reinforcements. But the deadliest operation he participated in was known as Latroun, a strategic hill on which sat a fortress dating back to the crusades called the Knights Tower, as well as an Abbey of French Trappist monks. The hill dominated the Haela valley that was, according to legend, where David fought Goliath, but more importantly, it controlled the road toward Jerusalem. The Arab Legion, composed of Bedouin military units under the command of the Trans-Jordan Hashemite Kingdom, was well implanted in the area and armed with canons.

All earlier Israeli attempts to capture the hill had ended in failure and cost of many injured and many killed. It was here at Latroun that Arik Sharon faced death for the first time. During an attack by a unit essentially composed of new Jewish immigrants and volunteers, he took two bullets to the stomach from a Jordanian sniper. Gravely wounded, he was evacuated by his comrades (among them was Cyrill Kern, today a millionaire in South Africa, always an important contributor to Sharon's election campaigns, and a figure in the criminal trial of Sharons's son Omry) to a hospital, with bullets whistling around them as they carried him. The battle for Latroun was the bloodiest of the entire war of independence, and in the carnage, Arik lost many close friends. His unit, hidden in the fields of wheat, had been decimated, the golden sheaves spattered with Jewish blood. He would long grieve this battle, and its consequences influenced his decisions later in life in no small way. But he never lost his confidence nor his ability to pursue combat with unshakeable optimism and enthusiasm. From his father Shmuel he had learned to turn the page, and always consider missions accomplished from a positive viewpoint. Never despair! Never accept defeat!

But carried by his ardor, Arik sometimes advanced too quickly and was known to have a heavy foot on the gas pedal, metaphorically as well as practically. One day he spun his jeep off the road and he found himself in a ravine, with only a few ribs broken, lucky to be alive.

Chapter 2

The Red Beret

Everyone, look! The Red Man is passing.
Victor Hugo

Hostilities with the Arab armies were declared ended on July 20, 1949. But an armistice is not a peace, and nothing on the horizon gave any real hope of starting a process of reconciliation. To the contrary: the larval state of war would persist for a long time to come. The length of the young nation's frontiers made it easy for the *fedayin* to infiltrate and sabotage kibbutz water supplies – leading to the destruction of crops – and murder Israeli civilians. The wave of incursions and attacks had but a single aim, the creation of a terror psychosis in the villages close to the border.

Israel felt obliged to respond in kind, and a series of retaliatory raids were launched into Egypt and Jordan. Ariel Sharon, already a captain in military intelligence, was sent to the Central Region Command where he patrolled the demarcation line with the Trans-Jordan and reconnoitered near Arab villages. Several months after his arrival, he fell seriously ill with malaria, and its symptoms – intermittent high fever and anemia – weakened Arik to the point that the heavy doses of quinine he took to combat the disease had less and less effect; his military doctor prescribed a change in climate.

After much reflection, Arik was given time off – as long as he could find the money he needed for airfare and hotels on his own – to travel to Europe and to the United States. His first stop was Paris.

This was the first time Sharon had ever left his land, and when he arrived in the French capital in December 1951, dressed in peasant clothing, he found himself in the depths of a particularly cold winter. His uncle Joseph, who lived in style in a luxury, sixteenth-arrondissement flat, took Arik under his wing. They began by visiting a made-to-measure clothier in the old Jewish Quarter of the city – *Le Marais* – where he acquired a stylish suit, leather gloves, and a rakish hat. Uncle Joseph also provided spending money, and the young man, warmly dressed now, set out to discover the City of Lights at its most lovely, in the weeks before Christmas. Christmas trees, lights, and decorations abounded, and as Arik walked up the Champs-Elysées and the great boulevards of Paris, he could not help being impressed by the well-stocked shop windows, and the elegant and attractive French women.

The beginning of the trip seemed to have the desired effect on his state of health. With his malaria now in remission, Arik set out for New York on an ocean liner. Accompanied by his aunt Sarah, he visited Manhattan, Washington, and Palm Beach. When he returned home a month later, he was motivated and full of energy. Something in him had changed. His ocean crossing and his discovery of new continents had put his Israeli reality into perspective, and for the first time, he began to call into question the career in the military that until then had seemed to him inevitable. He decided to attend university, but in truth, had no idea what to study. Perplexed by all these decisions to make, he requested and was granted an extended leave by his immediate superiors. Tempted first by agronomy and then by law, he in the end registered at the Faculty of Middle Eastern studies at the University of Jerusalem, where he met his future wife, the love of his life, Margalith – "pearl" in Hebrew.

He had known this young woman before, some years earlier, in his native village. She was then a newly-arrived immigrant from Romania, just sixteen, who had been brought over to Israel by the Youth Movements. Slim, olive-skinned, with a soft look to her and hazel eyes, she wore her hair in two plaits that framed her elegant neck. Arik was struck dumb with love, and often took her for moonlight walks around the kibbutz. But with general mobilization and the confusion of war, he had lost track of her. And then he found her again, in Jerusalem, finishing a degree in nursing. She had just turned twenty. A year later, blessed by a military rabbi, and promising themselves to each other for better and for worse, they married and moved into a tiny furnished flat. But space was not a problem; they were in love.

Several months later, just when Arik was preparing for his end of year examinations, he received an urgent summons from his military commanders. Arab attacks were on the rise, creating new victims every day. More than one hundred sixty Israeli civilians had been assassinated in the previous few months alone at the hands of the *fedayin*.

The situation was intolerable. Reprisals seemed to be the only way to check the murderous incursions and special unit was created in the paratrooper brigade for just such missions - Unit 101. Sharon would become its uncontested leader. He recruited volunteer commandos, scouts trained in all-terrain, day and night combat. These fighters needed to have an innate sense of orienteering, know the topography of the terrain by heart, and possess an iron esprit de corps. They often behaved with savagery, possessed rough and brutal ways, but Arik considered this an advantage: he knew that fighting the barbarism and cruelty of their enemies required more than lace curtains and doilies. They needed to strike deeply and strongly and put the Jordanian authorities on notice that they needed to stop the *fedayin* from infiltrating Israeli territory. The unit chose to act with an exemplary strike on the village of Kibbya, in the Trans-Jordan. While its residents slept, Arik and his unit entered the village armed with ten kilos of TNT.

The results were tragic: sixty-nine dead, including women and children hiding in shelters, and close to a dozen Jordanian soldiers killed in hand to hand combat. Unit 101 had blown up forty homes, not knowing that in the basements innocent lives would be lost.

The operation was universally condemned. But it served its purpose as a warning, and represented a turning point in the policy of reprisals adopted by the IDF.

The following day, Captain Sharon was summoned to the office of the Minister of Defense and Government Head, David Ben-Gurion. It was to be a meeting – their first – that would determine a great deal in the young officer's future career. The Prime Minister appreciated Arik's hot-blooded temperament and the dissuasive anti-terrorist methods used by Sharon's Unit 101. The direct channel from Sharon to the highest levels of power was without precedent. It did not go unnoticed by his fellow officers who were not all pleased by the turn of events, to say the least. Arik would from then on be singled out, and to some extent, marginalized. But to Ben-Gurion, the military operations led by Sharon which led to the suppression of Arab attacks in the region could have a snowball effect, and even if the foreign embassies and the United Nations condemned this policy, and had to be taken into consideration, future Israeli governments would maintain this line: imperative military operations could never be dictated by non Israeli interests.

In December 1953, Moshe Dayan was named Israeli Chief of Staff. The eye-patch wearing general enjoyed the full confidence of Ben-Gurion, and this shored up Sharon's position in the armed forces. Dayan integrated Unit 101 into the 890th Paratrooper Battalion, and named Sharon as commander. In taking this step, Dayan, well known for his lack of tact and his brutal methods, created much resentment in the Red Beret brigade. Revolt was in the air as Arik took control of these forces. During the ceremony, he was booed and interrupted by whistling and cries of derision. A significant number of officers, and many of the soldiers, preferred to remain with their former commander. It was a rebellious gesture never before seen in the IDF, and illustrated just how controversial Sharon was, even as a twenty-six year old soldier.

Promoted to the rank of lieutenant-colonel, Arik proceeded to shuffle and reconstitute his forces, introducing the methods developed in Unit 101, and shaping the Red Berets into a unified fighting machine which would become Israel's attack force for operations outside the borders of the country. The paratroop battalion became a close-knit unit under Sharon's leadership, and Arik became, incontestably, the most admired commander in the armed forces. Many, many soldiers now chose to follow him into battle, and, inspired by his confidence and pride, the paratroopers handled the majority of their missions with great success. Very quickly, the media cottoned on to Sharon. Flattering articles about him in the press mushroomed. Military correspondents were allowed to accompany the paratroopers on some of their missions and would describe the soldiers' exploits in superlative terms. Ben-Gurion himself was effusive in his admiration for this insolent fighting Sabra, a native son of the land, and quite obviously, the Prime Minister's favorite.

As Minister of Defense, Ben-Gurion would often personally invite Sharon to take part in meetings of the general staff, to the dismay of the senior officers. A proud man endowed with a sharp cynicism, Arik would often irritate his peers and elicit jealousy and animosity. He was known for believing that he could safely ignore direct orders from his military superiors and take decisions on his own. How wrong he was! His every move, every gesture, every word were scrutinized in detail. One day, it was discovered that Sharon had slapped a warehouse officer who had refused to obey a direct order. This led to a military hearing during which Arik was severely reprimanded. Everyone accepted the fact that the paratroopers formed an elite battalion, but they were also a part of the army, not an independent fighting force. They were not to enjoy special status nor use unapproved, audacious methods, even if these resulted in spectacular success, such as the raid on Egyptian Army Headquarters in Gaza on February 28, 1955 that inflicted such great humiliation on that country's strongman Gamal Nasser that he was obliged to go begging in Moscow for arms to defend himself.

Sharon held on, and succeeded in proving to Ben-Gurion that these raids were justified. Israel had to inflict heavy losses on the enemy, and through the use of arms make the Arabs understand that they could not vanquish the Jewish state on the battlefield. Israel no longer feared Arab threats and intimidation.

Dayan, as chief of the armed forces, found Sharon's direct line to Ben-Gurion less and less tolerable. He could not permit Arik a free hand with the Prime Minister. Military hierarchy would just not allow it. Impulsive as ever, Dayan decided to relieve Sharon of his command, but when Arik learned what had been done, he went directly to Ben-Gurion, raging. The Prime Minister answered philosophically, telling his protégé, "Patience and time will win out over force and anger." These were prophetic words.

Sharon returned to his unit and pursued his operational plans. But during a night-time raid in the Sinai desert, his jeep hit a rock and overturned, trapping him beneath a vehicle that could explode at any moment. Only the most strenuous and desperate efforts by his comrades succeeded in freeing him, and he was rushed to hospital. Several days later, he had fully recovered, and the crisis with Dayan had abated. Ever the pragmatist, Moshe Dayan had reversed his earlier decision. Tensions were fast rising on the border with Egypt and a joint operation with England and France was being planned. Sharon would be a key player in the historic effort to secure the Suez Canal and protect vital shipping lanes from Nasser's threats.

French paratroopers arrived in secret to study Israeli utilization of French arms and especially troop transport aircraft. Sharon received them warmly on behalf of the IDF, and they returned to their country impressed, convinced that a Franco-Israeli strike against Egypt was operationally feasible.

In October 1956, the Suez Invasion was launched. Sharon and his soldiers from the 202nd brigade parachuted into the Sinai and executed a striking and successful attack on the Mitla Pass. Despite a number of mistakes that resulted in the deaths of many Egyptian and Sudanese prisoners, Sharon's brigade soon arrived triumphant on the shores of the canal.

Meanwhile, British and French aircraft were bombing throughout Egypt and paratroopers from the two countries landed in Port Said. At the same time, in an extraordinary meeting, the United Nations Security Council demanded an immediate cease-fire. It was a race against time. The Soviet Union, furious and feeling exceedingly threatened by the Hungarian uprising now taking place in its zone of influence, sent a series of alarming signals with Defense Minister Marshall Bulganin going as far as threatening the use of atomic weapons. The Suez campaign had suddenly become a world crisis. Paris and London backtracked, and "Operation Musketeer," whose aim was to secure the Suez Canal, ended in catastrophe. It was a total humiliation for England and France. Israel, between a rock and a hard place, finally withdrew its troops from the Sinai Peninsula. Nasser declared his military defeat a political victory, and moved Egypt closer to Moscow. Sharon was beside himself. In a confrontation with Dayan and Ben-Gurion, angrily beseeched them not to abandon Gaza, which he considered a major staging point for terrorists.

But a different decision was taken, primarily for political reasons. It would be impossible for Israel to remain alone, isolated in the international arena and the cause of grave tension between the world's two superpowers of the period, the U.S.S.R and the United States. World peace was at issue, and the Israeli-American special relationship was still young and fragile.

Sharon found respite from the shifting political winds of the military in his family life, filled with its own swirling emotions. There was love, and joy, and happiness, but also sadness and melancholy. After Arik had buried his fallen comrades from the Sinai battles, his first son, Gury, was born. The joyous event was overshadowed by sadness when Sharon's father Shmuel, passed away three days later in another hospital bed. Arik felt so terribly alone all of a sudden: he was twenty-eight, a young father, with his own father gone and his elder sister Dita now living far away in the U.S.A.[1]

Some months later, Arik decided to pursue his studies at the British Royal Military Staff College at Camberley. He took up residence in London with his wife and their child. It was a strange time for him, with the vivid memories of violent combat in the Sinai sand now pushed aside by theoretical battles with tin soldiers and ordnance survey maps. He took a stab at improving his English, but had little success. His thoughts were back in the harsh Israeli reality, with his comrades and their combat. Sharon realized then that he was not only a career soldier, but a true Sabra career soldier.

When he returned home, a new team was running army headquarters; he was kept far removed from the paratrooper battalion he loved so much, and just as far away from military operations. Instead, he was named to head the School of Infantry. It was a position he accepted with no complaints. After all, his protector Ben-Gurion was in hot political water, and Moshe Dayan was now out of uniform.

Sharon periodically requested - and was denied - a position at the nerve center of the IDF. His attempts to be transferred to a tank division fell on equally deaf ears, and his field of action seemed to shrink by the day. It was a price paid for his direct relationship with Ben-Gurion. Arik's undisciplined and domineering, self-assured nature had seemed to close more doors than it opened. He was now thirty, less involved, and impatiently waiting for better days to come.

David Ben-Gurion was by now a mere shadow of his former self, and had left politics, retiring to his kibbutz in Sde Boker, in the Negev Desert.

Sharon somehow held himself in check, and took advantage of the downtime afforded him by this reversal of fortune to study constitutional law and take care of his little family. His wife held a position in the Health Ministry, a sinecure that promised the Sharons financial stability. Then came tragedy: one day, driving alone on the road to Jerusalem in a little Austin she had brought back from London after the family returned from Arik's studies, she was struck by a heavy truck and killed instantly. Sharon learned the terrible news while he was playing with his five year-old son, Gury. In the midst of the tragedy, Margalith's younger sister Lily took over the role of mother to the young child. Later on, Lily and Ariel fell in love, wed, and formed a happy couple for life, salvaging something good from the terrible events that had befallen them.

Note

1. Dita (Yehudit) Scheinermann married a surgeon in 1941 and left Palestine a year later, an exile her family never forgave. Her relationship with her young brother was brutally cut off when their mother Vera willed the entire Kfar Malal farm to Omry, the eldest son of Ariel's second marriage. She offered a consolation gift of twenty-five thousand dollars to her daughter, but it was spurned. Arik had little direct contact with his sister, and she refused to speak with him on the telephone. From the time he became Prime Minister of Israel to the day he fell ill, Sharon did not meet with her a single time, even though he visited New York often. Childless and still a beautiful woman at eighty-one with a forceful personality, Dita lives in Manhattan, alone.

Chapter 3

A General's Ruses

A brave general never surrenders, even in the face of the inevitable.
Jean Cocteau

On December 15, 1963 – a Sunday – at ten in the morning, the new Israeli government of Levy Eshkol named general Yitzhak Rabin head of the army general staff. Rabin, upon Ben-Gurion's warm recommendation, appointed Arik Sharon chief of staff for the Northern Command. Sharon was to be second in command to general Avraham Yaffe and form an operational team with him. It would be "mission accomplished."

Arik and his second wife Lily had settled with son Gury in Nahalal, an agricultural village near Haifa that was also home to Moshe Dayan. Nine months after their arrival, their own first-born arrived, a chubby little boy they named Omry, after an ancient king of Israel. The Sharons bought a small farm and settled into country living and crop raising.

But in the greater Middle East things were on the boil. The military had seized power in many Arab capitals, and positions with regard to Israel were stiffening. In the North, tension with Syria acute: border incidents had become a daily occurrence. The Arabs announced a decision to divert the waters of the Jordan River, which represented fully one third of Israel's needs. Worse, the diversion was taking place at a fever pitch. Israel considered this an act of war, which demanded an immediate and forceful response. Sharon was put in charge of solving the problem. He sent bulldozers into the border areas near the demilitarized zones, to construct fortifications. Syrian response was predictable and immediate: their artillery pounded the construction sites, and the kibbutzim of Upper Galilee were attacked.

This was a serious escalation of an already tense situation. The curious thing was that President Bourguiba of Tunisia had at the very same time suggested the Arab states adopt a more conciliatory and positive stance with regard to the Jewish state. In fact, in a quite remarkable speech he gave in Jericho on March 3, 1965, he declared that, "In Palestine, the Arabs have rejected any notion of compromise solutions. They have refused to share resources, and will have cause to regret this in the future. If we, in Tunisia, had rejected the notion of autonomy within the French Empire in 1954, our country would even today have remained under France's dominion. This 'all or nothing' Palestinian policy has led us to defeat and to endure the sad lot in which we find ourselves today." These were wise and sincere words, and were followed in April 1966 – a year before the Six Day War – by Bourguiba's solemn appeal for the recognition of Israel based on Resolution 181 of the United Nations concerning the sharing of Palestine.

Several weeks later, General Yaffe retired as Chief of the Nazareth-based Northern Command since at that time, and since 1954, retirement had been mandatory at age forty-five. Today, the chief of general staff and his generals remain in charge well into their fifties. Yaffe was replaced by General David Elazar, popularly known as "Dado." Elazar, born in Yugoslavia, had a prudent temperament. Less impetuous than Sharon, Dado's every move was calculated and his actions thoughtful and broad-minded. Dado's vision took into consideration all the strategic and political consequences of military action. Arik, by contrast, saw everything through the lens of the battlefield, and was known to be trigger-happy.

It was hardly a meeting of soul mates. Suspicion was the watchword and the two seldom agreed, with Sharon thinking that Elazar lacked confidence in him and conspired against him. Arik was completely wrong. I myself worked closely with Elazar for two years, and have a profound understanding of the man. I can state without hesitation that Sharon's conclusions about Dado were unfounded. Elazar was a man of great personal integrity, a man of strong convictions. There was no way he was going to support the kind of risky adventure touted by Sharon in a region abounding in farming villages, where the slightest spark could spawn an inferno. Elazar decided to rein in the wild ambitions of Ariel Sharon, thinking rightly or wrongly that the better part of valor is prudence.

Dado's decision to put an end to the collaboration meant that overnight, Arik found himself out of military employment. He took an unpaid leave of absence and decided to take an extended tour of Africa. It was to be a lengthy journey that took him through the natural wonders of Kenya, Ethiopia, and Uganda. On his return, Rabin, to Sharon's great surprise, named him in charge of military instruction at general staff headquarters, and promoted him to the rank of brigadier-general. It was, in fact, an elegant way of permanently losing him in the bureaucracy: a military burial with full honors...

No longer in charge of any military operations, Sharon could now only exercise his abilities in the field in the case of a general mobilization for an imminent conflict. The situation hardly fit his character, and it was certainly not in line with his career aspirations. He was still aiming for the top: his dream was to become chief of staff of the IDF, nothing less, but he did not yet see that the effect of the appointment was to sideline him.

In frustration, he decided to move from the farming village of Nahalal to Tsahala, a suburb of Tel-Aviv populated by IDF officers, and several months later, welcomed his third son, Gilad, to the world. As a father, he felt completely fulfilled. But dramatic events were soon at hand. On February 22, 1966, Hafez al-Assad, the chief of the Syrian Air Force, seized power in a Damascus coup d'état. His first acts were to provoke violent incidents in the Tiberiad area, and resuscitate the diversion of the Jordan Rivers waters affair. Syrian troops shelled border farmlands, and Israeli troops raided the Jordanian village of Samoa, an act that resulted in riots breaking out between Yasser Arafat's Palestine Liberation Organisation and the Jordanian Army. Jordan's King Hussein was accused of being soft on Israel, and of showing lack of foresight.

The situation on the border seemed to be deteriorating by the day. The nadir was reached on April 7, 1967, when Israeli fighters shot down six Syrian Migs. Assad placed a desperate call for help to Egyptian dictator Nasser, convinced that the Israelis were about to launch a massive attack. Nasser's response was to immediately place his troops on full alert.

One month later, as Israeli soldiers paraded through the streets of Jerusalem in celebration of the nineteenth anniversary of the State of Israel, Nasser, in an obvious preparation for combat, expelled the United Nations observers from the Gaza Strip.

At Bor, the Tel-Aviv underground nerve center of the IDF, Prime Minister Levy Eshkol was presiding over a meeting of his top generals. The atmosphere was heavy. Yitzhak Rabin, chief of the general staff, was nervously chain-smoking, and appeared to have lost control of the situation. One after the other, the generals offered their analysis and declared in favor of a pre-emptive strike, but without suggesting a specific date. Rabin was hesitant, as was Eshkol. The Prime Minister, who was also Minister of Defense, nervously stuttered through a speech broadcast at the time by Israeli radio, Kol Israel. He stumbled over his words, reading from a hastily-typed script full of spelling and syntax errors. The consequences were disastrous: listeners, who had tuned in to be reassured, now feared the worst. Their leader no longer inspired confidence, and obviously lacked the self-assurance the situation demanded.

Arik Sharon, and many generals alongside him, were by comparison diametrically opposed to this climate of pessimism, and exhibited an unshakeable confidence and belief in victory. Sharon's view was that the politicians had their role, which was to define objectives, and that the military had its role also, which was to achieve those objectives without political interference. Neither should step on the toes of the other.

In the face of the Prime Minister's evident lack of leadership, and of the hesitation of Rabin – who fell ill soon after – Sharon took the initiative. He prepared operational plans for a pre-emptive strike. The goal was ambitious: wipe out the Egyptian forces, and limit Israeli casualties to a strict minimum. Sharon, and generals Weizman, Tal, Yaffe and Peled considered that the Israeli Defense Forces – Tsahal – were much stronger than they had been in the 1956 Suez conflict, and would be able to achieve a brilliant victory with no foreign involvement. Sharon refused to even consider a limited operation, a step-by-step campaign like the one previously used in Gaza. Instead, he pushed for a strike similar to the one Israel had mounted during the Suez crisis. Dayan, for his part, was categorically opposed to an invasion of Gaza. "Gaza is a human bomb. We'll be trapped in quicksand! We need to defuse the bomb, not conquer it."

On May 22, 1967, Egypt's Gamal Nasser closed the Straits of Tiran to all shipping coming from or going to Israel. Tiran dominated the Gulf of Aqaba, and thus the Israeli port of Eilat was threatened with asphyxiation. This declaration was considered by Israel to be an act of war.

Abba Eban, Isarel's Foreign Minister, flew at once to Paris, nominally Israel's strong ally. But to his amazement and disgust, President Charles de Gaulle told him that France did not want to see a new armed conflict in the Middle East, and immediately placed an embargo on arms shipments to the region. What this really meant was that France had no stomach for a fight. The Israelis called France's position "capricious and shocking," and Israel felt quite isolated, with the United States mired in the Vietnam War, and the Russians solidly backing – and arming – the Arabs.

The country was plunged into a state of anxiety. Wild rumors abounded: Rabin had fallen into a state of depression, Ben-Gurion had painted an apocalyptic scenario for the IDF generals, and the most worrisome, that General Weizman, egged on by Sharon, was planning to seize power and declare a state of emergency. In normal times, such whispers would have been unthinkable in democratic Israel, but these times were not normal, with the Arab nation threatening to throw the Jews into the sea.

There was pressure put on the politicians by the military though, and it resulted in a government of national unity. For the first time in the history of Israel, the left-wing Labor party and the right-wing nationalists would sit together in Cabinet. Moshe Dayan, a Laborite, was appointed Defense Minister, while future Prime Minister Menachem Begin was named Minister Without Portfolio. It turned into a nightmare for Ben-Gurion, who quickly concluded he should never have allowed his political adversary Begin to sit at his table. But it was too late. Eshkol, more pragmatic, felt there was no other choice. Dayan, in the meantime, went on calmly and masterfully preparing his plans for war.

On June 5, 1967 at 0744 hours, the hostilities, quickly to become known as the Six Day War, began. Sharon had a strategic objective and carried it out successfully, employing a ruse. He first sent out units to reconnoiter, then used motorized infantry to open a direct route through the Sinai to the Suez Canal and Sharm-el-Sheikh. The operation demanded flawless, round-the-clock coordination between tanks, infantry, and paratroopers. The combats led by General Sharon in the Um Katef and Abu Angela regions would be in later years studied at military academies as monuments of strategic planning and execution. They quickly entered into the annals of classical modern warfare as legendary battles. Sharon's own tank division, the 138th, was the first to reach the shores of the Suez Canal.

Arik was a polished survivor of many desert conflicts, and his division alone, and in only three days, destroyed more than sixty Egyptian tanks and one hundred pieces of field artillery. The Egyptians lost one thousand soldiers, and hundreds more were wounded and taken prisoner. The victory was sweet, and spectacular, but for the Egyptians, it was an abject defeat. Triumphant, the thirty-nine year-old Sharon declared himself ready for any other missions.

The Six Day War was without precedent in contemporary history. At the cease-fire, Israel controlled three times the territory it had held but a week earlier. But the territory came with a population of one million Arabs, who, added to the three hundred thousand Arabs already living in Israel, came to be later understood as a long-ignored demographic time bomb which could constitute a veritable danger to the Jewish state, Today - forty years later - the Arab population of Israel is about 18%, roughly one million, while the population of the territories is about two million two hundred thousand, of which one third is made up of Jewish settlers.

Israel had won a remarkable victory on the battlefield. The Arab air forces had been annihilated on the ground. Israel had seized territory that could be used as a buffer zone or a bargaining chip. But the diplomatic battle had just begun, and that was a whole other story. The Arabs seemed undiscouraged by their military defeat, and unwavering in their opposition to the Zionist state. Hardly forty days after the war, Nasser gathered the Arab leaders - with the notable exceptions of the Tunisian leader Bourguiba, and Hassan, the King of Morocco, who both refused to embark on a policy blinded by fanaticism and sent their Prime Ministers in their place - in Khartoum. The communiqué at the end of the meeting called for no recognition of Israel, no negotiations, and thus, no peace.

The period immediately after the Six Day War is a remarkable illustration of the asymmetry in the history of the Arab-Israeli conflict, the former nations hostile intransigence contrasting sharply with the ardent desire on the part of Israel to compromise and reach a lasting peace with its neighbors.

The day after the Khartoum meeting, the Egyptians began systematic shelling of Israeli positions all along the length of the Suez Canal. It was the beginning of the War of Attrition, which lasted from 1967 until 1970, and, fostered by the delivery of new, modern weapons from the Soviet Union, it resulted in 1414 Israeli casualties. There was to be intermittent activity on this front – and another 673 Israeli victims – from 1970 until the October 1973 Yom Kippur war.

To respond to the challenges of this new armed conflict, Arik Sharon drew on all the lessons he could from the battles of the Six Day War. Placed in charge of troop instruction, he reconstituted the details of each battle, then, in order to demonstrate the facts on the ground and to show an active presence in the field, he decided to move the military schools to the West Bank, despite the reticence of the General Staff. Moshe Dayan, on the other hand, was in favor of the move, and so it was done. Sharon's aim was to safeguard the urban areas of the country and guarantee the security of Jerusalem. He argued successfully that a military presence on the hills and strategic crossroads of the West Bank was vital to the security of Israel. His plan could not have been clearer: it was a combination of military strategy and a new, massive Jewish presence in the ancestral Kingdoms of David and Solomon.

The first step would be to set up a military presence to be able to guarantee security for Jews who could settle in a safe environment. Sharon's watchword was a simple one: "creating a series of facts on the ground will ensure the future." By the establishment of a complex set of situations, when the right time came, long-term solutions corresponding to the needs of Israel would be easier to find. But there were difficulties. Eshkol's government was pragmatic in nature and unable to plan for the long-term. The future was essentially far off; it was also beyond their ken. Eshkol wanted quick and efficient solutions that would avoid another war and not shock the Arab population under Israeli control. Patience was required. Under no circumstances could a massive Israeli civilian population be allowed in the West Bank, which along with Gaza was considered a military zone. Arik was constrained to put his plan away for a while, but nothing changed in his mind.

Then another blow struck Arik, a hard, personal blow. On October 4, 1967, while Israelis were celebrating Rosh Hashonah, congratulating each other and exchanging compliments and best wishes for the New Year, Sharon was at home with his children, when suddenly a shot rang out from the courtyard. Rushing outside, he came upon a horrible scene. His eldest son, ten year-old Gury, lay prone on the grass, covered in blood, an old rifle by his side. In shock, Arik picked his boy up and rushed him to hospital, but it was too late: Gury was dead. The child, killed accidentally by a bullet from a rifle everyone thought unloaded, was buried next to Sharon's first wife, Margalith.

Of all the terrible things Arik had to confront in his life, there was nothing more atrocious and difficult to face than this. He was inconsolable, and blamed himself for the death of the only child he had fathered with his late wife. It was one more chapter in his life that ended with drama, remorse, and sad memories.

Chapter 4

Arik, King of Israel

As great as they may be, our kings are just like us.
Pierre Corneille

President Nasser of Egypt was determined to wage a war of attrition against the Israeli Army that since June 1967 was sitting on the far side of "his" Suez Canal. On the Israeli side, from IDF headquarters, General Bar Lev – the newly appointed chief of general staff – and his generals, were seeking an efficient way of silencing Egyptian artillery and countering any Egyptian attempts to cross the waterway. Many discussions later, and against the advice of Sharon, Bar-Lev authorized the construction of a kind of "Maginot Line," a series of fortifications commonly known as the Bar-Lev Line that ran to almost one hundred eighty kilometers and was linked by a communications network. Each position dominated the canal, had behind it a small support detachment of tanks, and was built with a stone-walled courtyard able to hold several tanks inside. A paved road along the line was protected by a berm whose role was to conceal Israeli troop movements from prying Arab eyes.

The avowed purpose of the line was to withstand Egyptian shelling and interdict the Arabs from sending soldiers across the canal. But for the first time in its existence, Tsahal had now to confront a static and defensive position war. Sharon was deeply set against this tactic, and taking into account both operational and psychological aspects of the situation, stated that to the contrary, given a line of defense that was remote from the populated areas of the country, it was necessary to organize a staged and highly mobile reactive ability which could launch tactical attacks and thus stop any Egyptian attempt to cross the canal in its tracks.

There was a raucous argument about the plan between Bar-Lev and Sharon in the presence of Dayan, an argument Sharon lost. Describing the plan as dangerous and stupid, he angrily left the meeting, slamming the door behind him. Bar-Lev was disgusted by this breach of military protocol and fired his "loose cannon general." In fact, Bar-Lev could not have invented a better occasion for ridding himself of a cumbersome rival. Furious when he learned of his dismissal, Sharon went to see Dayan and Golda Meir, the Labor Prime Minister. But he quickly learned they had no current desire to "intervene in the internal affairs of the army," and returned empty-handed.

It was a time for reflection in Sharon's life. Considering his future possibilities as a civilian, the fifty-one year old former general, much admired by his soldiers and a darling of the media, found himself quite attracted to the world of politics. It was a field in which he felt he could start a new and interesting career. He had been a long time member of Mapai, the left-wing Labor party that had governed Israel since its inception, but he quickly realized that his place was not in its ranks. So, while still in uniform, he tested the waters of Labor's adversaries, the Herut party, which was more liberal in its outlook than the Mapai, and fiercely nationalistic. He held a long meeting with party leader Menachem Begin, after which he believed, perhaps somewhat naively, that he would be welcomed as a hero, with cheers and salutes. Begin of course accepted Sharon's decision to join Herut, but proffered neither guarantees nor details of any future role the general might have. Innocent in the mysterious ways and traps of party politics, Arik was deeply disappointed at the way things turned out, but in any case, the country was in the throes of an election, and as everyone knows, campaign promises are a dime a dozen, and rarely kept.

The day after the Begin-Sharon meeting newspaper headlines screamed out in large type, "Arik Sharon to run for Herut!", setting off a political storm. There was supposed unrest in the armed forces and discontent at army headquarters, but broad satisfaction on the Right. Dayan, Bar Lev, and Elazar were furious while Sharon was accused of being the first general to bring politics into the armed forces. Well, no one could honestly deny knowing that party politics were alive and well in the IDF, and always had been, but since this involved Arik Sharon, the *enfant terrible*, things were somehow "different." The hypocrisy and double standard of the clamor were, to put it mildly, oppressive.

Since 1948, every single chief of staff of Tsahal had belonged to the Labor Party. Party politics were rife throughout the government and state entities, from the very bottom to the very top. The norms for career advancement, just like in the bad old days of Bolshevik Russia, from where many Israelis had emigrated, were based on holding the "little red membership card" of the party in power.

The Labor Party bosses decided in the end that it would be better to keep Sharon out of the election, and instructed Bar-Lev to renew Arik's contract forthwith. "Keep him in the army!"

The spin doctors of the time, working overtime, even found an ingenious way of accomplishing this task. Sharon would be dispatched to conduct an extended tour of the U.S.A. and the Far East, lecturing on the subject of the defense of Israel. Upon his return – after the election – he would be named in charge of the Southern Command of Tsahal. No, party politics was never at work within the IDF! Sharon presented his apologies to Begin for his tempestuous public declarations – which as a military man he was not allowed to make – that had caused no small embarrassment to the Herut leader, especially since the country was in an election period, and decided to wait for military retirement before jumping in to the intrigue-riddled political fray once more. But the next time there would be no uniform on his back to rein him in.

Meanwhile, the War of Attrition raged on. The feisty Sharon had to defend his forces against daily Egyptian harassment from static defensive positions, the construction of which he had vehemently opposed. He obeyed orders, ever the good soldier, but through clenched teeth, and with an angry heart.

Tsahal, the armed forces of Israel, had been conceived as an offensive fighting machine. It was not at its best in an immobile stance, stoically taking a pounding from the Egyptians. Something had to be done, and so Sharon ordered patrols and observation posts all up and down the canal. Commando units also raided Egyptian positions, sending a clear message to Nasser: "Watch your back. Israel has a long reach, and can strike at will into the very heart of Egypt."

Nasser was unbending, and master of the illogical. He ordered the pursuit of artillery duels all along the front, obviously caring little for the inhabitants of Suez, Ismailia and Kantara, who were fleeing in droves for their lives. Nor for that matter did he seem to care much that his oil refineries were going up in smoke. He only knew one thing, the war of attrition had to end with an Arab victory over the Zionists.

Sharon's forceful reprisal raids on Egyptian positions caused the Egyptian dictator, in the end, to propose a cease-fire. It would last hardly more than four months, time enough for both sides to shore up their positions. Nasser's intentions were obvious: the War of Attrition was part of a global strategy meant to weaken Israel materially and morally, until the time when the Arabs could successfully prosecute an all-out war against the Zionist enemy.

Confronted by declarations of war and massive artillery barrages, Israel reacted with all of its might. In September 1969, Israeli Air

Force fighter jets downed eleven Egyptian planes, and Commando Unit 13 sunk two hostile torpedo patrol boats. Infantry and tank units crossed the Gulf of Suez and destroyed observation posts, military encampments and radar facilities. One month later, a special forces commando unit, the Sayeret Markal, succeeded in bringing back to Israel a sophisticated new Russian radar installation, intact, operational, and ready to be taken apart by electronics counter-measures specialists.

Nasser flew to Moscow to demand reinforcements from the Soviet Union. He wanted Russian pilots, soldiers, and military advisers ... and got them. Soon, Soviet pilots were flying over the skies of Cairo, Alexandria, and Aswan. Russian artillery experts were manning SAM-3 missile sites, and the entire Egyptian Anti-Aircraft Defense network was now under Soviet command. More than ever, Israel seemed heading for an ineluctable, direct confrontation with the Soviet Union.

On July 30, 1970, over the Gulf of Suez, Israeli and Russian fighter jets got into a dog-fight, and four Migs were shot down. Sharon, following the events from his observation post, was jubilant. The Soviet War Minister immediately flew to Cairo. Washington tried to calm things down, not wanting any further escalation, nor direct Russian involvement in combat. Israel, after all, was not in a war with the Soviets and did not seek either air supremacy or a face-to-face confrontation with Moscow.

It was an incident that illustrates the level of Soviet intervention in Egypt. More than fifteen thousand Russian soldiers were stationed on Egyptian soil, and placed at the disposal of Gamal Nasser. The Middle East powder keg seemed primed to endanger world peace.

But Israel and the United States needed to combat the Russian moves, and Washington too delivered new and sophisticated arms to their ally, including Phantom fighter jets. But Tel-Aviv was cool to the idea of a direct U.S. presence, believing Israel could achieve military parity on its own. Meanwhile, the White House proposed renewing mediation to avoid further escalation, and the U.N. special envoy,

Gunnar Jarring, was dispatched to the area. Within a week, his diplomatic shuttle achieved a cease-fire, and after seventeen months of daily combat, the War of Attrition ended with a whimper; but it had cost many lives and engendered heavy destruction along the Suez Canal.

By September, Gamal Abdul Nasser was dead. The natural death and disappearance from the Arab scene of one of the most virulent proponents of armed struggle against Israel led to the opening of a new chapter in Egyptian history: with Anwar El-Sadat coming to power, the whole nature of Middle East politics would change.

Arik Sharon took advantage of the precarious Suez cease-fire to turn his attention to the problem of the Gaza Strip. He had long sought to avoid this coastal enclave becoming a haven for terrorism and long claimed that it was exactly that. The rise of Arafat and the PLO was disquieting, and the current bloody confrontation between the Palestinians and the Jordanian Army brought with it the real risk of Jordan being used as a trampoline for anti-Israeli terrorist incursions. But in Gaza the solution to the problem could not be simply military. In fact, it would have to be preponderantly political and humanitarian. The population was living in overcrowded squalor; conditions of life in the refugee camps there was intolerable, and Israel, as the occupying power, had a moral and legal obligation to help.

As was his habit, Sharon prepared a highly detailed plan of action, which would take place in several stages. First, he had to eliminate the terrorists. He divided Gaza into many grids, and the squares of land so demarcated were to be separate and autonomous. Israeli soldiers were to go over each area, street, and building inch by inch, and to know all the topographic details from top to bottom. In order to control the terrain and make the soldiers' tasks easier, bulldozers were sent in to cut broad access roads through the warren of alleyways in the camps, and to flatten the orchards, cactus hedges and orange groves that served as hiding places for the terrorists. Patrols were on duty twenty-four hours a day, and spotters – the slimmest of the soldiers – were stationed in the trees to observe the comings and goings in each area. Still other soldiers disguised themselves as Arabs. Anyone who sheltered terrorists would see his home dynamited by the Israelis, and his family expelled. But for those who wanted to live peacefully, working the fields and living by the sweat of their brow, there was the offer of better housing, outside of the camps, and the possibility of a better life. Sharon wanted to solve, in his own pragmatic way, the problem of the Palestinian refugees, without waiting for the arrival of the Messiah.

A humanitarian solution of the refugee problem could also lead to an improvement in Israel's diplomatic status. Instead of waiting for a global political solution, which was obviously, despite the Palestinians' prayers, not going to happen, here was a plan that addressed the problem of human suffering. It was quintessential Sharon: practical, quick, and yes, brutal, but in Arik's eyes, efficient. And he was right. Little by little, life in Gaza returned to normal, and for many months the incidence of terror diminished to the point of being practically extinct. But unfortunately, the plan to relocate refugees in new housing was a crushing failure. The Israeli government refused to get involved in the internal affairs of the United Nations humanitarian organizations. The Arab states, for their part, had no interest in seeing the sensitive question of the Palestinian refugees, "chased from their land," resolved by Israel, as this would effectively close the file on the still burning issue of the right of return. The question was unresolved then, and it remains unresolved to this date.

In January, 1972, Dado – David Elazar – became the new chief of staff of Tsahal. The appointment infuriated Sharon, who took great umbrage at his rival having squeezed him out of the position he had long sought. The nomination, approved by Moshe Dayan and Golda Meir, was, as usual, a political one. Sharon considered that he had missed his rendezvous with IDF History, and was obliged to definitively abandon his military career. He was forty-five, the customary retirement age in the armed forces, and Dado encouraged his quick departure. Twenty-five years of service and an astonishing military career were marked by a solemn ceremony. It was a formal good-bye, but Sharon, even out of uniform, retained the rank of Reserve General, and remained on call.

While awaiting the next election campaign, Sharon had to see to his family's welfare, and went back to the land, buying an abandoned farm in the northern Negev. The owner, an Australian Jew, was pleased to sell to Sharon, who used the proceeds of a two hundred thousand dollar loan from a friend and a four hundred thousand dollar loan from an American bank to finance the sale. There was every expectation of Arik's being able to reimburse the loans from the farm's revenue. It was a dream come true for him, and tied into the previously unfulfilled hopes of his agronomist father. Sharon could breathe here, on his land, in his country, surrounded by the herds of sheep, cows, and horses. He felt free, happy, and had the time and space to ponder what political life might bring. In his mind's eye, he was already Prime Minister of Israel...

A year went by, the seasons following one upon the other in the natural rhythms of pastoral life. But it was if the moment Arik found peace, the Arab-Israeli conflict found a way to crush it. Tension escalated rapidly with Damascus after fourteen Syrian Migs were shot down by Israeli jet fighters. The Egyptians, showing solidarity with Syrian strongman Hafez al-Assad, brought reinforcement to their side of the Suez Canal. Israel now faced a force of many divisions hardly a stone's throw away across the narrow body of water. The Russians, once bitten, twice shy, were unwilling to supply the highly sophisticated arms that Sadat wanted, and in a furious reaction, the Egyptian strongman expelled all the Soviet soldiers and their advisers from his country. The Israeli leaders concluded – and in this they were almost catastrophically wrong – that Sadat was signaling his inability to wage an all-out war with the Jewish state. As it was, Sadat's feint and secret planning with Syria for a coordinated attack had consequences that were grave enough. The attack was planned for the feast of Ramadan, when Muslims around the world were celebrating.

In spite of alarming secret information obtained by the Mossad and a warning from King Hussein that serious moves were afoot, Golda Meir's government waited until October 4, 1973, to mobilize Israel's reserves. On that day, Sharon, even though he was no longer in active service, was called urgently to army headquarters. He was mobilized together with his entire armored division, the 143rd. With war thought to be imminent, all the dusty tactical maps that could be found were pulled out of the desk drawers to help make urgent plans. Sharon, always ready to take on the most ambitious tasks, was prepared to attack and occupy the Arab capitals.

The next day, while all the Jews of the world were marking *Yom Kippur* – the Day of Atonement –, the most sacred day in the Jewish tradition, Egypt and Syria launched a co-ordinated, massive attack on an incredulous Israel. The sheer size of the offensive was without precedent in Middle Eastern history. The Bar-Lev line, like the French Maginot line before the Nazi offensive in 1940, collapsed like a house of cards, as the Egyptian forces ran through it. Sharon's apocalyptic predictions had been unfortunately proven correct. Combat was pitiless. Dayan, referring to the First Temple of Jerusalem – destroyed by the Babylonian King Nebuchadnezzar in 587 B.C. – and to the Second, flattened by the Roman Emperor Titus in 70 AD, openly spoke of the imminent destruction of the Third Temple. It was an evocation of the catastrophic situation faced by the country in the first days of the Yom Kippur War, comparable to the destruction of the Temple and dispersal of the Jews.

But Sharon was not in a talking mood. Without informing his superiors of his plans, he stubbornly went on the offensive, attempting what no one believed could be done, crossing the canal and taking the battle to Egypt. It was Mission Impossible; but after several unsuccessful attempts and heavy losses, his forces established some bridgeheads and crossed the waterway, first in canoes. A raft-borne tank brigade followed quickly in their wake. After a bloody battle that took hundreds of lives, he broke out behind the canal and, like a sly old fox, completely encircled the Egyptian Third Army. Sharon, wounded in the forehead and bandaged, gray hair messed by the hours of sleepless combat and fatigue, eyes red, was still standing, now before the gates of the city of Ismailia, ready to charge into Cairo, hardly one hundred kilometers away. But as in the later First Gulf War, political masters ordered the advance stopped. Cairo was forbidden territory!

Dayan feared the consequences of capturing an important Arab capital. Still, thanks to the determination of General Elazar, the army's operational commander, and the courage of Sharon and his troops, the fortunes of the Kippur War – also known as the October or Ramadan War – took a decisive turn in favor of Israel. Egypt was defeated, a cease-fire agreement was signed, and the Israeli forces disengaged.

The military victory had come at a terrible cost; the Jewish state had never before suffered such grievous losses. A political and psychological earthquake was rocking the soul of the country. Golda Meir and Moshe Dayan were in scalding hot water. Many IDF generals were replaced. As for Sharon, he emerged triumphant from the terrible events, his opinions sought by the international press. Perhaps the most notable interview appeared in the *New York Times* on November 10, 1973. In it, he was publicly unforgiving of the generals' laxism and refusal to annihilate the Egyptian forces, thereby abandoning the opportunity to score a complete victory over the enemies of Israel. The interview provoked an outcry at army headquarters and led to a bitter conflict among the top brass. Sharon, you see, was still in uniform, even if he was in the reserves, and the military were not used to washing their dirty linen in public. No one, his opponents maintained, could allow himself to draw such devastating military and strategic conclusions and set them out for judgment by the entire country. The October War victory, crushing as it was, did not belong to a single general, no matter how important he might be. Sharon seemed to be posturing for political reasons, trying to gain a strategic advantage on the eve of new elections to the Knesset. His adversaries among the general staff would not easily, nor soon, pardon his "betrayal"; the rancor was to remain for years to come.

Then yet another dramatic event occurred: David Ben-Gurion, the founder of Israel, passed away at age eighty-seven. The entire Jewish nation was in mourning, paying tribute to the "old lion," who symbolized, in the minds of many, the soul of a people. A rich page of Israeli history was being turned, and a new chapter being written, a chapter inspired by confidence, in which Arik Sharon, Ben-Gurion's disciple and admirer, would have a significant role to play.

PART TWO

Chapter 5:

The Political Vision

Politics is the art of creating facts, in order to control
– and toy with – events and people.
Beaumarchais

There was notable effervescence among the dozens of reporters, photographers, and cameraman waiting impatiently in the great hall of Beth Sokolov, the media center hardly a stone's throw from the headquarters of the Israeli army. The man they were to interview and film was of course Arik Sharon, former general now, and savior of the nation during the October War.

Wearing a white shirt with rolled-up sleeves over beige pants, Sharon walked decisively to the podium and immediately came to the point. To the journalists and the sea of microphones shoved in his face, he declared, "I have decided to unite all the liberal and Zionist forces in the country and form a united political bloc whose purpose will be to assemble the opposition parties for the coming elections under a single banner."

Sharon, who had proven himself to be a great military strategist, turned out to be only an average speaker. He answered the many questions posed by the reporters, but there was something missing in his responses. The journalists would have liked to know, for example, how, having hardly whet his whistle in the political arena, he felt he could single-handedly unite the splinter opposition parties into a single, structured and solid alliance built around him. Given the facts of Israeli politics, his plan sounded utopian, even somewhat irrational. The next day, the newspapers published unenthusiastic accounts of the press conference; columnists were divided as to the opportunism of the neophyte politician's project. But Sharon moved forward with his plan and was well-positioned on the common electoral list of the Likud, which had been formed as a result of the union of the Herut and Liberal parties.

The January 1974 elections took place, and Likud, with Sharon in its midst, increased its representation in the Knesset by seven seats, but this was not sufficient to dislodge the Labor Party from power. It seemed that neither the evident malfeasance within Labor, nor the earthshaking lapses surrounding the October War had been enough to convince a timorous Israeli electorate to throw the country into the hands of political unknowns. Despite the presence of Sharon the war hero, the Likud had proved unable to attract the necessary votes; Golda Meir and Moshe Dayan continued to govern, at least for the time being.

Sharon the elected Member felt ill at ease in the – to him – foreign world of the Knesset. He sat on the Foreign Affairs and Defense Committee but rarely spoke, and in fact, his parliamentary activity was quite limited. He preferred to keep his mouth closed and put up in silence with the one-note chattering, bored with the "galuti," milieu steeped in the mentality of the European Jewish Diaspora. Sharon was out of step with this ghetto universe of superficial politeness and back-stabbing intrigue. He felt he was from a different place, the world of the Sabra, the peasant soldier, characterized by honesty and forthrightness. Not the world of public stage acting. It would be some time, and after much trying experience, before he learned to faultlessly play the parts required by the many scenarios of Israeli political theatre.

Not quite a year later, Arik resigned from the Knesset, a rare act in any democracy, especially so in Israel. The new Prime Minister, Yitzhak Rabin, offered him the position of personal adviser on security and anti-terrorism, and it was an offer he enthusiastically accepted. He was back in his element now and Rabin, as opposed to some of the other IDF generals, inspired confidence in Sharon. Rabin was, like Arik, a true Sabra and like Sharon, he was a man who was uncomfortable in the political circus of the Knesset, an unpretentious leader devoid of ideological fanaticism. Designating Ariel Sharon had, in Rabin's eyes, two advantages. On the one hand, it would handicap Shimon Peres, the "perennial intriguer," (Rabin's own words); and on the other, Sharon was the ideal man to oversee the delicate relationship with the settlers, especially the fundamentalist *Gush Emunim*.

Rabin, the hero of the Six Day War, had been Israel's ambassador to Washington for three years, a posting that added diplomatic knowledge and *savoir-faire* to his font of military experience. He and Sharon seemed primed to see things eye-to-eye. For eight months – June 1975 to February 1976 – Sharon studied the arcana of Israeli politics from its heart, the Office of the Prime Minister. His own office, out of sight, but right opposite Rabin's, was well situated to receive important visitors and to allow him to take part in meetings with various world leaders. It was during this time that he would acquire a new, broader vision of national and international politics, and travel widely.

Nothing seemed to last long in the roller coaster of Israeli politics, though: Rabin's government soon fell on a non-confidence motion, and new elections were called. Under the circumstances, Sharon felt he could not remain as Rabin's advisor, and, after considerable reflection but little enthusiasm, he threw himself into another election campaign.

The elections were held in early 1977, a year that began with a cascade of scandals unprecedented in the history of Israel. First, a highly-placed official was convicted of defrauding a Swiss bank in which the Rothschilds were involved. Then the Governor of the Bank of Israel was charged with embezzlement; and if that wasn't enough, the Housing Minister committed suicide by blowing his brains out. The climate was unhealthy, the citizenry troubled, and the unease caused by the October War still hung like a dark cloud over the nation.

The Labor Party, never out of power since the creation of Israel, was on the wane, losing its grip on the electorate. More than ever, it seemed, Sharon was in a strong position to move forward with his plans to unite the opposition around him. Theoretically! But in reality, in yet another disappointing move, the nationalist conservatives found Sharon's plan of pulling together all the splinter parties too ambitious, and vetoed it. In response, Sharon created his own party, the *Shlom Tsion* or "Peace be upon Zion" Party.

The public opinion surveys initially gave Sharon's party fifteen seats in the Knesset, but this soon fell to two seats, and with the decline came disenchantment among the party activists. Sharon himself fell into a funk, and seriously considered giving up. His party was new-born, under-funded, and facing well-oiled, well-financed, well-structured, and experienced political machines. Lily, his wife, encouraged him to hold firm, as did many family friends. She reminded him of his own motto, "General Sharon never abandons a project, never admits defeat..."

Unconvinced, and with little conviction, he left for a fund-raising tour of the United States. When the electorate finally spoke, the surveys proved correct. Sharon's party won only two seats. Voters had stuck by their traditional party affiliations, and punished Sharon just as they had previously punished Ben-Gurion, Dayan, and Ezer Weizman in similar circumstances. But the ground in the Land of the Jews had shaken, and Sharon's defeat was under the radar of a larger event, the first Conservative victory in the history of Israel.

In what was called a "revolution in the annals of the Jewish state," on Tuesday, May 17, 1977, the political hurricane struck and swept into Opposition the Labor Party, which had run Israel since 1948. Menachem Begin was the new, all-powerful leader of Israel, and with his accession to power, a new chapter would begin in the political career of Arik Sharon.

Begin appointed this son of the Russian agronomist Shmuel Scheinermann, Minister of Settlements and National Development. It was a dream come true for the man nick-named "the bulldozer," and now, in charge of the Israel Lands Administration, he dusted off his detailed plans for new housing and settlements in Judea and Samaria (otherwise known as the West Bank), Gaza, and the Golan Heights. At Cabinet meetings he underlined the strategic and purely military importance of his plan, which combined the "Allon plan" (In 1969, Ygal Allon, head of the *Palmah* before Independence, proposed a compromise peace with the Palestinians based on territorial concessions by Israel, and no retreat from the 1949 armistice borders. On a March, 1972 state visit to Israel, then-President of France François Mitterrand called the plan "the most realistic, global, and pragmatic" chance for peace.) – which insured an Israeli presence in the Jordan Valley – with the construction of roads and a new residential and industrial belt on the hills overlooking the Jerusalem region and surrounding coastal plain.

Encouraged ideologically by Begin, and spiritually by the National Religious Party or *Mafdal*, Sharon launched a massive program of construction in the West Bank and the Jerusalem surround, easily obtaining the budgets and authorizations he needed to move it forward. The country became a gigantic construction site, the pace of work accelerating as Israel withdrew from the Sinai Peninsula. Over the course of the next few years, Sharon criss-crossed the entire region many times and personally supervised the construction of new roads and towns. Sixty-four new settlements were added to the twenty-seven previously authorized by the Labor governments. To create a counter-weight to the swelling birth rate among Israeli Arabs in Galilee, Sharon authorized fifty-six new settlements in the North, many of which were built on the Golan Heights. Thousands of settlers moved into comfortable homes and enviable conditions of life here, especially since "the bulldozer" had ensured the communities came equipped with a well-developed infrastructure.

It was a dream come true for General Sharon, as well as for Sharon the Sabra. The right of Jews to live within their historic frontiers was now compatible with the security and the defense of the country's urban population. Menachem Begin, who was deep into peace negotiations with the Egyptians, gave Sharon a free hand until Washington warned against accelerating the building of new settlements in the Territories. In fact, satellite photos in hand, the Jimmy Carter presidency demanded a freeze on construction. Begin acceded, and in response, proposed Palestinian autonomy. Moshe Dayan – Minister of Foreign Affairs – and Ezer Weizman – Minister of Defense – encouraged Begin, but exasperated by the snail's pace of events, eventually left the government, fed up with their advice being ignored. Negotiations bogged down over Begin's refusal to broaden the areas of Palestinian autonomy he was ready to accept. Elections were – again ! – approaching and Begin the parliamentarian had no intention of losing the electorate, or power. The apparently inevitable crisis looming with both Egypt and now the United States seemed graver with the departures of Dayan and Weizman, and there was a real risk of the government falling.

The campaign was rough-and-tumble. Begin, retaining power but politically weakened and personally ill, gave the Defense portfolio to Sharon, and the Foreign Affairs portfolio to Yitzhak Shamir. Begin, who had a sarcastic penchant, had one day publicly commented that General Sharon was a man quite capable of sending in his tanks to surround the Prime Minister and his Cabinet. It was an offensive statement and Sharon would long resent Begin for the insult. But personal feelings were left aside: Begin named Sharon Minister of Defense because he felt that Arik was probably the only man in the Cabinet capable of the courage and brutality required to expel the settlers from the Sinai peninsula, and flatten the desert towns of Ophira and Yamit, all required under the circumstances of the Israeli retreat from the Sinai.

The "hawks" of Israel were now in charge of an intransigent and harsh policy. The irony of Sharon – who had been denied the position of Army Chief of Staff – finding himself the overnight head of the all-powerful Tsahal with a free hand to implement strategic plans he had himself developed and which had long-since ripened - was lost on few. Once he had removed the Sinai settlements, Arik Sharon acted on his own, according to three major principles.

Firstly, military and civilian implantations had to be shored up in the Territories, especially in Judea and Samaria, and he authorized the construction of two hundred thirty new settlements in the Territories and in Galilee in less than seven years.

Secondly, a strategic agreement needed to be struck with Washington, and he signed the first accord on military and strategic cooperation with the Reagan administration in November 1981.

And finally, the Palestinian question had to be settled, by force if necessary.

His vision required, in the short run, evicting Syria and the PLO from Lebanon and allowing the Lebanese Christians to govern that country, then, creating a Palestinian state in Jordan that could absorb the far-flung refugees. The March, 1979 Peace Treaty with Egypt and the wiggle room it gave seemed to offer Sharon a propitious moment to settle accounts with some other Arab states. Israeli aviation was sent to take out Saddam Hussein's Osirak nuclear reactor near Baghdad on June 6, 1981, stifling the dictator's taste for atomic weapons. Shortly thereafter, war broke out between secular Iraq and its Shiite neighbor, Iran, temporarily restricting the trouble-making abilities of both. But the Western democracies were facing crises of their own, as Argentina seized Britain's Falkland Islands in the South Atlantic, and war broke out between the U.K. - governed by Margaret Thatcher's Conservative Party - and the military dictatorship ruling Argentina. A more serious problem seemed the Polish revolt against the Communist government. Led by Lech Walesa of the Solidarity union movement, from the Gdansk shipyards, this was a movement that had the potential of seeing the Red Army invade Poland and touch off a conflict with likely grave - and certainly unpredictable - consequences between the Soviet Union and the NATO Alliance.

Chapter 6

The Lebanon Syndrome

King Solomon, having finished the construction of the Temple, brought in panels of cedar from Lebanon for the inner walls.
Kings 1, verse 6.

On November 26, 1981, Menachem Begin slipped in his bath-tub and broke his hip. In great pain, he was urgently brought to the Hadassah Jerusalem Hospital, where he convalesced while closely following the details of political events. His Cabinet ministers came to meet with him in his hospital room. Each morning, Yehiel Kadishai, Begin's loyal secretary, brought the state papers he needed to read, and documents he needed to sign. Begin read all the newspapers, and listened to the news bulletins on state radio, The Voice of Israel. But his morale was at a low. His wife Aliza was ill, Moshe Dayan had just passed away, and Egyptian President Sadat had been assassinated, shot by Muslim extremists. The future of the Egyptian regime seemed tenuous, and if it fell, the Middle East could teeter over into a state of war once more.

The Sinai had been definitively returned to Egypt, but Begin wanted to show his people that there would be no giving back the occupied territories, nor the Golan Heights, and especially not the West Bank, "cradle of the Patriarchs."

He turned up at the Knesset in a wheel chair, in considerable pain, and asked to speak. Everyone was astonished when he immediately called for a vote to officially annex the Golan. There was no debate, no discussion on the motion; none of his allies had been advised of his intentions, not even Sharon, who was in fact favorable to the decision.

This was an obviously provocative act that was quickly condemned throughout the world: Damascus strongman Hafez al-Assad threatened a new war to recover the territory he had lost during the Six Day War. Syria, which had been physically present in Lebanon since the beginning of the Civil War in that country, ratcheted up its pressure on Lebanese Christians, who immediately turned to Israel for political and logistic assistance.

Already, in 1976, as adviser to Yitzhak Rabin, Sharon had fiercely opposed letting Syrian troops get a foothold in Lebanon. In fact, he proposed sending Israeli warplanes in to thwart any incursion on the part of Damascus, but Rabin, pressured by Jimmy Carter, who saw Syria as a part of the stability equation in the area, and by French president Valery Giscard d'Estaing and Prime Minister Jacques Chirac, backed away from that idea.

After some vicious inter-communal fighting in Beirut, a tacit agreement between al-Assad and Arafat was made in May 1976, in Ryad, Saudi Arabia, during a meeting of Arab leaders. Arafat promised non-intervention in internal Lebanese affairs. But the Lebanese Christians were panic-stricken, and turned to Israel and Sharon for help defending themselves. It was not the first time they sought aid from Tel-Aviv, either. Right after the civil war broke out, Lebanese Christian leaders close to former President Camille Chamoun and the Gemayel clan came to the Israeli Embassy in Paris for a discrete meeting. They needed arms to combat the Palestinians, who had set up a virtual state within a state – Fatahland – in the South, near the border with Israel. Six months later, an Israeli delegation landed at the port city of Jounieh, north of Beirut, in the heart of Christian Lebanon. Among the Israelis were IDF officers and Mossad agents, whose role was to prepare an historic public meeting between Yitzhak Rabin and Camille Chamoun. Chamoun, who ruled Lebanon from 1952 through 1958, now presided over the Christian Lebanese Front, and ran the Tiger Militia. Since then, despite the many meetings with Pierre Gemayel and his sons Amine and Bashir – who subsequently died in a car bombing before acceding to the Lebanese presidency – contacts with the Chamoun clan have also continued without interruption.

In 1978, on March 11, an Israeli bus had been bombed on the Haifa-Tel-Aviv coast road. The toll was heavy, thirty-five dead, and eighty-two injured. Israel responded with the Litani operation that created a security zone of some seven hundred square kilometers, running from the village of Shaba in the east, right to the west coast of the country. Major Haddad, a Maronite Christian, commanded this zone and was tasked with maintaining security for the Israeli villages near the Lebanese border. The move reinforced Israel's relationship with the Christians of Southern Lebanon and the zone served as a staging area for attacks on PLO positions.

With the blessing of General Rafael Eitan – nicknamed Rafoul (no relation to the author) – Sharon established fruitful contacts with the Christians, and following detailed Mossad planning, he landed by helicopter on the Lebanese coast, escorted by Israeli fighter jets and Naval units. It was late at night, and combats were raging all around when Arik landed at Jounieh where Bashir Gemayel, the military commander of the Falangists, waited impatiently. They left in a convoy of armored Mercedes-Benz limousines for a working dinner at a secure villa, followed by a contingent of security guards and rough-looking armed "gorillas." During the meeting, Sharon put an official stamp on the friendly relationship with the Christian militiamen, and prepared a joint operation against the PLO. Dinner was followed by a tour of "Beirut by night," and Arik, dazzled by the beauty of the city, flew back to Israel for a debriefing by Begin. He forcefully set out his impressions of what had just taken place, and what might take place, to the inner Cabinet, seemingly in complete charge of the agenda.

In 1982, on February 16, surrounded by an impermeable wall of secrecy, Bashir Gemayel met with Menachem Begin at his Balfour Street Jerusalem residence. The operations proposed by Sharon were given the green light, and emboldened, Arik began preparations for a broad military action against the PLO and the Syrian presence in Lebanon. General Eitan, bent over the yellowing maps from army headquarters, pondered all the possibilities, including the capture of Beirut itself. All that was needed was a provocation at the right moment, a reason to launch the attack.

Washington needed to come on board, but was hesitant, deciding instead to send an emissary, Phillip Habib – a man of Lebanese descent – to calm things down. But despite his fruitful meetings with al-Assad and Arafat, and despite their promises of a cease fire, the attacks on Israel continued, causing many civilian casualties. Jerusalem was in no way going to tolerate these flagrant and systematic attacks on Israeli citizens and southern Lebanese Christians; matters were made worse by the Paris assassination of Mossad agent Yacov Barsimantov on April 3, 1982, and by a Palestinian attack in Athens.

Not three weeks later, in a patent warning, Israel sent in its air force to bomb PLO bases in the south of Lebanon. But tensions remained high, with attacks and violations of the supposed cease-fire accord more and more frequent. Events were now quickly moving forward. On May 16 – a Sunday – Ariel Sharon briefed the Israeli Cabinet on his military plan, code-named *Oranim*, "pines" in Hebrew.

Its immediate objective was to shield Israeli border villages from PLO artillery fire, which meant pushing the Palestinians forty kilometers away from the line, outside the range of their Katyusha rockets. Debate within Cabinet was highly animated, and many, including Housing Minister David Levy, demanded more precise information. It was clear that *Oranim* would result in an inevitable confrontation with Syria, especially in the Bekaa Valley, and could lead to a new war. Sharon was obviously perplexed, and replied honestly, "There is no possible way to guarantee that there will be no Syrian intervention."

Levy obviously rattled, responded, saying, "So we're knowingly heading towards a new conflict which will set the whole Middle East on fire, is that what you mean? Don't you think we ought to distinguish between our permanent war on Palestinian terror in South Lebanon and full-scale war with Syria?"

Sharon's reply was forthright. "Well, attacking the PLO terrorist camps will serve as a severe warning to Damascus, whose army is in the Bekaa, and Syria, anyway, controls most of Lebanon."

Levy went on, "But are we capable of convincing the Syrians to voluntarily withdraw from the country?"

"Only by force of arms, David."

At this point, Menachem Begin intervened and ended the discussion: "The cease-fire in Lebanon must be absolute, and so must our response to its violation. The PLO is an abject organization of terrorists. Every single day it threatens to destroy Israel and kill Jews all over the world. There is no way we can live under the threats of these "bastards." They're nothing more than two-legged monsters, and we will not accept any arbitrary interpretations of the cease-fire. No free nation can remain indifferent to such threats, and every state has the right of response in the protection of its citizens."

One week later, on May 24, 1982, Sharon left for Washington and urgent talks with Alexander Haig, Ronald Reagan's Secretary of State, and Caspar Weinberger, Secretary of Defense. They were both cool to his plans as he set them out. The United States was not in a mood for dealing with a new crisis in the Middle East, and preoccupied with events in Poland and tension with the U.S.S.R., neither desired to include attacks on Jews in Europe as violations of a cease-fire that was meant in their view to apply only to the Israel-Arab borders. Sharon insisted that there was an unshakeable osmosis between Israel and the Jews of the diaspora, and in the end, brought Haig on board, but the general, always a prudent man, sent a letter to Menachem Begin demanding patience, and cautioning against actions that could escalate the conflict throughout the region. Begin was outraged at the condescending tone of the letter. He responded in the dry, patriotic, and undiplomatic style he was known to adopt whenever the safety of Jews was called into question. It was a regrettable error of judgement, for, far from being a distant foreign leader mouthing hypocritical lessons in political morality, Alexander Haig was an unconditional friend of Israel, and an admirer of Tsahal and its brave generals; a leading member of this elite group was Arik Sharon.

Despite the unabated tension in the field, and waiting for events to move forward, Sharon flew to Europe in early June. Journalists were informed that he was on a secret mission. But in fact, he and his children accompanied his wife Lily on a trip to Romania, where she was received as an honored guest. Lily wanted to visit the land of her ancestors, and took her husband and their two boys to Brasov, the town where she was born. The trip was emotion-filled, especially when they visited the Brasov synagogue and the house in which Lily spent her first years.

It was perhaps not the ideal moment to leave on personal business. Sharon's critics castigated him for a lack of judgement. Surely there were better occasions than this to traipse off for an epicurean and nostalgic tour of Ceaucescu's Romania?

In any case, two days later, while Sharon was still abroad, Shlomo Argov, the Israeli Ambassador to London, was grievously wounded in an assassination attempt openly claimed by the PLO. The British arrested three agents of the Abu-Nidal group, who were convicted and sentenced to thirty-five years in prison, although the unit's leader, Naef-el-Rousan, benefited from early release for "good behavior." Ambassador Argov remained in a coma for twenty years before finally passing away on February 23, 2003.

There had to be a response to this heinous act. Not wishing to wait for Sharon to return to Jerusalem, Begin called a Cabinet meeting to decide on a reprisal. It would be inadmissible for Israel to do nothing when one of their diplomats had been gunned down by Palestinian thugs. A forceful reaction was called for, to head off further assassination attempts that could take place – who knows? – in Paris, or in Athens perhaps. Rafael Eitan, Israel's Chief of Staff, proposed an air force attack on the PLO infrastructure in the suburbs of Beirut, and on their military camps in the south of Lebanon. Begin signed off on the proposal and the attacks took place. PLO response was to immediately shell Israeli villages in Galilee. Artillery duels went on throughout the Sabbath. Meanwhile, Sharon was still in Bucharest, out of touch. But he took the first plane he could back to Israel, and headed straight to Tel-Aviv, where he requested a full briefing from the Chief of the general staff. Once he was brought up to date on the state of operations, he went right to Jerusalem and a Cabinet meeting held exceptionally at sundown on the Sabbath.

His intentions were clear: he wanted the to Cabinet to immediately authorize the Peace in Galilee operation. The picture he painted for members of the Prime Minister's Office was an alarming one. The Syrians, he told them, were preparing for a broad new war. And the PLO was feverously organizing to intensify the bombardment of Israeli villages in Galilee. Terrorist activity was unprecedented. Tunnels were being dug, underground shelters and bunkers too, all out of reach of Israeli air force attack capability. The situation required troops on the ground, but it was to be an intervention limited in time and in size. The surgical strike would go no further than forty kilometers into Lebanon, and last at the most two or three days. Begin and his ministers, though enraged by the Palestinian attacks, were not military men, and the many little green and red arrows on the army maps meant little to them. They found it difficult to distinguish between the forces in the field, and harder still to fathom how the operation might evolve.

In the end, as was customary, the Cabinet simply instructed Tsahal to proceed with the mission, and keep losses to a minimum. There was little taste for a polemic on the details of military and strategic questions, since the majority of its members were not experts in these fields. Begin and his Ministers were simply not able to always master the confidential documents provided by Israeli Intelligence and hence, unable to micromanage the generals. When the vote was taken, only one hand was raised in opposition to the plan. Yitzhak Berman, Minister of Energy and Infrastructure, proposed delaying the operation so that they might order a serious study of all possible military and diplomatic consequences...He was greeted with hoots and laughter, a lightweight compared to Sharon.

Generals Sharon and Eitan were happy with the green light given to their plan by the Cabinet. They had shared a long history as paratroopers, evolved in similar ways in Israel's recent conflicts, and made an excellent team, respectful of one another, but also maintaining some critical distance. General Eitan was a frank and straightforward man, of the rough-and-ready school, whose life ended tragically in November 2004, when at age seventy-five, he was carried off by a wave on the breakwater of the port of Ashdod. Not one to be intimidated by Sharon, he would always have the last word; it was often a crude one.

The two generals had long been working on an ambitious plan that echoed the Suez Campaign of 1956. This "grand operation" was to start by a major Israeli landing at Jounieh, from whence the Tsahal troops would advance to the South and join up with other infantry and motorized forces in a pincer movement. At first, the plan drawn up by Sharon and Eitan was limited in scope, but then they received the OK from Begin to enlarge the zone within which military operations would take place. It was a significant asset, enabling them to scale their plans and add flexibility to the parameters of the action.

Begin informed the leaders of the opposition of the imminent military action. Shimon Peres and Yitzhak Rabin gave their approval, but asked that care be taken not to provoke the Syrians. Begin gave his word on that, and Sharon flew that same evening to the headquarters of the Northern Command, to give final instructions to his field commanders.

The next day, at ten in the morning, watched by astounded United Nations UNIFIL forces – the "blue helmets" – three Israeli tank columns crossed the border into Lebanon. International reaction was swift and vigorous in condemning the move. The United Nations Security Council demanded an "immediate and unconditional" retreat of the Israeli troops. In Paris, French President François Mitterrand, presiding over the Summit Meeting of western leaders, was forced to abandon his well-prepared agenda to deal with the crisis. Even U.S. President Ronald Reagan tried to convince Jerusalem to back off. All in vain. Begin would hear no talk of retreat, convinced he was on a sacred mission to guarantee peace in Galilee for forty years to come.

One of the harsh truths about military conflict is that you can always know when a war will start, but never when it will end. History is sadly replete with examples of this truism. The Lebanon operation, initially limited in scope, quickly escalated into a total war with Syria and the PLO. Far from lasting mere days, it went on for more than three months, going well beyond its announced objectives and carried with it grave consequences for Israel itself. The fighting with the PLO, complicated by the topography and demography of the area, was bloodier than predicted. Population density was high, with many different minorities living one on top of the other, and the pace of the fighting consequently slowed to a crawl, causing heavy losses among the IDF forces. In fact, from the date of the initial invasion in June 1982 until October 11 of the same year, Israel suffered three hundred sixty-eight fatalities and two thousand three hundred eighty-three wounded.

On June 12, 1982, Israeli forces besieged Beirut. For the first time since the founding of Israel, an Arab capital was occupied by Jewish tanks. The French were outraged, with their Foreign Minister Claude Cheysson in a state of panic. The Russians, despite Ronald Reagan's attempt to calm them down, considered the situation to be extremely serious. The "limited operation" had taken a very bad turn indeed, and there was a serious risk of it degenerating into a larger war.

Sharon was at the head of his army, on a hilltop overlooking Beirut, watching through field-glasses as the action unfolded. His stubborn preference – in the light of the order to co-ordinate with the Lebanese Christian Phalangists and his rage at the double game that came with this dependence – was to command alone as solitary master of the situation. The Israeli government was not always kept informed as events evolved. Nor was Prime Minister Begin. It was a way for Sharon of using his own judgement without officially disobeying orders.

There was much hatred in the Beirut air. The Christians despised the Palestinians and wanted nothing less than to expel them from Lebanon with the help and the benediction of Tsahal. Jerusalem sought to avoid this trap, and made a clear-cut distinction between terrorists and refugees: only men under arms were to be legitimate targets. Refugees constituted a humanitarian problem whose solution could only be achieved by diplomatic means. For the more than a quarter of a million Palestinians living in the squalor of the camps and the ghettos of Beirut, often with not even a roof over their heads, it was a very tangible problem indeed – and one needing an urgent solution.

Sharon ordered his forces to shell armed Palestinian positions and to try and keep tabs on the comings and goings of Yasser Arafat. Elite snipers were put in place and readied to take out the head of the PLO as soon as a clear shot could be had. But then Begin, who had originally agreed to the elimination of the Palestinian, changed his mind at the last second, and demanded instead that France and the United States somehow arrange to evacuate all the PLO fighters from Beirut – with Arafat first in line.

It was not a vision Sharon shared. He wanted to settle the Palestinian problem in his own way, and for good, by liquidating all the PLO combatants. He still remembered the encirclement of the Egyptian Army during the October War, and the consequences of having succumbed to international pressure – and pressure from Israel's politicians too – not to carry the fight all the way to Cairo. There now existed a unique opportunity to shake things up the in the Middle East for a long time to come, and he – the man some called Israel's Napoleon – was uniquely placed to modify the strategic and political situation in the interests of the Jewish state. He had a global strategic vision that included the entire Arab/Islamic bloc of countries, from Mauritania to Pakistan that aimed at countering Soviet expansionism in the region by empowering – with the help of the Americans – moderate and pro-Western regimes in those nations.

Eliminating Arafat and his men under arms could pave the way to an equitable settlement of the Israel-Arab conflict, with Jordan as Palestinian homeland playing a model role. In Beirut, meanwhile, there seemed to be no end to the raging revenge killings and political assassinations. On September 14, 1982, Bashir Gemayel, head of the Lebanese Christian Phalangists, was blown up in a successful assassination in the middle of Beirut's Christian zone, almost within sight of Israeli troops and tanks. With all the "what if?" scenario planning, no one had ever considered the possibility that such a powerful and well-protected man could be taken out. Jerusalem had hoped to soon see him as president of a new, free, and democratic Lebanon. But the assassination, ordered by Damascus as a move against Israel, made an already complex situation explosive. All of Sharon's well-laid plans began to fall apart, collapsing like a house of cards. Serious doubts were now raised about his audacious move into Lebanon, which in the light of events now seemed "too ambitious." Had he really thought through all of the possible hypotheses and taken into account the "powder keg" mix of the local minorities with their conflicting interests, weaknesses, customs, and whims?

Within seventy-two hours the calls for revenge made themselves heard throughout the suburban Beirut Palestinian refugee camps of Shatilah and Sabrah. In a fury, the Christian Phalangists led by Elie Hobeika committed a savage and indiscriminate massacre of four hundred men, women, and children. The Israeli commanders were in a state of shock, dumbfounded at the unrestrained killings. According to a Lebanese witness, an enraged Sharon confronted Hobeika, screaming, "You were not supposed to do this. I never asked you to massacre people in the camps. If I had wanted this to happen I would have gone in myself with my tanks. Believe me, you will pay for this![2]

Israeli public opinion was in consternation. The Labor Party opposition cynically chose to exploit the tragedy for partisan political reasons. Large protest demonstrations were organized in Tel-Aviv to demand the resignation of Begin and his government. For the first time, Sharon was called an "assassin," while all the while in Beirut, combat was ongoing, and Israeli soldiers falling. The wave of protest, though, went on, unprecedented, recalling America during the Vietnam War. Sharon had to face this new front, for the most part, on his own. He was frustrated and full of indignation at the abominable calumny and out and out lies of the stories and political cartoons that filled the Israeli and international airwaves and newspapers. Menachem Begin, under overwhelming pressure from public opinion, denied that Tsahal or Sharon had any responsibility for the Beirut massacre, but felt compelled to order a judicial inquiry to ascertain the facts of the Sabrah and Shatilah killings. The inquiry concluded that Israel had no direct responsibility for the tragedy, but it was nonetheless severely critical of Begin's government. Sharon, in the hot seat, hired legal counsel to defend himself from the accusations against him, but in 1983, lost his case, and in March of that year was forced to resign.

"Peace in Galilee," which had as its military objective the destruction of the PLO command structure, was an unmitigated success: Arafat and his troops were tossed out of Beirut. The political objective of the operation, on the other hand, failed. There was to be no new, moderate, and pro-Western regime in Lebanon. It was clear that Arik Sharon was a brilliant military strategist and a valiant general. But it was as evident that his ambitious plans could not be realized by simple force of arms. In the complex quicksand of the Middle East, nothing could be accomplished without a political settlement. It was a bitter lesson about which Sharon would have occasion to long ponder. The Lebanese adventure would haunt him through his years wandering in the Israeli political wasteland.

Note

[2] Quoted in *Dans l'Ombre d'Hobeika,* by Robert M. Hatem, page 59. Jean Picollec éditeur, Paris, 2003.

Chapter 7

The Wasteland

How wonderful it is to give orders, even if only to a herd of sheep.
Miguel de Cervantes

It was eleven-thirty in the morning, and the coalition ministers, gathered in the Cabinet meeting room, were impatiently awaiting the arrival of the government leader. Finally, Menachem Begin arrived, wearing a dark suit and white shirt open at the collar, tieless, accompanied by his secretary. His pace was slow, his body bent over his walking stick. The Prime Minister was no longer the orator whose speeches made the walls of the Knesset tremble, the magnetic leader so admired by his supporters, so feared by his adversaries. Menachem Begin had become a tired, sick old man, disgusted by the political life he had once cherished. The death of his wife Aliza and the quagmire of the Lebanese adventure had worn him out. That he had become a mere shadow of himself was obvious to all, an awful and unwelcome development.

The members of his Cabinet stood and saluted him with deference; he merely nodded an acknowledgement then everyone sat down, acutely aware that their leader was suffering terribly. Begin adjusted his thick-lensed glasses that had a habit of slipping down his nose, and in a weak and broken voice, got right to the point:

"I have decided to resign. My decision is irrevocable. I would ask you as a courtesy not to try and make me change my mind. It would be useless. I have thought long and hard about this, and have come to the conclusion that I can no longer govern as before. I can't take it any more. I must leave. From the bottom of my heart I thank you for your long support. Thank you. Now please do not disturb yourselves further on my account."

And with that stunning declaration, Begin rose from his chair, leaning on his cane, and, accompanied by his faithful secretary Yehiel Kadishai, left the room. A solemn silence fell over the room like an omen casting a doomful spell. Menachem Begin would never again set foot in this chamber where he, like his predecessors, had taken such important, crucial, historical decisions. This is where the future of the nation had been so often played out, and now one of the main actors was abruptly exiting the stage. The curtain had come down, and in dramatic fashion.

Everyone awaited the next act, but not impassively. The elbowing in the corridors of power was brusque, and energetic, the challenge weighty. Yitzhak Shamir and David Levy seemed primed for the job, each claiming to be best positioned and most able at governing the country. The political battle was on; it was rough-and-tumble, and at times disgracefully base, with low blows in abundance.

Sharon stood in the wings, watching the cockfight. He had decided to support Shamir -- who would win out in the end - but kept his counsel for the moment, observing events and waiting for an opportune moment to weigh in. Hurt and humiliated by the mess the Lebanese invasion had turned into, he had no intention of losing another political round. So he played a waiting game until he could confront his own adversaries at a time and place to his advantage. For months, damage control was his main preoccupation. He intended to shore up his tarnished image and expose the accusations still being made about him as unfounded. He crisscrossed the country seeking support, especially among members of Likud; sued *Time Magazine* for libel - and easily won –; and demanded a counter-enquiry into the way the Lebanese war was prosecuted. It was a time when he struggled furiously to clear his name and recover both his honor and the prestige he once enjoyed.

The political fury helped plunge Israel into a deep economic crisis, with inflation running at four hundred per cent. Early elections became inevitable: millions of dollars were still being poured into the settlement program, and Lebanon was sucking up one million dollars a day, while the country was in a state of virtual bankruptcy with a foreign debt cresting the forty billion dollar level. It was a real dog's breakfast.

More and more Israelis were turning to extremism. The police had discovered and dismantled a new "Jewish Resistance" network that had planned to attack Israeli Arabs and blow up the Dome of the Rock, also known as the Mosque of Omar, in Jerusalem, Twenty-two Jewish fanatics were arrested and the country was slack-jawed.

The war in Lebanon raged on with tragic losses, even after Israeli troops redeployed to the Chouf mountains. In Saida, seventy-five soldiers were killed in an accidental natural-gas explosion at the Tsahal Northern Command headquarters. In Beirut, two hundred forty-one U.S. Marines died along with sixty French soldiers, in truck bomb attacks on their barracks in the fall of 1983.

On November 23, 1983, the Yitzhak Shamir government decided to free four thousand seven hundred Palestinians in exchange for six Israeli POWs in a delicate operation overseen by the French. The price was heavy, for some of the freed prisoners went right back into terrorism, the most spectacular example of which took place on April 12, 1984, in the middle of the election campaign. Four terrorists took control of a bus on the Tel-Aviv-Ashkelon road. A female soldier on board was shot. Tsahal attacked the bus, and killed two of the Palestinians. The other two died during a harsh interrogation by Shin Beth, the Israeli intelligence service. Somehow, a photographer was able to snap a picture of the dead terrorists, and despite military censorship, the photograph was published. In the wake of the scandal, a commission of enquiry was established, resulting in many middle-level Shin Beth officers losing their jobs. Avrahom Shalom, the head of Shin Beth, was forced to resign.

The July 23, 1984 elections gave comfort to no one. Despite the departure of Begin, the Lebanon misadventure, and the economic crisis, Shimon Peres and the Labor Party were unable to elect enough members to the Knesset to form a government on their own, even with the usual splinter-party coalition alliances in play. Things had reached an impasse, and Sharon, looking at the situation, felt very strongly that a national unity government was the only solution to the problem.

He met with Shimon Peres for extended discussions. The two men had known each other for many years, and despite political and personality differences, there was mutual respect between them. Sharon had a strong card to play: as a former member of the Mapai – the Labor Party – he was a favorite of Peres' spiritual father, David Ben-Gurion. An expert strategist and tactician, the blustery general was always ready, in complicated situations, to use his abilities in the "interests of the nation." Peres was won over by Arik's analysis, and the two worked out a power sharing plan to govern Israel, based on a rotating primeministership.

Sharon was enthusiastic at the accord, and ran the plan by Shamir, who for his part was less than ecstatic. As new head of Likud, he was naturally suspicious of Peres, and reticent to move in this direction, but in the end, he ceded to Sharon's arguments. Arik the "bulldozer" had once again carried the day.

Shimon Peres thus became Prime Minister of Israel for two years, beginning on Friday, September 14, 1984. Shamir would automatically succeed him at the expiration of his mandate. The arrangement satisfied Sharon: his advice had been heeded, he was finally taken seriously by the leaders of both the Israeli Left and Right, and he was now the official point man on national consensus. His presence in government was now assured, in the greater interests of Israel.

For six years, he acted as Minister of Trade and Commerce. During that time he worked hard to help create and expand Israeli industry, and set up factories all over the country, including the territories. He signed a free trade agreement with the United States, and traveled widely. Many African states renewed diplomatic relations with Israel thanks to military and agricultural cooperation agreements Sharon signed, and took steps to implement. Even Egypt – initially reticent – accepted, in the end, General Sharon's good offices.

The enemy who had first crossed the Sinai Peninsula and then the Suez Canal in canoes during war-time to eventually encircle and capture the Egyptian Army, was now received with full honors in Cairo. A special plane was placed at his disposal and he flew over the expanse of the country, all the way to the Sudanese border. Concerned as ever with Israel's need for water, he visited the gigantic Aswan Dam, which had been built by the Soviets during the Nasser regime.

His generous offer of Israeli expertise in agriculture, though, proved a difficult nut to crack, despite the agreement he made with Youssef Walli, the Egyptian Minister of Agriculture. There was a lot of hostility among the Egyptian *fellahin* to the idea of Israeli advisers; cooperation with the Zionists, against whom the government had preached hatred for so many years, was a delicate matter. But the minister promised progress: Israeli know-how could be used for the betterment of Egypt.

At the end of each day's work, Sharon was in the habit of telephoning his mother, Vera – whose common-sense pragmatism he greatly appreciated – to get news and listen to her wise counsel. One evening, he enthusiastically recounted his memorable side-trip to the Valley of the Kings.

"I could not have imagined how grandiose, how magnificent it is. I tried to decrypt some of the hieroglyphics, but it was impossible.

And yet, it was our people who built the pyramids. I only wish you could have seen with your own eyes the human warmth with which I was welcomed. I was thinking, a few years ago, I was close to this place with my troops, fighting them. And now, we have signed an agreement on agricultural co-operation. Who could have foreseen this?"

Sharon's mother's response was of a typically practical nature: "Son, don't be fooled by appearances. Be yourself, don't believe in promises. Everything that glitters is not gold, and flowery words are not always followed by acts in kind. The hardest thing in the world is to bridge the gap between promises and actions."

On May 13, 1988, Vera Scheinermann passed away at age eighty-eight. Until her last breath, this strong-willed woman refused to be known as "Arik's mother." She was buried in a private plot in her village of Kfar Malal. Her words though, lived on in Sharon's mind, and he would meditate on their wisdom each time he faced a difficult situation. Vera Scheinermann had always played an important role in Arik's life. She had instilled him with a strong will, and influenced his most crucial decisions. If he had found the strength to follow a political career and persevere in the face of the swirling winds and currents of Israeli politics, it was in no small measure thanks to her. Her death was a significant blow.

During the post-Lebanese war period, Sharon stayed out of the spotlight, but was active in matters of defense. He expressed his opinions in Cabinet meetings but avoided making waves, leaving Shamir, Peres and Rabin to govern while he concentrated on running his own department, obtaining both political and budgetary approval for his new projects.

He especially wanted to gain sympathy among the Likud members, who constituted his future bastion of support. The Lebanese syndrome was still omnipresent in the minds of Israelis, and the majority of voters were still hesitant about handing the defense of the nation to an adventurer. Frustrated, Sharon felt an imperative need to regain the confidence of his people.

Opportunities were plentiful: he was handed the Housing portfolio, and the Chair of the Ministerial Commission on Immigration and Integration of new immigrants. He planned an airlift, notably, out of the Sudan, which brought thousands of Ethiopian Falasha Jews to the country. It was an extraordinary feat, put together in great detail by the Mossad that resulted in welcoming home the descendants of the tribe of Dan that had been thought to have vanished thousands of years earlier. Moreover, after Mikhail Gorbachev's *Perestroika* changed the U.S.S.R. for good, more than 570,000 Soviet Jews succeeded in emigrating to Israel. Sharon, who spoke a little Russian learned from his parents, quickly found the right tone with these newcomers, and helped them to successfully assimilate into Israeli society. In fact, at a later date, Arik Sharon would be the first Israeli Prime Minister to officially visit Moscow. In less than eighteen months, Sharon had broken all historic records, building 144,000 new apartments and rehabbing twenty-two thousand apartment buildings. The pace of immigration from Russia and immigrant integration into Israel continued to intensify until 1992. During that period, more than one million Soviet Jews were able to settle in "the land of milk and honey."

On November 25, 1987, a Palestinian terrorist flew into Israel on a glider, landing in an Israeli Army camp, and killed six soldiers. There was stupefaction in the country, but the Palestinians felt encouraged to increase their attacks on Tsahal. Several days later, an Israeli truck collided with a Palestinian taxi in the Gaza strip. Four Palestinian civilians were killed, and rumor spread quickly that the incident had been a planned Israeli retaliation for the glider affair. The rumor was baseless, but it served as a linchpin for widespread demonstrations, which quickly turned into a veritable uprising: the first *Intifada*.

Israel possessed the means to break the back of the uprising. Sharon, recalling his anti-terror struggle in Gaza, counseled a forceful policy, but Yitzhak Rabin, who was Defense Minister, over-ruled that idea and issued strict orders to Tsahal: only in cases of self-defense could soldiers open fire. Judaic values and the rules of democracy were maintained in the face of illegal acts in which the Palestinians did not hesitate to use women and children as front-line shields. The balance, and the mission, were extremely delicate. Arafat, from his refuge in Tunis – where he had lived since the summer of 1983 – watched as the uprising grew, unable to control the crowds. Washington attempted to calm things down, but was ineffective, and could hardly remain stolid as images of "the war of stones" captured the imagination of television watchers around the world. George Schultz, U.S. Secretary of State, proposed a plan aimed at the establishment of a full peace agreement at an international conference where Israel and a joint Jordanian-Palestinian delegation would negotiate face to face.

Arafat's PLO would be sidelined under this plan. Peres and Rabin, convinced that this was the ideal moment to put an end to the *intifada,* demanded that Israel accept the American proposal. Sharon and Shamir countered that Israeli concessions must be balanced by reciprocal concession on the Arab side. And there could be no question of opening things up to an international conference at which other, less friendly or even hostile foreign powers like the U.S.S.R. would be able to weigh in.

King Hussein of Jordan was profoundly vexed, and decided to cut off all links to the West Bank and let the PLO alone represent the Palestinians in future discussions with Israel. It was a snub for Jerusalem, but especially for Shimon Peres, who saw the American peace plan – but also the Jordanian option for a global arrangement with the Palestinians – go up in smoke. It was yet another missed rendezvous with History.

The next elections to the Knesset brought losses to both the Likud and the Labor parties. But the extremist splinter parties gained representation, and Shamir, forming a new coalition government, named a hawk, Moshe Arens, as Foreign Minister. Peres was demoted to the role of Finance Minister, while Arik Sharon kept his portfolio. On November 14, 1988, Arafat announced the creation of the sovereign State of Palestine from Algiers, and a number of governments gave immediate political recognition to the self-proclaimed state. The following month, now in Geneva, Arafat stated publicly that he "recognized Israel's right to exist in peace and security, and that he was completely renouncing terrorism."

While the declaration was received positively by the nations of Europe, and even by the U.S.A., Yitzhak Shamir furiously proclaimed that the West had fallen into "the trap of lies" set by the PLO leader. Arik Sharon declared that as far as he was concerned, "Arafat is a pathological liar and an assassin who should be tried for crimes against humanity."

Arafat's new posture, recognizing Israel's right to peace and security presented a new PLO face to the world, apparently more moderate and responsible now that terror had been publicly disavowed. Respected Israeli politicians like Ezer Weizman and former Foreign Minister Abba Eban, stood up in support of the creation of a Palestinian state. In Paris, Arafat was received with full official honors by French President François Mitterrand. The French Jewish community protested what they saw as an outrage, but in vain. To calm things down, Arafat, at Mitterrand's request, termed "out of date" the part of the Palestinian Charter that called for the destruction of the Zionist state. From thence forward, he said, that paragraph was to be considered null and void. But in the streets of Gaza and on the hills and towns of the West Bank, the crowds of masked youths were still throwing stones, and the IDF responding with rubber bullets. The *Intifada* was apparently not reading the news from Paris.

Israel denounced Arafat's duplicitous stance and on November 15, 1989, Shamir flew to Washington to restart peace plans. One goal was to push the PLO off its perch as self-appointed and sole representative of the Palestinian people. During sometimes heated discussions with Shamir – obstinate in his refusal to even consider recognizing the PLO – U.S. Secretary of State James Baker suggested elections be held in the occupied territories. "People tell me you are a pragmatist," Baker said to Shamir. "Don't fool yourself, the world has changed. You will have to give up your dream of a Greater Israel."

"Like yourself, Mr. Secretary, I am a man of principles," Shamir replied, "but I am also pragmatic and can be flexible when necessary, according to circumstances. Those who say I'm dogmatic are wrong. But I sincerely believe that the creation of a Palestinian state has within it the seeds that could lead to the destruction of the State of Israel. Is it vital to pursue our efforts to achieve a comprehensive peace with our Arab neighbors? Of course. Ten years have passed since we signed a treaty with Egypt based on the Camp David accords, and this peace is the cornerstone for building peace right across the region. But we must now put an end to the violence in the streets, the boycott of Israel, and armed conflict."

Shamir's words were voiced with great care, methodically, his thick eyebrows moving up and down as he spoke to underscore his position.

"But Mr. Shamir," Baker replied. It does no good to be needlessly stubborn. The situation requires a new way of thinking. I think it is important to first engage in negotiations with the Palestinians; after that it will be much easier to sign non-aggression pacts with your Arab neighbors. We are prepared to offer you the guarantees you need for your security. The United States stands squarely with you."

Satisfied at what he had obtained from the Americans, but of prudent temperament, Shamir returned to Jerusalem to present the peace plan proposal to the other members of Cabinet. Peres and Rabin were in favor, but six ministers, including Sharon and Levy, were strongly against it. Fearing more U.S. pressure on the Prime Minister, they called a meeting of Likud members and prepared to join hands and contest Shamir's leadership, demanding he unequivocally abandon any plans for elections in the territories with the disastrous potential for a PLO victory.

This was a new tactic for Sharon, who until then had supported Shamir's government. Now, he was prepared to foil any new initiative proposed by the Prime Minister, and do everything he could to shake the Shamir-Labor coalition. In his view, the party of Shimon Peres was unduly hasty in its desire to achieve an "at any cost" settlement with the Palestinians. It was vital to unite all the conservative forces in the country to block any move considered contrary to the interests of the nation. Sharon's view was that it was first imperative to end the Intifada, and only then could productive negotiations be held with the Palestinians in the Territories. He was a proven expert in the anti-terror struggle, and could produce a detailed and efficient operational plan at will.

In the international arena, the closed borders of Eastern Europe clanged open, the communist dictatorships chased from power. The Berlin Wall of shame was taken down – concrete block by concrete block and by hand in many places – and Germany was on the road to unification. The South African apartheid regime was on its last legs. The European Community moved toward political and monetary union. In this context, the Middle East could not remain the last major foyer of endless conflict. Sharon needed to understand that a peaceful solution to the Arab-Israeli conflict was becoming more imperative by the day. Unless Israel took the diplomatic initiative by launching its own plan for peace, it could expect to be ever more isolated in the world, and to come under more and more pressure. Shamir had gotten that, and moved forward, if not entirely pleased with matters.

At the conclusion of the Baker-Shamir meetings, the American had proposed a five point plan. In it, Washington gave Israel satisfaction on a number of issues but was irritated by the subsequent tentative moves and hyper-sensitivity of the Shamir government. Inside the Likud Party, Sharon's own anti-Shamir "Intifada" was continuing, the revolt decrying the government's capitulation in the face of American demands. The administration of George Bush – the father – declared that it saw the settlers' colonies in the Territories as illegal, and made all new American loans conditional on an Israeli promise not to install new Soviet immigrants in these communities. Shamir agreed to this, but Sharon, the Housing Minister, refused to kow-tow to what he considered to be ill-advised interference in Israeli internal affairs. "Facts on the ground" had an immense role to play in the future of the occupied territories, and would doubtless be important bargaining chips in any future negotiations on a final status.

"How could I continue to sit as a member of a government that has begun to auction off parts of the land of Israel?" he proclaimed on

February 8, 1990, addressing Likud members come to protest at an extraordinary meeting of the central committee of the party. "This road leads straight to catastrophe, it is a mortal danger to the Jewish people."

The confusion at the meeting held in the Cinerama amphitheatre in Tel-Aviv, was complete. Sharon physically grabbed the microphone from Shamir and took the floor by force, welcomed by thunderous applause. With people screaming and shouting, insulting each other at will without really knowing why or apparently caring much about the ideological motivations of the objects of their rant, the scene soon deteriorated into a caricature of a Middle Eastern bazaar. The strongest shouters, or the ones who got hold of a connected microphone, carried the day. This deplorable, chaotic spectacle dishonored the Likud, but it was soon to become the norm in public political meetings across the country, a reflection, really, of the chaos that reigned within Israeli public opinion.

The evening of the raucous meeting, Sharon submitted his resignation and ostentatiously left government. The split in the Likud party seemed to be inevitable, and the governing coalition's fall very probable. But Shamir had nerves of steel and the patience to wait for the storm to subside without publicly confronting Sharon or his two allies, David Levy and Yitzhak Modai, who would soon become Finance Minister. Shamir was quite conscious of the fact that the goal of Sharon, Levy, and Modai was essentially electoral, and that the posturing of the former had in reality but one objective: taking over the Likud Party. Internal opinion surveys showed he was likely to succeed. At that point, the old conspiratorial fox Shimon Peres jumped into the fray, showing as usual his political flair. While still acting as Finance Minister, he conducted secret negotiations aimed at setting up his own governing coalition and even went as far as demanding a non confidence motion in the Knesset. In the topsy-turvy world of Israeli politics, this normally absurd act - a sitting minister calling for the defeat of his own government - was not only possible, but, incredibly, a historical fact.

Sharon, however, by a combination of logic and arm-twisting, managed to convince enough conservative members of the Knesset not to follow Peres, and he was denied a majority, giving Shamir some breathing room. He continued to govern with the support of the extremist parties on the Right, appointing David Levy as Foreign Minister and Benjamin Netanyahu – Shamir's new favorite – as his deputy.

The Baker plan was cold-storaged and a jubilant Sharon, now in a stronger position than before, held on to his Housing portfolio. Construction cranes were seen everywhere in the country, with new sites springing up in the North, the South, and in the occupied territories.

In the Middle East, the expression "Never a dull moment" is an almost daily fact of life. In the midst of the brouhaha over the coalition and the Baker plan, on August 2, 1990, Iraqi dictator Saddam Hussein sent his army into Kuwait. American forces soon arrived in the area, headquartered in Saudi Arabia, leading a coalition meant to expel the invading Iraqi troops and restore the Kuwaiti ruling family to power. A lot was at stake here. Saddam threatened to attack Israel with Scud missiles, and the menace was taken extremely seriously by the IDF high command. Shamir convened a meeting between his Cabinet ministers and the Tsahal generals. Many scenarios were discussed, including a preventive strike and the assassination of Hussein. When Sharon's turn came to speak, to no one's particular surprise, this tactical and strategic expert, using a long pointer, outlined his plan for a new military campaign against the Iraqis. From his point of view, this was classic warfare, and all classic battles resembled each other:

> "We need to first attack and destroy Saddam's air force, as a preventive measure, then send in our paratroopers to stop a Scud retaliation. Finally, we need a large-scale cleanup operation using our tank forces in the H2 and H3 zones of the Iraqi desert."

Sharon always looked at the big picture; his ambitious raids had been proven both audacious and spectacular. From a purely military standpoint, his plan was, according to him, quite feasible, but required the co-operation of the Americans, and military coordination. Without Washington's accord, the plan could not go forward. In addition, Israeli tanks would need to establish a corridor through Jordan to reach Iraqi territory.

Many thought this a goal beyond reach. Shamir, ever the incarnation of placid strength, and supported by David Levy and his close advisor Avi Pazner, rejected the military option. He took Levy's judicious counsel and adopted a low profile in the conflict, agreeing to U.S. requests to show restraint in the face of Iraqi threats and let the Americans take the front row. But who could calculate the risks of inaction? The Jewish state might be running right into imminent peril; for six weeks beginning on January 18, 1991, the entire Israeli population was issued gas masks, and plastic to set up airtight shelters in their homes where they were to remain during the night, protected from Hussein's Scuds and the threat of poison gas warheads. The entire country showed a remarkably calm spirit, tending to its anxiety in private. For the first, and perhaps last time in Israel's history, the defense of the country was not in the hands of Tsahal, but of a foreign coalition of armies led by the United States of America.

Sharon was revolted by the decision, which he saw as a grave and profound mistake, likely to weaken the dissuasive power of Tsahal in the eyes of Arab countries and tarnish Israel's sovereign reputation. And all to just satisfy the Americans. Shamir was unconvinced, though, especially when his policy of restraint began to bear fruit.

On October 30, 1991, a Middle East peace conference began in Madrid. That the meeting was held at all represented an important diplomatic victory for Israel, but now, seventeen years after the Geneva Peace Conference, and for the first time, Jerusalem's position was validated: direct negotiations with the Arab states began, with no preconditions. But as always, Israeli internal politics had a considerable impact on the government's ability to negotiate with a free hand. Shamir had to deal with Sharon's demands, and with the caprices of the members of the extremist splinter parties in the Knesset. Though only seven in number, these elected representatives had a considerable impact on the coalition's ability to govern. In fact, they held the balance of power and could topple the government at will. The Likud was seriously weakened by, on the one hand, General Sharon's stance, and on the other, by the demands of the extremists – whose constant refusal to compromise infuriated Shamir, of whom it could never be said that he had anything but unshakeable love in his heart for the Land of Israel. Some of the more centrist Likud Cabinet members came out strongly against what they saw as a fanatically-inspired attempt to cause their party to self-destruct. They also accused Sharon of feeding the anti-Shamir revolt.

Sixty-three days after the opening of the Madrid Peace Conference, the seven ultra-nationalist representatives resigned their seats in the Knesset, depriving the now lame-duck Likud coalition of a working majority in parliament. The consequences were immediate: Shamir was forced to resign and call new, early elections.

The centrist Likud members were not wrong: Sharon had indeed discouraged the ultra-nationalist splinter party members from supporting the overly flexible policies of Yitzhak Shamir, which would, in his view, lead to the creation of a Palestinian state. Sharon also believed the Madrid conference had been a colossal mistake. But his obstinate refusal to cede any terrain to the Americans – or to the Arabs – had resulted in the weakening of his own political party. The very public pushing and shoving between Sharon and the extremists on the one hand, and Shamir and his allies on the other, had simply opened the door wide to a Labor comeback. For the next four years, Ariel Sharon and his Likud comrades would sit on the other side of the Knesset, in the Opposition.

Chapter 8

The Long Wait

These words like daggers enter in mine ears.
William Shakespeare, Hamlet, Act III Scene 4

On July 13, 1992, Yitzhak Rabin presented his new government to the President and the people of Israel. Shimon Peres was once again Foreign Minister, and Rabin kept the Defense Ministry for himself. The Labor Party victory was met abroad with sighs of relief. Rabin and Peres had received the approval of their nation - and the support of foreign governments - for moving forward in a serious manner on peace negotiations, giving priority to settling the Palestinian question. Additional settlements, which Sharon had fought so hard to maintain, would be now suspended. The Americans unfroze ten billion dollars that had been withheld because of the "Shamir government's intransigence." It was a sum destined to ease the integration of Soviet Jews into Israeli life, and to reward Israel's good behavior during the Gulf War. Looked at from this point of view, the George Herbert Walker Bush administration had been somewhat less than fair in its relations with Shamir.

One month after it was sworn in, the Rabin administration decided to release eight hundred PLO prisoners from Israeli detention, and undertook to work towards an equitable solution for all Palestinians. While on an official visit to Cairo, Rabin openly called for beginning the resolution with Gaza. Peres quickly added, "to be followed by Jericho." From that point on things would move swiftly.

In secrecy, a small group of Israelis began serious discussions with PLO leaders. Several months later the Oslo Accord in Principle was signed, by which Israel, in exchange for official recognition, would begin a staged evacuation of the territories conquered in the 1967 war. What followed, with the beginning of the Intifada, is well known.

During this period, a bitter Arik Sharon had to be satisfied with sitting on the Foreign Affairs and Defense committees of the Knesset, unable to influence in any way, shape, or form the ongoing negotiations with Yasser Arafat. His comments to Israeli and international media first and foremost concerned his own party; in particular, he compared the weakness of the current government unfavorably to the Shamir administration which had the backbone to stand up to pressure from Washington. Still, in Sharon's view, the Likud had, *de facto,* opened the door to the creation of a Palestinian state. The Labor Party was subsequently able to apply the Oslo Accord without constraints.

Contrary to Ben-Gurion, Begin, and Shamir, who had concentrated their efforts on defining the kind of peace agreement that could be made, the Rabin-Peres duo had succumbed to the temptation of immediate – but not necessarily optimal – peace. With great ceremony, and in the midst of general euphoria, they simply signed, in the process breaking many long-held taboos, and revealed all the cards they held in their hand. "A new Middle East" was promised. But the cart, in this instance, came a significant way before the horse, and many were lulled to sleep by their hopes and dreams. Nightmares were soon to follow.

It was evident that all the previous Israeli administrations had desired peace with their country's neighbours... but not at any price. In the first place, no prior government leader could have imagined a scenario that moved so quickly, since there was certain to be a snowball effect resulting from the irreversible nature of such official accords. Rabin and Peres had all of a sudden breathed new life into a moribund and thoroughly discredited – even among Arab states – PLO, and rehabilitated Yasser Arafat – who was now imbued with renewed personal prestige – by offering him an economically viable country supported by the international community. But there were no comparable undertakings on the Palestinian side, no guarantees that the accords would actually be implemented nor that Arafat would definitively suppress the anarchy, violence and terror that reigned in Gaza and the West Bank.

In an astonishingly short time, Israel made numerous errors, losing the fruits of a fragile peace it had paid so heavy a price to win on the endless blood-soaked battlefields of its history. Rabin, but especially Peres, had been intoxicated by the "romantic left wing" and made promises and signed agreements that would carry the country into uncharted waters. There was a Hollywood-like spectacle of media-rich interaction between the actors of History at work here; on the ground of day-to-day confrontation, however, people were tuned to a different channel.

Following a short period of relative calm, the suicide bombers struck again. No Israeli could put up with this permanent nightmare, but in practical terms, what could be done to stop the homicidal maniacs? Many were convinced that the problem had no solution. The Jewish state had known bloody conflict before, and had confronted and defeated the armies of a united Arab world. But this was different. A new generation of cat's paw terrorists was ready to seek martyrdom and wear explosive vests stuffed with nails and ball bearings whose only intent was to cause havoc and kill as many Israeli civilians as possible wherever people gathered, whether on public transport, in restaurants and hotels, or in the marketplaces. These young, naive, and desperate "true believers" were generally sent by hardened, older activists, whose cynicism was apparently boundless...for they never went in themselves. Finding disaffected and depressed young men – and soon women – was not very hard. There was even a theatrical nature to this horror, as they videotaped the messengers of death, and often dressed them as Orthodox Jews or women to avoid being searched by Israeli police or IDF patrols.

This battle played out on the front pages of the newspapers and on television. The photographs of Israeli victims and the horrible views of the carnage caused the government to be much more sensitive to its critics now. In the Knesset, debate was fierce: Sharon termed the Oslo Accord a "colossal error" and accused Rabin and Peres of a naiveté bordering on social death wish.

Within the Likud Party though, Sharon was not in the ascendancy. Shamir and his supporters preferred to look for a younger man, smooth, talented, and a powerful orator, who could bring Likud back to power and preserve the dream of Eretz Israel - Greater Israel. Their choice was Benjamin Netanyahu - nicknamed "Bibi" - who was Israel's former Ambassador to the United Nations, Vice-Minister of Foreign Affairs and a man the party stalwarts were convinced was right for the job. Sharon was left to flounder on his own.

Peres and Rabin had intentionally left a fog of imprecision surrounding many of the detailed points of the Oslo Accord with the PLO, infuriating the settlers who were now in a state of complete confusion. Street demonstrations and confrontation with Israeli police were inevitable. Kicking, punching, and barricades with the ensuing dispersal charge into the crowds by police and the use of tear gas, water cannons and paddy wagons, all elements of a classic scenario for street demonstrations and the imposition of law and order, were common.

In the great Zion Square in Jerusalem, a celebrated site of electoral rallies and great political assembly, thousands came to register their opposition to the Oslo Accords. Rabin was in the hot seat, accused of treason, even compared to Pétain and to Mussolini. In a show of horror and abasement, many demonstrators carried posters depicting Rabin wearing a Palestinian keffiya or even a Nazi uniform.

Opposition leaders followed each other to the balcony overlooking the square. Soft on the extreme Right, Netanyahu and Sharon both spoke, and violently condemned the agreements signed with Arafat, calling for new elections to be held. Fanatical and bizarre rabbis holding black candles took part in ceremonies that harkened back to Middle Ages obscurantism. They cursed Yitzhak Rabin with the *Poulsa de Noura* – "ball of fire" in ancient Aramaic, – condemning "the damned" Rabin to a violent end. Only a few weeks later, during a peace rally on November 10, 1995, Rabin was in fact assassinated, in the Kings of Israel Square, by a Jewish fanatic who was a law student and partisan of the extremist Right. For the first time in the history of Israel, a Jewish political leader was to be killed by one of his own. Verbal incitement had finally led to murder. And even today, a minority of Israelis has still not learned from this tragedy, and continues to encourage hatred and violence against the leaders of the nation.

Following Rabin's killing and the ceremonies of national grieving, the country sunk into a state of total shock. New elections were held in a surrealist atmosphere punctuated by a growing number of suicide bombings perpetrated by Muslim fanatics willing to blow themselves up in the expectation of eternal bliss in Allah's Paradise. Fanaticism and blind hatred had taken over on both sides of the struggle. Neither Peres nor Netanyahu had any intention of conceding anything to the bombers or the faceless men who sent them to kill. There would be no question of the dignity and faith of an entire people being stolen by a few bloody attacks. The "dead-enders" would not be allowed to plunge the Middle East into another regional war. Israel's survival was not at risk, nor its strong democracy, but the nation's morale, influenced by the acts of terror and especially the way the sensationalist media played them up, was at a nadir. It was clear that the people would mandate as Yitzhak Rabin' successor whichever of the candidates they felt would offer the country and its citizens the greater sense of security.

The campaign saw Peres promise to apply the Oslo Accords, while Netanyahu came out resolutely against them, talking about "red lines" that could not be crossed. Sharon was still on the sidelines, far removed from the inner Likud circle, and not a part of major campaign or policy decisions. "Bibi" was keeping his distances from his rivals within the party. A skilled diplomat and brilliant public speaker, he sought to define himself as a pragmatist and a moderate, young and able to govern for many years to come. In his view, Sharon was the icon of the complex and controversial past, weighed down by military adventurism and the tragedy of war. By comparison, Bibi came across as a fresh hope, a man in whom the nation could have confidence. It worked. Benjamin Netanyahu won the elections and Likud was back in power.

Bibi presented his Cabinet to the nation on June 18, 1996. David Levy was back in his comfortable seat as Foreign Minister, and Yitzhak Mordecai was Defense chief. But for the first time since he joined the Likud Party, Arik Sharon was not invited to join the government. David Levy intervened on the infuriated Sharon's behalf, telling Netanyahu he was making a serious mistake, and demanded Sharon be brought back into Cabinet. Unless that happened, Levy told the Prime Minister, he was prepared to immediately resign. So an "arrangement" was made by the now considerably embarrassed Netanyahu: a new department of government was created especially for Sharon, the Department of National Infrastructures!

Once in power, Netanyahu changed his policy and contrary to his electoral promises, announced that Israel was irrevocably bound to the Oslo treaty, since the nation's word had to be good. Signed international agreements had to be respected. Sharon was displeased but kept a public silence. In private comments, though, he viewed Bibi as weak, and was convinced he should have found a way to cancel the accords and resist international pressure. Netanyahu had betrayed his electors and was now in an irreversible process of negotiations whose conclusion could only be the creation of a Palestinian state run by Yasser Arafat: "Bibi is a man who easily capitulates under pressure. He is an opportunist and an egocentric who has no respect for the Likud ideals."

Netanyahu assured King Hussein of Jordan of his good intentions, and informed Egyptian President Hosni Mubarak of his desire to pursue the peace process. He also reassured U.S. President Bill Clinton, and sent an upbeat message to Arafat. Change would take place in an environment of continuity. But despite the favorable reception in the international community, Bibi had serious problems within his own government. Security issues dominated ongoing discussions with the Palestinians and the parties profoundly distrusted each other. The Palestinian Authority, breaking its word, released prisoners formerly held by Israel and who had been transferred to detention centers in the West Bank and Gaza to serve out their terms. These men immediately returned to armed struggle, and the vicious and untenable cycle of violence continued. Netanyahu demanded reciprocity for each Israeli concession now, but nothing was forthcoming from the Palestinian side. The situation led to personal tensions within Cabinet and to the resignation of Foreign Minister Levy, a year and a half after he took up the post. Netanyahu replaced Levy with...himself, preferring to personally manage a department with which he was thoroughly familiar from his time as Plenipotentiary Minister in Washington, then U.N. Ambassador, and Vice-Minister.

While Israel celebrated the fiftieth anniversary of its independence, Netanyahu was still in negotiations with the Palestinians and, under American and European pressure, undertook to withdraw from ten per cent of the Occupied Territories, including the town of Hebron, home of the ancient Patriarchs of Israel. Various Cabinet Ministers, including Sharon, strongly opposed this concession and threatened to not sign the protocol. Bill Clinton, nearing the end of his second and final term in office, wanted to go out on a high note with the speedy signature of an interim agreement on the status of the West Bank, and made this a condition for receiving Netanyahu on a state visit to Washington. Painted into a corner and weakened by the resignation of Dan Meridor, his Finance Minister, the Israeli Prime Minister surprised everyone by reinforcing his position on the Right. He named Sharon Foreign Minister charged with negotiating a final status for the Palestinians. Arik, who had been for some time kept away from the crucial political decisions of the government, now found himself suddenly back in the thick of things, right at the heart and strategic center of the peace process. Aware of the importance of human relations in the functionality of a department engaged in such delicate matters, Sharon worked to win the confidence of the Israeli diplomatic corps, notably by not rocking the boat. Most ambassadors and senior staff, and notably Eytan Bentsur - the department's director - were kept in place.

Sharon was well-known for his intransigent opinions and personal aversion to Arafat. He used that to discipline the procedure for all negotiations: there would be in all cases reciprocity for any Israeli concessions, and a "Code of Conduct" was put together and put into practice by Bentsur. Netanyahu was in fact quite comfortable with the way things were going, and content to present a united and front to the Americans, supported by the blustery Arik Sharon. Ten days after naming Sharon as Foreign Minister, Bibi took him to Wye River, Maryland, to a meeting with Arafat set up by Clinton. The parties were to knock together a new accord. But never, not even in his worst nightmares, could the General who sent his fighter jets to bomb Arafat, and who had chased the PLO leader from Beirut, have imagined a face to face meeting with the keffiya-wearing man on U.S. soil. Worse, his mandate was to negotiate away a part of Eretz Israel, the land of the Jews, in exchange for peace and co-existence.

Seeing Arafat and Sharon in the same picture stupefied large parts of the Israeli public, but it only proved that Arik was beginning to change his views. Since he had been named Foreign Minister he had begun to develop a new and more pragmatic view of things, influenced by a global outlook. This evolution is, moreover, not uncommon among military men who later become political leaders. Once the warrior puts on the diplomat's clothes, he starts to understand that direct dialogue from a position of strength is the best way of reaching a peace agreement with a former enemy in today's geopolitical framework.

For one week, out of sight of the prying eyes of reporters, Clinton, Arafat, Netanyahu and Sharon, along with their delegations, combed through all the security issues and possible guarantees that could be given by each side. Sharon was dumbfounded when he learned that Bibi, without consulting him, had promised Clinton to give back thirteen per cent of the territories, not the nine per cent that Sharon had approved. Without obtaining anything in return, Netanyahu had given away part of the store. There was nothing he could do about it now, but Sharon, even though he continued the peace negotiations, was more and more careful.

He participated in the talks but refused to shake Arafat's hand. Whenever he spoke, he responded to the PLO man's proposals and presented his own point of view, without looking at Arafat, and referring to him always in the third person. A verbatim transcript of part of the discussions is illustrative of the prevailing climate:

> Sharon (exacerbated): "Mister President, chairman Arafat has just accused us of violating the Oslo Accords and being responsible for the deteriorating situation in Hebron. But I think he has forgotten that Hebron is the ancestral home of the Patriarchs of Israel, and Arabs committed atrocities there against Jews since the nineteen thirties, well before the creation of Israel."

> Arafat (looking around furtively): "Your excellency the President of the United States, General Sharon speaks of the past. But he has forgotten about the Jew who massacred tens of religious Palestinians come to pray at Ibrahim's Cave in Hebron."

Arafat was referring to the Baruch Goldstein incident. On February 25, 1994, reacting in his own way to the Arafat-Rabin Oslo Accords signed the previous September, this doctor, a member of the fanatical and racist Kâh movement, machine-gunned a group of Palestinians praying at the Cave of the Patriarchs in Hebron, killing twenty-nine. Goldstein was immediately killed by the crowd.

Three days after this acerbic exchange, on October 23, 1998, Ariel Sharon and Yasser Arafat were at the White House for the signing ceremony of the Hebron Accord. King Hussein of Jordan was there too, looking feeble, and with his skull shaven, the result of last-hope treatments for cancer. His presence was a gift to Clinton, because he should have rightfully remained hospitalized, as his days were numbered. The participants' faces told the tale: Arafat looked radiant, all smiles next to the dying king. Clinton, happy to have another occasion to forget the Monica Lewinsky zippergate scandal, was at his most unctuous. Netanyahu appeared - and was - tense, uneasy in the knowledge that any satisfaction he might be tempted to enjoy was illusory. Clinton's charming manner and U.S. pressure had obliged him to go along with the show.

Sharon fulminated, and alone among the celebrating party-goers, was fit to be tied. He observed the spectacle in silence, putting as much physical distance as possible between himself and the others, and refused to go on stage. He permitted himself no applause and looked on glacially as the speakers succeeded one other; under the circumstances he had little other means of expressing his disavowal of the proceedings.

Several weeks later, Bill Clinton left Washington for an official visit to Israel and the Occupied Territories. It was the first time in history that a sitting United States President had gone to Gaza, and he was received with enthusiasm and rejoicing. Hope abounded that a page in Middle Eastern history had been finally turned. To his astonishment, Sharon discovered that Netanyahu was secretly planning a meeting with Syrian dictator Hafez Al-Assad, using an American businessman as intermediary, and that Bibi was prepared to surrender large parts of the captured Golan Heights in exchange for a peace treaty with Damascus.

Enraged, he confronted Netanyahu: "The Golan is a strategic plateau that ensures the security of the north of the country, not a piece of merchandise to sell off," he fumed, "and besides, this is no way to conduct negotiations."

Sharon hardened his positions and encouraged the settlers to reinforce their numbers in the West Bank. He wanted to sate their anger at Israel's retreat from Hebron, prove his love for the Land of Israel and its ancestors, and demonstrate clearly that he had not changed his views, which were resolutely hostile to Arafat and to any territorial abandonment. Apparently declining any responsibility for the undertakings his government had taken with the Palestinians and seemed about to take with the Syrians, he played the part of powder-monkey, without going far enough to warrant resigning his ministerial portfolio. This was a tactical move from the old master of the game, and it was designed to garner support from both the Right and the Left. It's ambiguity worked, creating dissension in the Likud ranks, and weakened Netanyahu's government, leading to new alliances being formed in the ever-changing maze of Israeli politics. An irate Defense Minister Yitzhak Mordecai decided to form his own center-right political party. Bibi was ever more isolated, facing U.S. pressure and Palestinian demands on his own, and his government soon fell.

On December 21, 1998, after only thirty months in office, the government lost a non-confidence motion and new elections were called. It was a campaign in which Arik Sharon kept a low profile with regard to his party and especially as far as Benjamin Netanyahu was concerned. Sharon's standoffishness and Bibi's lack of stature created an opening for Labor, and under former general Ehud Barak, the party that had governed Israel longest was swept back into power.

After the election, Bibi retreated from public life somewhat to lick his wounds, leaving Sharon, in the official opposition now, paradoxically in a stronger position. On September 2, 1999 he was elected as uncontested leader of the Likud Party and set out to prepare for the next elections, quietly, but with considerable dynamism. His wife Lily, now ill with lung cancer, encouraged him in this, as did his two grown sons, Omry and Gilad, who would stand with him in the next electoral campaign. It would be a struggle marked by tragic events.

Shortly after he won the Likud leadership, an electrical short-circuit sparked a fire at the Sharon's Sycamores Ranch. A large part of the family residence was destroyed by the flames, along with photos, personal souvenirs, and hundreds of books. A Bible was one of the few books that survived intact, a fact Sharon attributed to Divine Intervention. Then, in March 2000, on the twenty-fifth of the month, Arik's beloved wife Lily passed away at age 73, carried off by the metastases from the lung tumors, leaving him tragically alone. During their thirty-seven years of marriage Lily had always been at his side, always smiling, radiant with life. She was buried on a grassy hillock near the ranch, in a field of red poppies, where she had loved to walk in happier times, and where her husband would gaze at her and speak to her of love. After Lily's painful death, Arik would often return to her burial site, to place flowers on her grave and speak with her in silent memory, timidly and tenderly, sharing memories of the happy times when they were a couple lost in bliss. To his close friends, he confided his desire to be buried – as far into the future as possible of course – next to his late wife, on that same hill overlooking their ranch, and not on Jerusalem's Mount Herzl – or in the case of Menachem Begin, on the Mount of Olives – as would have been customary for a leader of Israel. Sharon's desire, like that of Ben-Gurion – whose resting place is at Sde Boker, by his wife Paula – was to live forever in the Negev.

Arik Sharon had never allowed himself to by weakened by tragedy: a mission was a sacred trust, a solemn duty to be carried out. Lily had encouraged him – even from her death bed – to continue his quest to become Prime Minister – and hours before her passing had wished him success with all the energy she could still muster. In his moments of despair, he always succeeded in pulling himself up by his bootstraps, and this time was no different. He held on to his political ambitions now, with ever stronger conviction.

As leader of the official opposition in the Knesset, Sharon was present at all parliamentary debates, while he quietly pursued his contacts with the Palestinians and Arab leaders. He asked his son Omry and his diplomatic adviser Eytan Bentsur to meet in Vienna with Yasser Arafat's treasurer Mohamed Rachid, a man who enjoyed the PLO leader's confidence. He also bought a villa – rarely used – in the Arab sector of the old city of Jerusalem, a purchase seen as questionable and provocative, one that cost the Israeli public hundreds of thousands of shekels each year in upkeep and security. But it was the measure of the man.

Ehud Barak's decision to unilaterally withdraw Israeli forces from South Lebanon in May of 2000, and his intensive negotiations with Arafat and Hafez al-Assad could not leave Sharon indifferent. He launched a public relations campaign aim at showing that Barak's concessions represented a grave security risk for the nation. As was his habit, he employed an apocalyptic vocabulary in warning the Labor government, and the country, of his fears. After all, he had correctly predicted a catastrophe after the first withdrawal of IDF forces from the Sinai in 1975, declaring that the road to Tel-Aviv would be wide open for Egyptian tanks. While in Opposition in parliament he had consistently evoked disasters and tragic scenarios for the nation and felt no compulsion to see things differently now. In matters of defense and the security of Israel, Arik was convinced he was always in the right, and believed he alone knew what was best for the land.

As peace negotiations with the Syrians and the Palestinians brokered by outgoing U.S. President Bill Clinton bogged down, Arafat, seeking a tactical advantage, decided to instigate more violence - as much as he could manage - in the Occupied Territories. Now Barak, who had made an "arrangement" with Arafat regarding East Jerusalem and bartered away large parts of the West Bank, was confronted by a serious crisis in his government. Many Ministers resigned, including David Levy and all the members of Cabinet belonging to the ultra-orthodox Sephardic party, Shas. Then, with the departure of the Meretz, or extreme left-wing ministers, and that of General Yitzhak Mordecai, head of the center-right Merkaz Party, the Barak Labor coalition imploded.

Barak pleaded with Sharon to join him in a national unity government, but Sharon would not accept Barak's conditions even though he believed in the concept. In the end, his preference was to weaken Barak and take power on his own. In the face of the ongoing crisis, and bloody incidents involving Israeli Arabs, Barak resigned, announcing he would present himself again as a candidate in the anticipated elections.

Barak's time as Prime Minister of Israel had ended after twenty-one months. It seemed that no Israeli government could last out its full, four-year mandate any more before throwing in the towel. In any case, Sharon was ready to claim his place, and on September 28, 2000, in a daring and controversial move, visited the esplanade of Temple Mount, a sacred site for both Jews and Muslims, called Haram Esharif by the latter.

To reinforce his support from the diehard Israeli Right, Sharon chose to be accompanied by many Likud Knesset members and dozens of policemen and security guards. As he arrived at the pillars of the Dome, he was "welcomed" by an unforeseen rain of stones. Yet he had prepared this visit carefully. His son Omry, well-known for his moderate views, had advised his father against this, but Arik would hear none of it. He had obtained the accord of Barak and the assurances of Shin Beth that everything would go smoothly. It was Arafat, in fact, going against the advice of the Islamic religious authorities in Jerusalem, who decided to transform Sharon's visit into an excuse for symbolic revolt.

From then on, the two "provocateurs" would go head to head and dictate, each in his own way and for different and contradictory reasons, the path of history in the Middle East. Arafat and Sharon, two key figures in the story of the Arab-Israeli conflict would once again be at the center of anger that brought more trouble to the land.

Sharon had been at the least, imprudent, and should have given more thought to his son's advice of not visiting the Temple Mount. The United States and many European countries, as well as the Arabs, condemned what they saw as an obvious provocation on Sharon's part, and feared the consequences. French president Chirac went so far as to accuse Ehud Barak of behind the scenes scheming to allow the provocation to take place, which was absurd. Prime Minister Barak had no interest at all in pouring oil on the fire, especially during an election campaign.

The international media were in a frenzy, recalling the "provocateur general's" role in the bloody raids against Palestinian villages during the 1950s, and the more recent massacres in the Beirut refugee camps of Sabrah and Shatilah. The campaign to personally denigrate Ariel Sharon was now on, full blast. A Belgian court was even set to rule on an accusation of war crimes against him, comparing him to history's bloodiest dictators. The fact that this charge was a grotesque and ignorant mish-mash of historical fact and fiction seemed not to count, at least not on the front pages and in the editorial columns of many newspapers.

PART THREE

Chapter 9

Prime Minister

I am first among equals.
Menachem Begin, Prime Minister of Israel, 1977-1983

Sharon's walk along the esplanade of the Mosques in Jerusalem set off an angry reaction on the part of Muslims around the world, and re-energized the Palestinian Intifada. But it also shored up the general's popularity with the West Bank and Gaza settlers. The election campaign witnessed, for the first time in Israeli history, two former generals vying against each other for a mandate to govern. Ehud Barak was the outgoing Prime Minister and represented the Labor Party and the Left in general, although he was considered a "hawk." Ariel Sharon was an ex-laborite, now the uncontested leader of the conservative Likud Party. They shared a common strategy, but had significant personality differences and their tactics were diametrically opposed.

Barak was a man in a hurry. He believed he could quickly and definitively resolve Israel's problem with the Palestinians. Sharon, with more experience under his belt, believed in the importance of ruse, and preferred prudence in dealing with the adversary. "Little steps," preferably two forward and then one back was his preference. He felt the carrot would be more appealing to the adversary after it had suffered many blows from the stick.

Sharon's image makers and communications advisers, especially an American named Arthur Finkelstein, imported from the U.S. for the campaign, worked on presenting Arik as a benevolent and peaceful grandfather. Campaign television spots always showed him alongside his grandson Rotem, or playing with his grandchildren on the family farm. "The ideal zaideh" would no longer bluster, nor refer to the battle-grounds of history. They left that to their Labor opponents.

It was an efficient tactic, and quickly erased Sharon's reputation as an impulsive man and a pitiless warrior. The new Ariel Sharon smiled a lot and said little. His words were clear and concise, spoken in the Hebrew of the common man, and generously sprinkled with Russian expressions he had learned from his mother Vera, to gain support among the new immigrants from Moscow. Now he was seen on horseback, plowing the fields, and caressing the sheep or playing with his sheep dog.

For the average Israeli, who lived with war and terror on a daily basis, this was an appealing campaign. The peaceful images of a new and reassuring leader, a happy grandfather exuding quiet force and national consensus were hard to resist. Sharon's victory, on February 6, 2001, was a landslide. In what was to be Israel's last prime ministerial election by direct universal suffrage, Ariel Sharon won by a sixty-two to thirty-eight percent margin.

The unexpected – and to some inexplicable – victory shook Israel to its core; ripple effects were felt throughout the Middle East and around the world. Arab capitals were perplexed, with some Heads of State respecting Sharon and believing he was the right man for the moment, a warrior able to make territorial concessions from a position of strength; others were convinced Sharon had not changed and would never change an iota of his beliefs in a Greater Israel.

Whatever the case, Arik was back from political exile and in firm control of the destiny of the State of Israel. Triumphant, but carefully concealing his private emotions, he went to pray at the grave of his wife Lily on the morning after his victory. Then he returned to Jerusalem to say a prayer for peace at the Wailing Wall.

The national unity government formed by Sharon after he won the election made him Israel's all-powerful Prime Minister for the next two years. Labor and the splinter parties all gave their support to his coalition program. Shimon Peres was named Foreign Minister, even though he accepted the post with some reservations. He would in fact turn out to be Sharon's best advocate and follow Arik's policies almost to the letter, shelving his utopian plans for a "new Middle-East" and instead, pleading the cause of "peace and security." Unlike Sharon though, Peres believed that Israel had to deal with Arafat.

With the PLO strongman, Sharon was implacable, but he was prepared to be more conciliatory with other Palestinian leaders, and willing to renew negotiations with them on condition they succeeded in stopping new acts of terrorism against Israelis. His first official foreign trip took him to Washington, where he set out his peace plan to a sympathetic President Bush. The men quickly formed a strong friendship and determined not to negotiate under threat of violence and terror. Bush acceded to Sharon's request that the Palestinian Authority President no longer be welcome at the White House; in exchange, Sharon gave his guarantee that Israel would not touch a hair on Arafat's head.

But on the ground, things were getting worse. Human bombs were exploding all over the country. At nightfall, the cinemas, theaters, cafes, and restaurants were empty, and the streets of Israel now belonged to the soldiers and police who patrolled with guard dogs. Blackouts and curfews were enforced in the territories. Tsahal set up road blocks and checks on all possible ways into the country. Every single vehicle, and every single passenger was thoroughly checked, including pregnant women, the infirm, the blind, ambulances...no one and nothing could be exempt.

When terror struck the soul of America on September 11, 2001, only nine months after George W. Bush was sworn in as president, and the Twin Towers went down in rubble, there was total panic in the United States. That one airplane could be hijacked and turned into a flying bomb was frightening enough, but four? Two of the most iconic landmarks in the world were destroyed and more than three thousand lives extinguished in less than an hour. The Pentagon, symbol of American might and authority, was also hit and partially destroyed, and only by the courage of some passengers did United flight 93 crash in a Pennsylvania field and not on the Capitol. The crazed, messianic followers of Osama Bin Laden had achieved what no Hollywood screen writer could have imagined, penetrating the steel walls of fortress America and rolling over all norms of human behavior in an attempt to crush democracy and plunge the West into chaos and anarchy.

In Israel, these apocalyptic moments were seen through eyes accustomed to terror, but even so, the events were the absolute horizon of worst-case scenarios. Sharon imposed a state of emergency, and the military went on Red Alert. All Israeli sea and air space was closed, and the army went on a war footing. Only Israeli fighter jets were in the skies, the Star of David on their tails protecting the nation from who now knew what possible threat. Against the advice of Shin Beth, Sharon refused to abandon the Prime Minister's office and take refuge in the underground army headquarters shelters where he could be better protected.

As the hours passed, life began to return to some level of normalcy, but there was no way back to the way things were before. It was clear that from now on, the war against terror would be international. The Mossad intelligence services considered the attacks to be the beginning of the Third World War that would concern all countries. Concerted action and full exchange of information would be needed to press a war without mercy on the terrorists. The fundamentalist madmen would not be allowed to dictate the future of the world.

In Sharon's mind there was no significant difference between

Arafat and Bin Laden. Both were terrorist leaders who sought the staged destruction of Israel. U.S. President Bush did not share this vision completely, nor did Shimon Peres, who, encouraged by the Americans, met privately with Yasser Arafat in the spring of 2001. It was a meeting Sharon could tactically allow, but to which he gave no serious credit. He was convinced Peres was wasting his time. The wave of terror was ongoing, and Arafat was still in Sharon's sights.

And yet, Sharon was prepared to concede an independent state to the Palestinians. A mere twelve days after the Manhattan and Washington attacks, in an historic speech given to a gathering of educators at the Latroun amphitheater – on the very hill where he almost lost his life in the bloody battle of May 1948, hardly a week after the creation of the State of Israel – Arik Sharon said those very words.

> "I wish to offer the Palestinians what no one has ever done, not the Turks, nor the British, nor the Egyptians, nor the Jordanians: a Palestinian state on the West Bank of the Jordan River."

It was stupefying offer, coming from the leader of the Likud Party and the incarnation of the diehard Israeli Right. After fifty-three years, Sharon had come full circle. His words marked a fundamental shift in the foundations of his party, and heralded an historic new policy for Israel.

A month later, George Bush, satisfied with Sharon's policy, looking for support in the Islamic countries and sympathy in the West for his own anti-Bin Laden operation in Afghanistan, declared that the Palestinian problem was a separate issue from the threat of Al-Qaeda. On October 2, he declared for the first time that he supported the creation of a Palestinian state next to Israel. The quick reaction to his Latroun speech was something of a surprise to Sharon, though, as was the lack of coordination with the White House. Something of a disappointment too, since he had believed the American administration would be intransigent with regard to Arafat and refuse to negotiate with the PLO chief under threat of terrorism. In a flamboyant speech he warned the free world, and in the first instance the United States, against repeating the tragic error Neville Chamberlain made in 1938 by sacrificing Czechoslovakia to the Nazis.

"Israel is quite able to defend itself," he said.

The tone of his words was unappreciated in Washington, and Bush quickly asked for clarification. Sharon, unrepentant and unabashed, responded in writing, without excusing himself for anything he had said. History would not repeat itself here!

Three days later George W. Bush gave the order to U.S. forces to attack the Taliban-run Afghanistan regime and capture Osama Bin Laden, dead or alive. The Joint Chiefs of Staff were also well advanced in their plans to invade Iraq and overthrow Saddam Hussein. The Axis of Evil was now in the sights of the United States, and the trap was closing.

Sharon decided to aim directly at the sponsors and enablers of terrorist acts in Israel. It was a targeted campaign that saw many activists arrested, bank accounts frozen, and ships full of arms and munitions stopped on the high seas. It was part of an all out war, one that raged on all fronts, including retaliation killings from which Israeli politicians were not exempt. On October 17, 2001, Israeli Tourism Minister and former general Rehavam Ze'evi - known by his nickname of Gandhi since he refused to wear a bullet-proof vest or be surrounded by bodyguards - was assassinated by a Palestinian in his hotel on Mount Scopus. Tension ratcheted up, and Shin Beth, redoubling its efforts, was soon hot on the trail of the assassin. Marwan Barghouti, chief of the paramilitary Palestinian Brigades armed force, was picked up in Ramallah, but the cycle of violence was raging and no one seemed able to put an end to the terrorist attacks.

Bullet-proof vests were now worn at all times by the Prime Minister and his Cabinet. Sharon, not only the target of Palestinian gunmen and agents of Al-Qaeda and other Arab fanatics, but also of extremist Jews, was protected by a large contingent of bodyguards.

On January 10, 2002, Israeli marine commandos from the famed Unit 13 intercepted a cargo ship in the Red Sea laden with sophisticated weapons and ammunition - including shoulder-fired ground to air missiles - bound for Gaza. In spite of the importance of the seizure, and Israel's knowledge that the arms shipment had been secretly ordered by Arafat, and in spite of the horrifying wave of suicide bombings from one end of the country to the other, Sharon remained confident in the outcome of the crisis.

At a breakfast meeting with foreign newspaper correspondents, he declared with a smile:

> "In a few weeks I will celebrate my seventy-third birthday. I have accomplished everything I hoped for in my political career. Now I have only one last desire, one thing on my mind, the conclusion of a peace with the Arab countries and the Palestinians. That will be my last accomplishment, and once it is done I will happily retire to my ranch, ride my horses and tend to my sheep."

Sharon's birthday was in fact celebrated quietly with his family, in private, but his optimism was soon shaken by yet another horrible act, for on March 27, on the eve of Passover, a homicide bomber blew himself up in the ballroom of the Park Hotel in the seaside town of Netanya, killing thirty blameless Israelis celebrating the ritual feast. Thirty more names were added to the tragically long list of victims. In the month of March 2002 alone, one hundred Israelis lost their lives to Palestinian Kamikazes.

Israel's response was lighting-swift and sharp as a knife. Operation Homat Magen - Defensive Ramparts - sent thousands of soldiers into all the cities and towns in the West Bank. Every building was thoroughly searched, room by room, with no stone left unturned. What was found was stunning: tens of caches full of weapons, explosives laboratories, munitions, cartridges, shells...and tons of incriminating documents.

Many terrorists, including the assassins of Rehavan Ze'evi, had found refuge in Arafat's headquarters – better known as the Mukhata.

Sharon threatened to overrun Arafat's headquarters and arrest the killers; when Israeli tanks and artillery were visible from his window, Arafat went into a panic, and cried out for immediate international intervention. George Bush, preoccupied by his preparations for the Iraqi invasion, voiced concern and demanded that Sharon pull back Israeli troops from the immediate area. For once, the Israeli Prime Minister gave in to U.S. pressure, but left his forces around the town of Ramallah, to ensure that the terrorists could not flee. As for the assassins of Rehvam Ze'evi, they would be transferred to a Jericho prison by CIA agents, their Palestinian-guarded detention to be watched over by American and European observers (later, after the 2006 elections that brought Hamas to power, and after new Palestinian president Abbas was unable to guarantee the safety of the observers, Israeli troops entered the prison and seized the prisoners who were about to be released by their guards, and took them into custody and trial in Israel courts.)

Sharon's first idea was to expel Arafat from the West Bank. For his safety and for medical reasons, he could leave, but he could not return. Shin Beth and Mossad advice went counter to this plan, however, and both security agencies counselled keeping him in quarantine. "Better to have him in Ramallah, in his decrepit headquarters, than running free in the palaces and government offices all around the world, trailed by famished newshounds."

It was good advice, and Sharon listened to it. Arafat would be a prisoner in his own house, in a room with no electricity, cut off from the rest of the world. That did not mean Israel would do nothing, though. Shin Beth agents and paratroopers seized confidential documents from the Mukhata that clearly proved Arafat to be the principal patron of the acts of terror. Sharon was satisfied, declaring that "From now forward, and until the end of his days, Arafat would no longer be an interlocutor for peace between Israel and the Palestinians." He was, in Sharon's view, to be considered already dead.

On April 9, heavy fighting broke out during a total blackout in the overpopulated Jenin refugee camp in the northern part of the West Bank. During the night news filtered out that fourteen Israeli soldiers had died in an ambush in the narrow Jenin alleyways, and the army commanders decided to send in heavy bulldozers to clear a route through the camp, rather than send more soldiers into the mortally dangerous, narrow winding lanes. Many homes were simply flattened by the giant machines. In the confusion and panic that ensued, alarmist rumors flew in all directions claiming a massacre on the scale of the Sabrah and Shattilah killings near Beirut, leading Arab newspapers to speak of hundreds of victims, Despite a categorical denial by Israel, U.N. Secretary-General Kofi Annan named a Commission of Enquiry to get to the bottom of factual events. Sharon was livid, seeing in his mind the repetition of the Beirut scenario, with the international media accusing him of being the instigator of yet another massacre. Israel, and its armed forces – probably the most humane and careful army in the world when it came to taking precautions against collateral damage – were once again accused, tried and judged guilty of crimes against humanity, without any proof whatsoever being shown.

The United Stated pressed Israel to cooperate with the U.N. commission and Shimon Peres, in the end, offered discrete collaboration and succeeded in convincing Sharon to go along with the enquiry, which concluded that there had been no massacre at all in the Jenin refugee camp. Fifty-six Palestinians in all had been killed, half of them wanted terrorists on the Shin Beth arrest list. Sharon declared that "Israeli armed forces, alone in the world, took such risks to its own soldiers and put in place such checks as were required to avoid harm coming to the innocent."

But the cycle of violence did not abate. On April 11, the Gjriba Synagogue in Djerba, Tunisia, was attacked by an Al-Qaeda network. That the twenty-one victims were mostly German tourists and Tunisians made the crime, to the international media, all the more senseless. On June 23, Israeli fighter-bombers dropped a thousand kilogram explosive device on the Gaza home of Hamas leader Sheikh Sakah Shadeh.The entire building was destroyed by the blast, but among the ruins lay the bodies of fifteen innocent Palestinians, including the wife and son of the wanted man.

It was an enormous error of judgement, and it led to both Israeli and international media severely criticizing this new method of targeted assassinations of wanted terror leaders, although, ironically, it is precisely what the Russians do in Chechnya and what the U.S. Air Force does in Iraq. In the recent case of the elimination of Abu Musab al-Zarqawi, two missiles fired by F-16 jets destroyed the house where Zarqawi was meeting with his spiritual counselor, killing them both as well as four others, including an unidentified woman and a child.

This incident was the first and undoubtedly the last time the Israeli Air Force would use an F-16 fighter-bomber to liquidate a single terrorist. Sharon would pursue his attacks on the saboteurs of peace in the West Bank and in Gaza, but Apache helicopters armed with Hellfire missiles, and drones, would now replace supersonic airplanes in the struggle against terror.

As the date for the invasion of Iraq approached, a nervous and impatient George Bush invited Sharon for urgent talks at the White House. Remembering Minister Sharon's public criticism of the Shamir government's policy of non retribution – a promise squeezed from the Israelis by his father, President George Hebert Walker Bush, as the Scuds were falling on Israeli cities during the first Gulf War – Bush the son wanted to obtain a formal promise from Prime Minister Sharon to not retaliate against Saddam Hussein if missiles were to again be launched. There were fears of confrontation and verbal blows, but to the contrary, the meetings, prepared in advance down to the last details, went very smoothly. The two men quickly found a formula for agreement, and an interpersonal friendliness that augured well for the future. Sharon came with documents in hand that irrefutably proved Arafat's direct involvement in acts of terror: his signature was on the financing of arms purchases, as well as on the checks sent as compensation for their loss to the families of the *shahid,* the self-appointed suicide bombers, or so-called martyrs. It was enough to convince Bush. He promised Sharon that Arafat would no longer be seen by the U.S.

as a valid partner for peace and would have to be replaced by the Palestinian side.

Sharon was jubilant at the accomplishments of the meeting, and promised the Americans unlimited access to Israeli air space, and if needed, military bases. Bush promised to destroy on a priority basis the Iraqi Scud sites within range of Israel, and to send Israel the Patriot anti-missile missile system. Sharon affirmed that the attack on Iraq was not an issue of direct concern to Israel and promised to keep Israeli forces out of the fray, so as not to interfere with the ongoing operations of the coalition military forces. As a caveat, Prime Minister Sharon did leave open the possibility that under certain circumstances, a Tsahal raid could not be ruled out, though the Americans would have advance knowledge if such an event were to take place.

"I am even ready to send in commandos to take out the Iraqi sites," he commented, in his well-known sardonic style. Bush pretended not to hear this, and said no more, not wanting the conversation to bog down. But Sharon was quite serious, and relying on his own experience, he had no reason to rule out military options under the right circumstances, He ordered the Israeli Chief of Staff to consider all possible options and to again equip the entire nation with gas masks, just in case.

On November 29, 2002, a team of U.N. experts arrived in Baghdad. Their final report, issued after weeks of fruitless, intensive searching that discovered no trace of nuclear, biological or chemical manufacturing of weapons of mass destruction, was crystal-clear: Iraq had not reconstructed its ability to make such weapons. Bush was furious, but even though he could not backtrack on his preparations for war, he gave Saddam Hussein another stay.

The elections were back on in Israel, and the campaign took place in a climate of fear due to the ongoing suicide bombings and fear of imminent war with Iraq. The national economy was hurting, with unemployment rising to eleven per cent, and tourism was in decline, as was foreign investment. Many companies were pushed into bankruptcy by this situation with the foreign debt of the country exceeding twenty billion dollars, the balance of payments negative, inflation unchecked, and the Israeli shekel weakened. Something needed to be done, and quickly. Sharon introduced draconian measures to stabilize the economy, including major budget cuts to the Health and Family Welfare Ministry. But in Israel, as elsewhere, no good deed goes unpunished, and Sharon's attempts to bring the economy back to health provoked strong discontent in the Labor Party and in the ultra-orthodox Shas Party. They demanded a more equitable distribution of the budget cuts, and support for families with many children (who coincidentally happened to often be Shas supporters). If the pain was not to be equally shared, they said, they were willing to bring down the government.

Sharon, revolted by political blackmail, found himself between a rock and a hard place. Urgent measures were imperative to pull the country away from the brink of economic disaster, but his Labor and Shas coalition partners persisted and publicly condemned the budget cuts in the Knesset debates. Government ministers were now openly voting with the Opposition. Furious, Sharon decided on the spot to fire the turncoats and show Israeli public opinion that whatever the cost, he would never cede to base political maneuvering. In the swirling winds of total political confusion, the governing coalition collapsed. but Sharon, stubborn and sure of himself, succeeded in passing his economic cuts, including a last-minute supplementary amount of more than six hundred million dollars that was subtracted from the budget. Economic catastrophe was averted, but social disparity seemed to increase by the day. Still, as the election loomed ever closer, it was an issue that no one seemed to want to discuss.

David Levy, humiliated and vindictive, resigned and refused to even talk with Sharon. The Labor Party, with Defense Minister Fouad Ben Eliezer at its head also left the coalition, slamming the door behind it. Amir Peretz, leader of the Histadrut labor movement, threatened a general strike, which would paralyze the entire country.

Once Sharon had won the Likud primaries, and was that party's candidate for the position of Prime Minister, he offered Benjamin Netanyahu the position of Foreign Minister that had been vacant since the resignation of Shimon Peres. As for Defense, he gave it to Shaul Mofaz, a hard-liner who had only recently left the military.

But more turbulence was to come. Having adroitly succeeded in shoring up his support in Likud, Sharon was suddenly confronted with a financial scandal that seemed to implicate his sons, as well as himself, in a cloud of corruption. The elections were still weeks away, and his victory far from assured. The press lapped up the scandal like kittens in a bowl of cream (see Chapter Ten for more on this).

The Prime Minister issued a series of blanket denials, and his stonewalling succeeded in at least temporarily overcoming the accusations and focusing the nation's attention on issues of security. He also had to face the new head of the Labor Party, former general Amram Mitzna. Mitzna had been opposed to the Lebanon incursion led by Sharon in 1982, and commanded Israel's forces in the West Bank. His unequivocal view was that Israel should pull out of the occupied territories, and first of all, get out of Gaza. His statements had the merit of being perfectly clear, but at the stage things were at then, both Sharon and the nation seemed indifferent to his views.

Sharon replied to Mitzna's verbal attacks using an ambiguous vocabulary, talking about peace and security. To shore up his conservative support he played the "Jerusalem will be our eternal capital and the existing settlements in the territories must be reinforced" card. But playing to the mainstream, he spoke for the first time of "painful concessions" that would be required of Israel – without exactly stating when and how they might be put into place. Sharon's well-planned ambiguity adroitly let people speculate on his real intentions while avoiding irritating Washington, which was deep into preparations for the Iraq War. And if there was one thing Sharon wanted to ensure at this point, it was keeping Uncle Sam happy.

On February 28, 2003, two days after his seventy-fifth birthday, Sharon was re-elected Prime Minister of Israel. His 925,279 vote victory was an unprecedented landslide, an almost two to one margin over Labor, who garnered their lowest support since the creation of Israel, only 455,183 votes. The middle-of-the-road non religious Shinnui Party doubled its representation in the Knesset to fifteen seats, while Shas was reduced to eleven Knesset members, a loss of eight seats. The extreme left-wing Meretz Party only managed to elect six members. As for Labor, it was down to an embarrassing nineteen seats compared to Likud's thirty-eight. The people of Israel had spoken, moving to the right, and gave Ariel Sharon a clear mandate. Moving forward, Sharon could now govern the country with an iron hand.

Chapter 10

The Corruption Scandal

In affairs of state, a corrupt man is always more desirous than a simpleton, because the corrupt man cannot always allow himself to be directed by his conflicting interests, while the simpleton will be the toy of those who surround him.
Cardinal de Richelieu

Arik Sharon always rose at daybreak, an old habit going back to his youth and his time in the army. After eating an always-plentiful breakfast he would take telephone calls. Each morning at 6:30 on the dot, his faithful adviser and former army colonel Raanan Gissin - who speaks faultless American English - would call to read his boss the day's newspaper headlines and sum up the major stories of the day.

Sharon would listen attentively, and usually make no comment. As a child, he had taken the habit of parking himself at his father Shmuel's knees so as not to miss a syllable as the elder Scheinermann read the news from Davar, the Labor Party's paper, out loud. Things were not that simple any more, and Sharon, a man with much to accomplish, always had a crowded agenda which precluded him from personally reading the many national and international newspapers; in any case Sharon preferred to concentrate his mind on the daily confidential briefings prepared for him by his staff.

On the morning of January 7, 2003, Arik was in a particularly bad mood as his adviser read him the sensationalist story on the front page of *Haaretz*. According to the newspaper, Israeli police suspected him of personally receiving a 1.5 million dollar loan from a multimillionaire foreign Jewish friend, the proceeds of which were to reimburse questionable contributions received by Sharon's sons to help finance the recent Likud election campaign.

The foreign millionaire was Cyril Kern, an eighty-year-old British citizen and resident of South Africa who had made a fortune in the textile business. An old comrade-in-arms of Sharon, Kern had saved the Prime Minister's life by evacuating him quickly to a hospital after Arik had taken a bullet to the stomach during the 1948 battle of Latroun. Kern had since been an intimate friend and supporter of the Sharon family. The money in question had been wired from the Austrian Bawag Bank, and was in fact a five year loan bearing interest at three per cent.

There was nothing especially newsworthy about foreign Jewish millionaires contributing to Israeli election campaigns, nor for that matter financing the career of Israeli politicians: it was done all the time. The legal issue seemed to ride on whether or not Israeli law, which set a contribution quota and specified clear and aboveboard reporting, had been broken. Even then, most political parties regularly broke the quota ceiling and gladly paid the fines that were levied on them. Sharon's filing was all in order, but he had been kept from knowing that his son Omry had also pulled in considerable amounts, which he transferred to the Likud Party coffers using shell corporations and undeclared accounts based essentially in the United States. These sums, it turned out, were seven times the amounts authorized by the law on party financing during election campaigns.

Omry, an obese thirty-three year-old who affected dark sunglasses and shaved his head completely bald, drove a chrome motorcycle and was often seen in bars or on cafe terraces, chatting with his buddies and with Likud Party members. His political opinions were liberal, and moderate, and although he was married with three children, he had eschewed a religious wedding sanctioned by a rabbi. Since his mother Lily's death, Omry had become his father's intimate confident and a grey eminence of the Likud. Always discrete, a seasoned adviser but mediocre public speaker, Omry was one of the party's chief rainmakers. Always accompanying his father, even on foreign trips, he was his father's shadow. But when the news broke of the scandal, the shadow was suddenly much darker, less welcome, and cast much farther.

This affair was a complicated and embarrassing one, with consequences never before seen in the history of the country. Israelis recalled that years earlier, in 1977, Prime Minister Yitzhak Rabin had been forced to resign when it came out that his wife Lea had maintained a U.S. dollar account in a Washington bank, in clear violation of Israeli regulations. Now, officers from the fraud and corruption section of the police secretly visited Sharon at his home and questioned him at length about his knowledge of the facts of the case. The Prime Minister maintained that he knew absolutely nothing of these matters, and had never been advised of the details of his son's business affairs.

"I had other things on my mind during the campaign," Arik told them. "My focus was on political matters as I criss-crossed the country giving speeches. Administrative business, money transfers, that was not my business. Omry had taken on the management of this aspect of the campaign."

"But Prime Minister," the inspectors pressed, "given the considerable amounts in question here, and that you were the president of the Likud Party, how could you have been kept uninformed of these transactions?"

Sharon responded with a smile: "Believe me, gentlemen, my son Omry is old enough to manage his business on his own."

But Arik was very conscious of the gravity of the situation, smile or no smile, and called a press conference at eight pm, taking advantage of the evening news that broadcast his words live to the nation. In the final run-up to the elections, this was a huge story, and the press conference was carried by practically every radio and television station in Israel – despite the media law forbidding candidates' declarations from being broadcast outside of the framework of regular campaign propaganda.

"I have come," Sharon began, taking a decidedly aggressive opening stance, "to answer the grotesque lies that have been spread about my family. This calumny has only one reason for existence, to try and seize political power through insult and injury. Unable to attack me directly, my adversaries have decided to try and get to me by aiming at my sons. Now, for my children to want to help their father out during the election campaign, that is a natural and legitimate thing. And yet the media is clamoring about this as a scandalous crime of treason! Some have even gone so far as to talk about "organized crime" and the Mafia reaching into the upper echelons of our political life. Have they lost their minds, fallen on their heads?

Sharon went on, speaking with conviction as he explained in detail what had happened and why he had in fact requested the loan using his sons as intermediaries:

"The State Controller's office had obliged me to return to the original contributors more than one million dollars – the surplus from my earlier election campaign – but I did not have it. I cashed in all my savings as well as those of my wife Lily, blessed be her memory, but this only came to 150,000 dollars. I asked my son Gilad to somehow find the rest, in order to proceed with the repayment as required. My farm was mortgaged, and we raised enough to settle down to the last penny. As far as I am concerned, this is a closed file, as the State Controller knows perfectly well."

Sharon had been speaking for ten minutes already, and was in the middle of further explanations when suddenly, the news anchors of all three television networks broke into the live transmission, stunning a slack-jawed nation. "Following a Supreme Court order we are now interrupting the Prime Minister's press conference and will resume our previous news program."

What was behind this last minute move by the Supreme Court? Was the election law being broken? Were Sharon's explanations not important enough to merit being carried live on television and radio? Why had the media initially responded favorably to the Prime Minister's request and given him a "free" hour to explain himself before the people of Israel? Could this mean some kind of back door conniving was going on, a monopoly over radio and television as there was under totalitarian regimes? The on-air questions were flowing fast and furious, reflecting the thirst for answers of a perplexed and divided public opinion.

One thing was certain: Sharon's message came through loud and clear. The press conference had clarified his position and reinforced his credibility among voters. In the wake of the Prime Minister's outraged words the government legal adviser, a sort of state prosecutor, demanded an immediate police investigation to uncover what, or who, was hiding behind the Israeli "deep throat", the pseudonym that was being given - in a throwback to the Nixon Watergate affair - to the person who had apparently divulged to the press these private Sharon family matters.

What followed was even more astonishing. The journalist who had first published the information was arrested, and his mobile telephone with all the confidential numbers used for his work sitting in its memory chip, confiscated. After many hours of interrogation and threats of criminal charges being filed, he decided that indiscretion was, in this case, the better part of valor and came clean, revealing that his source in this case came from the State Prosecutor's Office. This was an incredible development, as no Israeli journalist had ever before denounced a source to the authorities. Unthinkable in a democracy!

Liora Glat-Berkowitch, a lawyer working in the prosecutor's office, admitted being the source of the information, self-righteously claiming that she acted to embarrass the Prime Minister. "I felt I had do everything I could to stop his re-election," she avowed. Israelis were conflicted, trying to resolve the moral and political issues involved. But then a second scandal – the Greek Island – crashed into the eyes of the public, implicating Sharon's other son, Gilad.

In 1999, a wealthy Israeli real estate developer and prominent Likud Party member by the name of David Appel had hired Gilad Sharon on a consultancy basis to explore the tourist potential of the Greek island of Patrokelos in the Aegean Sea, not far from Athens. Appel, a bon vivant in his fifties, had made a fortune in real estate and was ready, apparently, to invest hundreds of millions of dollars to develop vacation complexes on the island. It was a gigantic – some said utopian – idea, but Appel nonetheless paid Gilad Sharon a $400,000 retainer plus $20,000 a month for his services in support of the development. Ariel Sharon, still in the Opposition in the Knesset, was aware of the general plan of the development, but not informed of the details of the project. Still, he attended a lavish reception in Jerusalem hosted by Appel in honor of the mayor of Athens, and when Appel – who had contributed substantially to the Likud war chest – asked Arik if it was possible to intervene with the authorities to help various development projects advance through the bureaucratic maze, Sharon listened.

The police were listening, too. They had been wiretapping Appel for some time in an investigation of some other suspicious business in which he was supposedly involved, and learned that Ariel Sharon had personally intervened to support an important real estate development in the Lod region, near Ben-Gurion International Airport.

Gilad Sharon was the younger son, well educated, looking the part of the intellectual, and holding degrees in agronomy and market economics. He had met his future wife Inbal when she was a high school student and he already a soldier. Seven years later they were discretely married in a religious ceremony without informing either Arik or Lily. Since 1989 Gilad and Inbal ran the family ranch where they lived privately with their two children, refusing all media inter-

Random scenes from the life of Ariel Sharon

Ariel Sharon surrounded by exhausted, celebrating soldiers after action in Syria, 01/12/1956. Photo: Government Press Office

Prime Minister Levy Eshkol, Defence Minister Moshe Dayan, General Haim Bar Lev and Lt. Col. Shlomo Lahat during their visit to army camps on the West Bank, September 20, 1967. Ariel Sharon is at the far left. Photo: Ilan Bruner, GPO

Prime Minister Yitzhak Rabin listens to his adviser Ariel Sharon, in the helicopter flying them to the Golan Heights. Photo: Ya'acov Sa'ar, 11/12/1975 (GPO)

Former Prime Minister David Ben-Gurion listens to explanations of Southern Command O.C. Ariel Sharon during a visit to Israeli positions along the Egyptian border near the Suez Canal, January 27, 1971. (GPO)

General view of the desert Sycamores ("Shikmim") ranch of Housing Minister Ariel Sharon. Photo: © Tsvika Israeli, 27/08/1990 (GPO)

Housing Minister Ariel Sharon and his wife, Lily, host Prime Minister Yitzhak Shamir at their Sycamores Ranch in the Negev Desert. Photo: Tsvika Israeli, 27/08/1990(GPO)

Knesset Member Geula Cohen on her way to attend the housewarming party at Ariel Sharon's new home in the Moslem Quarter of the Old City of Jerusalem. Photo: Maggi Ayalon, 15/12/1987(GPO)

Ariel Sharon laying a hand on the body of 5 month-old Yehuda Haim Shoham, who was murdered during a stone throwing attack near Shilo. The photograph was taken on 11/06/2001, at the beginning of the funeral. Photo: Avi Ohayon(GPO)

Defence Minister Ariel Sharon on the banks of the Suez Canal, returning by motor car from his official visit to Egypt. Photo: Moshe Milner, 21/01/1982(GPO)

August 6, 1981 ceremony at the Defence Ministry marking Ariel Sharon's taking over as Defence Minister from outgoing Prime Minister Menachem Begin. Mrs. Lili Sharon is at her husband's side, as always. Photo: Yaacov Saar, 06/08/1981(GPO)

Cabinet Ministers (right to left) Ezer Weizman, Rafael Eitan and Ariel Sharon during a break after the opening address of the 11th Knesset, Jerusalem, 13/08/1984. Photo: Chanania Herman(GPO)

Defence Minister Ariel Sharon and his wife Lili at at an Israeli Air Force Base during a military ceremony and aerial display. Photo: Baruch Rimon, 15/07/1982(GPO)

Egyptian President Anwar el-Sadat and his party dine with the Israeli negotiating team at the King David Hotel in Jerusalem on September 11, 1977. Photo: Ya'acov Sa'ar(GPO)

President Anwar el-Sadat shakes the hand of Israeli Defence Minister Ariel Sharon in Alexandria. Photo: Chanania Herman 25/08/1981(GPO)

(L-R) Prime Minister Menachem Begin and Ministers Burg, Sharon and Shamir walk from their lodgings to attend the funeral of assassinated Egyptian President Anwar el-Sadat, held on the Sabbath. Photo: Chanania Herman, 10/10/1981(GPO)

Ariel Sharon with Ambassador Eytan and Mauritanian Foreign Minister Dah Ould Abdi seated before the Chagal mural at the Foreign Ministry in Jerusalem on May 22, 2001. Speaking discretely in Hebrew, Sharon is asking Eytan to please get him an invitation to Mauritania, as he has heard "they have the most fantastic fish barbecues in the world." Photo: Gil Hadani views, keeping well out of the limelight. Gilad's political views were diametrically opposed to those of his brother Omry. He was a staunch and intransigent conservative, and a brilliant businessman, specializing in the sale of breeding bulls raised on the Sharon ranch.

Ariel Sharon was questioned about Gilad's involvement in the Greek Island project. He responded with a ringing endorsement of his son:

> "Believe me, my son Gilad is a very talented man. He is competent in business, and very much up on new technology, and I'm not saying this just because he's my son, you know. Frankly, he's really a "brain" with a lot on the ball."

"But Prime Minister," the police investigators persisted, "are you saying your son never spoke with you about his projects?"

"Never," replied Sharon with a laugh. "One day he said, 'Listen, dad, you take care of the Arabs and the rest of the world, and I'll take care of business. You have your field and your problems, and I have mine.' "

The truth was that Ariel almost always followed Gilad's advice. He was in the habit of listening in admiration and attentively to his son's every word. Gilad could reach his father at all times, even during raucous Knesset debates or Cabinet meetings. His calls were always taken by Sharon, who especially enjoyed hearing happy news from the ranch, a new birth, for example would invariably touch the Prime Minister who loved playing with the yearlings. Whenever the two men met, Ariel would take out his little notebook and write down his son's advice. And as a rule, whatever he wrote in his little books would sooner or later be acted on.

Initially, Gilad refused to cooperate with the police, but eventually he realized stonewalling was useless and handed over whatever documents he possessed. The police were already in possession of incriminating tapes made through phone taps. As the police investigators reminded him, his own father had fired Naomi Blumenthal, a Deputy Minister in his own government, for refusing to talk in an minor graft scandal. Was Gilad now a partisan of the double standard?

This scandal, like others, did not directly implicate Ariel Sharon and no criminal accusations seemed forthcoming as far as he was concerned. But many delicate questions emerged from the affair, questions which needed to be treated with frankness and transparency. For example, what did David Appel expect when he hired Gilad Sharon as a consultant? Was it a clever way to conceal a bribe? Was malfeasance involved? Did Ariel Sharon use the Greek Island affair to get around the laws governing politicians and state employees? Did he have the moral or legal right to get involved in sensitive files like the Lod development project? And why did Gilad accept six hundred thousand dollars in consultant's fees for a project that never got off the ground?

Arik responded to all the questions put to him during the lengthy police investigation, but remained vague, sardonic, and without seeming to take the interrogation seriously, which suggested that his conscience might not have been entirely clear in the matter. The State Prosecutor recommended corruption and perjury charges be laid, but Menachem Mazuz, the man responsible for the government's final decision in the matter, found no valid proof and closed the file, taking a considerable weight off the Prime Minister's shoulders.

Omry Sharon, however, was not so fortunate. Despite his status as an elected member of the Knesset he was charged in the matter of the unlawful contribution to the Likud Party and specifically accused of falsifying documents, bearing false witness, and illegal financing of a political party. The documents accompanying the charges included wiretaps and handwritten notes by the accused, purporting to show that Omry Sharon used shell corporations to launder money which served to finance his father's political campaign. But there was the question of his parliamentary immunity. If he resigned to face the charges, would this be the end of his political career? The risk was a maximum of five years in prison, but in all likelihood, with good lawyers, the sentence would be a reduced one, to be served in social work "in the public interest." After much reflection he pleaded guilty but claimed that the law regulating the financing of political parties was invalid, since the maximum for permitted contributions, given the lengthy Israeli campaigns, was ridiculously low. Few Israelis disagreed with him.

While malfeasance is common in most of the countries of the world, including Israel, and was not invented yesterday, its existence means that politicians need to be exemplary in their behavior and demonstrate prudence in their dealings, avoiding cupidity and the traps set by others. In this respect Arik Sharon should have behaved differently and shown a better example, even though he was only targeted on the basis of slight suspicion. Israelis need their leaders to conform to the highest standard of ethics and morality, and Sharon's actions did not meet that test. In wanting to defend and protect his sons at all costs, he was late in reacting to events, often finding himself playing catch-up with the media and its apparently never-ending revelations.

Chapter 11

The Roadmap

"This is a practical and fair formula for making peace."
Ariel Sharon, March 10, 2003

At the beginning of March, 2003, Ariel Sharon presented his new Cabinet to the Knesset. The majority of his Ministers were from the Likud party, with the selection process and distribution of portfolios heavily influenced by Sharon's elder son Omry, who had advised his father against taking the Sephardic Shas religious party into Cabinet. Instead, he recommended the coalition ministers come from the lay Shinnui party. Some said it was unfortunate that the business of state in a democratic country be decided this way, within the Sharon family and between the father and the son, but that is what happened. Shaul Mofaz remained at Defense, Silvan Shalom was now Foreign Minister, and Bibi Netanyahu was at Finance. David Levy and Dan Meridor, respectively outgoing Foreign Minister and Minister of Finance and Justice, were no longer part of the Executive branch of government.

Sharon's platform had nothing remarkable to it, no revolutionary measures to lift the nation's hopes for a better future. Political change had led to continuity; it was more of the same. The world was focused on the Iraqi crisis. In the territories, Arafat remained isolated in the Mukhata, and named Mahmoud Abbas – otherwise known as Abu Mazen – to become the new head of the Palestinian government. Abbas found himself in a difficult position, with suicide bombings continuing, Arafat still unwilling to call off the Intifada, and Sharon, resisting American and British pressure, continuing to send the military to comb through the West Bank and Gaza looking for wanted men and the exploding belt wearers they tried to send into Israel.

On March 23, the Second Gulf War began despite no unconventional weapons having been found in Iraq. The goal of President George Bush was clear: finish what his father had begun during the First Gulf War; take Baghdad, capture Saddam Hussein and undertake regime change. A new and pro-American government was to take power in a democratic Iraq.

President Bush called Sharon several hours before hostilities were to begin to advise him of the imminent events. Preliminary contacts took place between Tsahal and the Pentagon, but no formal operational coordination was set up. Inside Israel, most commentators, and even the intelligence services, initially thought that the U.S. invasion would take place in favorable circumstances. In fact, with the heart of the war not six hundred kilometers from Jerusalem, things were remarkably quiet in the Jewish state. No hostile fire was taken, and not a single Scud missile was launched against Israel. The apocalyptic predictions of some Israeli generals proved to be in error. Sharon had personally ordered the mobilization of all army reserves and the distribution of gas masks to the population, but as he was convinced that the Iraqis were essentially no longer capable of attacking, the measures were preventive in nature and designed to focus attention away from the situation in the territories.

As is well known, the Americans quickly overwhelmed the Iraqi armed forces; combat was often broadcast live on television. Baghdad was taken without much difficulty, the Americans welcomed with the enthusiasm reserved for liberators; but the euphoria would not be a lasting one. The forces of Bush's coalition had in fact fallen into a hornet's nest, and their initial victory – capturing the country and ousting Hussein, now fleeing from spider hole to spider hole – only marked the beginning of a war of attrition in which insurgent forces used ambushes, improvised explosive devices (the country was afloat in unprotected munitions seized wholesale and stashed away by remnants of Hussein's Baath Party and other groups) and assassination to try and make organized chaos, not disorganized democracy, the source of political power in Iraq. The provisional regime proved to be not up to the task of restoring order. With each passing day the list of fallen American soldiers grew longer, climbing beyond the 2,400 mark by May, 2006. The wounded in action count was much, much larger. The British lost more than one hundred dead and fifteen thousand wounded. Iraq was an ungovernable anarchy and talk grew louder of splitting the country into three: a Kurdish North, Sunni Center and Shia South might be the only alternative to civil war. Political and revenge killings were on the rise and would grow to frightening levels by 2006. Gangs of criminals found that non-political kidnapping was a lucrative and low-risk enterprise. Soft targets were everywhere, from well-off Iraqis to foreign male and female journalists, engineers and aid workers; even those employing bodyguards were vulnerable in an environment where life was truly a cheap commodity.

Terrorists seemed able to strike at will, especially in the so-called "Sunni Triangle" near the towns of Fallujah and Ramadi, and President Bush appeared unable to offer his tiring nation a quick fix. Americans were used to thinking short-term, but the battle against terror, as was becoming painfully obvious, would be a long and relentless one. Once basking in broad popular support and enjoying amazingly high ratings, Bush now saw his credibility sinking to all-time lows, and with it, his power to act with a free hand was ebbing.

In this context, Ariel Sharon seemed to be an ideal ally for George Bush. The men shared a vision of the use of power politics where the threat of force doctrine was in the ascendancy. The U.S. invasion of Iraq reinforced America's presence in the Middle East and weakened the influence of Europe. The Arab world was divided, and governments had taken a new tack since the fall of Baghdad. Hardly a one protested the invasion, or spoke up in Defense of the Hussein regime, which was remarkable since Iraq was a full member of the Arab League. Syria was now completely isolated as the "Eastern Front" was broken. Damascus was publicly accused of fomenting terror, and Iran was fast moving into America's sights. The obscurantist regime in Tehran was considerably more dangerous than Saddam Hussein had been. It sought nuclear weapons, possessed long-range missiles, and called for nothing less than the annihilation of Israel. The ayatollahs' followers, Hezbollah (Party of God) were well established in Lebanon and represented a clear threat to the Jewish state. "Jerusalem Day" was celebrated each year in Beirut by throngs of Hezbollah faithful. Their leader, Hassan Nasrallah, treated the crowds to inflammatory and bellicose rhetoric, calling for the destruction of the Zionist state, imploring the wildly applauding believers to march victorious on Al Quds, the Arab name for Jerusalem.

In responding to these threats, Sharon, ever the adroit tactician, preferred to take decisions in concert with the United States, while keeping his hands free to act in hot pursuit against the men who ordered terrorist attacks, be they Palestinian or Iranian-controlled Shia. He maintained ongoing and fruitful contacts with President Bush, contacts that gave positive results, and his plans for advancing the peace process with the Palestinians were taken quite seriously.

After lengthy discussions, on September 17, the Middle East Diplomatic Quartet – the United States, the EEC, Russia and the United Nations – issued a draft "Roadmap" with the intention of putting the peace process back on the rails. The document was based on the vision of President Bush as set out in a June, 2002 speech – before the Iraq War began – and had been painfully arrived at after detailed, point-by-point discussion among the signatories, then carefully examined and analyzed by Sharon. The Roadmap when officially published on May 1, 2003, proposed three essential phases in the march towards peace. (See document 2 in the appendix).

Phase One called for the end to terrorist acts and violence in all forms, the implementation of security measures and a return to an environment of calm. Israeli forces in zones occupied after September 28, 2000 – the beginning of the Intifada – were to be withdrawn, outposts were to be dismantled, and there was to be a freeze on new settlements in the territories.

Phase Two was to be a transitional phase, involving preparation for a final status agreement, democratic elections in the territories, and an International Peace Conference.

Phase Three was expected to see the final accord signed in 2005, signalling the end of the Israeli-Palestinian conflict.

From the start, Sharon refused to accept the international community's right to dictate the manner and timing – and substance – of the accords. He wanted no part of a Roadmap that was precise as to timing, and preferred to resolve the problems then in abeyance directly with the Palestinians, having first reached a friendly understanding as to substance and methodology with the American president. As he put it, "Too many cooks spoil the broth."

Two issues were particularly thorny for him. The status of Jerusalem, which for Sharon could never be less than the united capital of Israel, was the first, and on this the Prime Minister was intransigent. The second, equally egregious to Sharon, was the Palestinian so-called Right of Return that would have permitted Palestinians displaced in all conflict since 1948 to go back to their original homes, drowning the Jewish state in a wave of hostile voters. These two points, Sharon stated categorically, would never make it past the Knesset.

But the Americans were not moved by his efforts, and pressured by them, he decided to walk a political tightrope right to the end in a high-wire act that put his reputation on the line and threatened to overturn his government. It was a remarkable display of strength of character, and in the end, he carried the day.

First, at eight am on May 23, 2003, Ariel Sharon convened a

meeting of the Likud ministers of the Government of Israel to listen to their points of view. This was followed by a full extraordinary Cabinet meeting. Circumstances made the meeting very tense: several terrorist attacks the previous evening had resulted in many casualties, breaking the ongoing unofficial truce – *hudna* in Arabic (ten days later Abu Mazen would promise a formal truce during meeting in Aqaba). Outside in the streets, hundreds of demonstrators from the extremist Right were screaming epithets at the "traitor Sharon."

Inside, the atmosphere was heavy. Many of those present held the morning papers in their hands, with photographs of the victims of the attacks on the front pages. Ariel Sharon was seated at the center of a long mahogany table, nervous, and impatient. As usual, he opened the meeting with some banal remarks concerning the agenda. The tension was palpable as he began to speak, electricity in the air.

He stated his positions immediately, convincingly, and during more than six hours tried to convince the Cabinet to accept the Roadmap, vowing to oblige the other signatories to accept modifications at a later date:

"This is a very difficult day for me," he began. "I completely understand your apprehension, and I will do everything in my power to change the points that we are all concerned about, regarding the status of Jerusalem, the Right of Return, and not returning to pre-1967 borders. At this stage, I don't want to confront the Americans, who are our closest friends and allies, nor let the world conclude that we reject the peace process. Believe me, I know very well what is good for Israel and for the Jewish people. Everyone can speak his mind today, but before the meeting ends we have to take a vote."

Fifteen remarks were added to the document before it came to a vote. After long and fractious debate, the Israeli Government accepted the Prime Minister's plan, with, among other important modifications, a clause stating that it was the responsibility of the eventual Palestinian government to itself find a solution to the problem of refugees, including their integration into the new State of Palestine. This of course was tantamount to an outright rejection of the Right of Return.

The vote was taken on this basis, and carried, twelve for, and four abstentions, including Benjamin Netanyahu. The following day, during a meeting with the Knesset Likud Members, the party hawks went on the attack, denouncing the Roadmap and its supporters. It was, according to them, a more dangerous document than the Oslo Peace Accords. It was a real slap in the face for the Prime Minister, but Sharon, always at the top of his game in adversity, responded in a voice replete with *gravitas*, a caustic smile on his lips: “What would you suggest? That we continue to dominate and control a population of three and a half million Palestinians that is growing by leaps and bounds? How will we deal with that? You might not like to hear it, but I am telling you that we must put an end to the occupation. This occupation is ruinous for Israel!”

This was not one of the leaders of the extremist Left speaking, this was the blustery and forceful general whose actions may have saved Israel during the October War. And people listened.

The next day, Sharon, acting upon the advice of his legal counsel, tried to mollify his critics. He would not talk about the “occupation” any more, but instead, the “disputed territories.” Still, decidedly on a roll, Arik continued to surprise the members of his party by clearly stating that he intended to arrive at a peace accord, no matter how much headwind and high tide he had to fight to get it. Then he added, “Besides, I have no intention of asking the Knesset to vote on the Roadmap. It is not a peace accord to be officially sanctioned, only a framework for the peace process.”

The table was now set for George W. Bush to arrive in the Middle East, and he did just that, in the Jordanian port city of Aqaba, hardly more than a few hundred meters from the Israeli border, on the 4th of June. The American president was received with full honors and grand pomp by Jordan’s King Abdullah. Ariel Sharon and Abu Mazen were also present at what was to be the ultimate Middle East summit meeting. President Bush arrived convinced that time was ripe for him to impose a *Pax Americana* and be done with the problem. Bush's vision was clear: the Holy Land had to be divided into a Jewish state and a Palestinian state. He had already set this out in his June, 2002 speech, and this vision was, according to Ariel Sharon, one of the most significant contributions to the process of attaining a benevolent future for the Middle East. Sharon had in fact come to share this view of things, but had a different take on the means to attain it. Once in power, he had realized the necessity of giving up part of the territories in the greater interests of Israel. The occupation had to end!

But ever the pragmatist, he employed the carrot and the stick to good effect. In Aqaba he was conciliatory with Abu Mazen, believing he could reach a compromise with him without abandoning either his relentless struggle against terrorism or his decision to maintain Arafat in isolation until the end of his days. The American plan could be implemented in stages. But the *sine qua non* condition to let the peace train move down the line would be the ending of all terror, violence, and incitement of hatred for Jews among ordinary Palestinians. Faced with American and European pressure on this point he stood his ground, brandishing this argument in response to each initiative, each proposal.

When George Bush demanded the dismantling of all outposts and illegal, hastily-constructed colonies in the territories, Sharon agreed. When Bush asked the Prime Minister to accept the principle of contiguous borders between Gaza and the West Bank, Sharon agreed again, but insisted that this particularly thorny issue be settled within the framework of the final status accord.

Abu Mazen showed himself to be fairly conciliatory at the Aqaba meetings, not wanting to follow the high stakes rules of negotiation Arafat had always followed at the risk of seeing everything collapse. In front of the television cameras beaming his image out to the peoples of the world, he forcefully denounced terrorist acts and proclaimed "the end of the military uprising" as such methods were contrary to the principles of Islam; besides, he added, they were dangerous, and an obstacle to the establishment of a Palestinian state. Showing no little personal courage, he recognized – and it was the first time a Palestinian leader had ever done this – the sufferings of the Jewish people throughout history.

Sharon's acceptance of the Roadmap had surprised the Israeli public. Diplomatic circles were ecstatic at the dramatic change in the position of the Prime Minister. Less happy were the members of Likud: revolt was in the air, and ferocious discontent seemed to be the order of the day. The malicious gossipers suggested it was all a ruse on Sharon's part, a maneuver to make people forget the corruption scandal and the ongoing police investigation of his family.

Sharon was, as it happens, quite at ease with the principle of a "roadmap." He had already concluded that this solution, which he had been ready for some time to apply in his own way when circumstances were right, was ideal because it was phased, and not tied down to any set dates. More importantly, the roadmap formula unequivocally stated that there could be no final peace negotiations until terror had been finally and completely eradicated. The Palestinians would have to lay down their arms if they were serious about opening peace talks with Israel. It was a primordial and existential condition for the Jewish state.

On June 6, back in Jerusalem, the Aqaba Summit behind him, it was time for Sharon to pacify the right wing of his party. He called a plenary session of the Likud at the Jerusalem Convention Center. The meeting was, to put it mildly, raucous. Arik faced catcalls and hoots of disapproval. His speech to the meeting was constantly interrupted by booing and whistling, and his efforts to convince the members of his party fell far short, even when he quoted Menachem Begin, the Likud Founding Father. His reasoning was to no avail. In his own fiefdom, Arik Sharon had become an undesirable.

He was publicly accused of running the country with an iron fist, of giving no consideration to the Likud program or the views of party members who had, lest he forget, welcomed him and elected him.

Then he was criticized for deciding everything on his own, or together with his sons. It must have brought back memories of his parents' conflict with the members of Kfar Malal over collective versus individual decisions.

Stoic in the face of the attacks and the abuse, he kept calm and observed the crowd placidly, fully convinced he was in the right, and deeply believing that no one could force him to backtrack now. Ariel Sharon was past master in the arts of self-control and emotion-free governing, but it was difficult not to react to the loud, insulting criticism. In the recent past he had himself been a noisy and forceful opponent of other Israeli Prime Ministers. To appease the party hawks, he took the tactical decision to harden his positions and his demands with regard to the Palestinians and the Roadmap. This entailed reinforcing the struggle against terror, even at the risk of breaking the truce agreed to at Aqaba and confronting President Bush. Conscious of the fact that Abu Mazen was in no position to attack the fundamentalist Hamas movement, Sharon took the initiative - and the fight - right to the enemies of peace, targeting Hamas leaders with blood on their hands.

Only four days after the Likud meeting, he sanctioned the killing of Doctor Abdel Aziz Rantisi, the insolent Hamas spokesman. But Tsahal missed its target; Rantisi emerged relatively unscathed from his charred vehicle and pursued his attacks on Israel from clandestine locations, nonetheless somehow managing to regularly appear on Arab television. This assassination attempt provoked an American protest, but it especially infuriated the Palestinians and a revenge attack was not long in coming. One week later, a homicide bomber blew himself up in Jerusalem, killing seventeen civilians.

Hamas was now Israel's Public Enemy Number One. With the support of the American Jewish Lobby, the United States Congress passed a resolution recognizing the right of Israel to defend itself against terrorists and their sponsors. President Bush was shown Shin Beth documents proving Israeli assertions concerning the intentions of the terrorist chiefs and gave Sharon the "green light" to liquidate the "human bombs" and their sponsors. The U.S. President had finally understood that Hamas was the main saboteur of the Roadmap peace process. From now on he would close his eyes to the targeted Tsahal strikes. At the top of Israel's list was Abdallah Kawasme. His life ended in Hebron on June 20, 2003.

Abu Mazen watched the events, powerless to do more than watch what was taking place. In order to stop the cycle of violence and apply the truce he so badly needed to run the affairs of the government-in-waiting of the State of Palestine, he had to act quickly. After difficult negotiations with Hamas he obtained the promise of a six month truce, on condition that Israel stop its targeted killings. In response, Sharon muted his threats, but called Mazen a "little chick," adding that Israel would pursue its fight on terror until such time as the little chick grew its own feathers. The Palestinian leader put up with Sharon's vexed comments, the United States seemed content that the Roadmap was on, and hope was born again. But the truce, sadly, would only last a few weeks.

On August 19, 2003, another bomber hit Jerusalem; twenty-three victims lost their lives in the attack. Sharon then re-started the targeted killings and this time, going against advice from the head of Shin Beth, also decided to expel Arafat. As he expected, the United Nations protested, as did foreign powers. President Bush intervened and asked Israel to leave Arafat be, requesting restraint even after Sharon showed the American proof that Arafat had personally been behind the recent attacks. Now Abu Mazen decided to loudly resign from his position as head of the Palestinian government, and Arafat replaced him with Abu Alla. Sharon refused to meet with this man, brutally referring to him as "a puppet of Arafat" in a conversation with Bush. "I'll take my time," he told the U.S. President.

The sides were back at an impasse, the Roadmap stalled, and the carefully drawn plans of the players disintegrating. George Bush, immersed in the interminable Iraqi war up to his neck, seemed disappointed by the decision of his faithful ally Ariel. The Middle East was plunged back into the anxiety of the unknown, with the cycle of violence once more raging. The economic situation in Israel was worsening; in the territories, it was catastrophic. A perplexed Sharon cast around for a solution, a lifebuoy, something to hang onto. Yossi Beilin, a former Minister from a leftist party, and one of the architects of the Oslo Accords, met with Arafat confidant Abdel Rabbo in an attempt to restart the peace process. Encouraged and financed by the European Community, they prepared the "Geneva Initiative" and submitted it as an alternative to the Roadmap, which now seemed to have been transformed into a road block. The new plan, to which the Swiss committed six million U.S., was enthusiastically received in the capitals of Europe and gained much support in Israel itself - only not from Sharon, who along with the Israeli Right fiercely opposed the initiative.

The Prime Minister, recalling the left-wing demonstrators in the streets of Tel-Aviv and Jerusalem while he was Defense Minister during the Lebanon War, accused Beilin of collaborating with the enemies of Israel while Tsahal was trying to stifle terrorism. The political storm within Israel was worrisome, Sharon was more and more isolated, and a directionless anarchy now reigned among the Palestinians. A new plan began to take shape in Sharon's mind, a plan for unilateral disengagement, starting with the Gaza strip. But the Israeli Prime Minister led a fragile coalition with intransigent partners, and his ability to manoeuvre was limited. To find a way out of the impasse, Arik called on his old friend Shimon Peres. Peres, like Sharon a veteran of Israeli political infighting, had just been re-elected as head of the Labor Party at the ripe old age of eighty, celebrating his birthday with a star-studded list of personalities from around the world. Now he once more entered government at Sharon's invitation, in an attempt to jump-start the new plan.

Peres and Sharon were men of the same generation, knowing and respecting each other since the time when David Ben-Gurion had taken a liking to Arik Scheinermann and given the young officer his new Hebrew name, "Sharon." Their personalities were completely different, and their opinions often diametrically opposed. Sharon was a hardened military man and an adroit tactician. Peres was a fine diplomat with a vision for the future. Ironically, these differences in the end meant the two men completed each other in a way. There was no disagreement between them concerning the general outlines of the plan, which had to be moved on very fast to be successful. In the past, Peres had worked in a similar way with Yitzhak Rabin, but Sharon had an advantage over his predecessor: he knew how to put any project, even the most audacious, into practice. It wasn't for nothing that he was nick-named "the bulldozer."

Chapter 12

The Disengagement Plan

When a diplomat says "yes," he means "perhaps;"
when he says "perhaps," he means "no,"
and when he says "no," it means he isn't a diplomat.
English Proverb

Ariel Sharon was seated at a table in the Knesset restaurant before an assortment of delicious oriental dishes including one of his favorites, meatballs in a thick and spicy sauce. Always blessed with a good appetite, he wore a white napkin around his neck and ate with gusto. Around him were many of his collaborators including his faithful legal adviser Dov Weissglass, a lawyer who had been with Sharon for a long time and was in charge of many of the Prime Minister's legal matters. Weissglass was recounting his latest meetings with the Americans, preparing Sharon for a forthcoming trip to Washington.

The Prime Minister listened, his mouth full, seeming distracted. He was a man who appreciated good food, a true *aficionado* of the art of eating who was quite capable of ordering his convoy of vehicles to suddenly stop at a roadside falafel stand, and, standing up like any other ordinary Israeli, wolf down a large pita stuffed with the delicious deep fried chick-pea dumplings covered with tahini sesame sauce. His bodyguards, vigilant and severe as a rule, smilingly bent to the P.M.'s culinary excesses, usually taking advantage of the stop for a couple of falafels of their own.

No one in Sharon's entourage seemed able to get his snacking under control. Hunger makes the best man deaf, as the saying goes. For many years, Sharon's wife Lily had tried - and failed - to reign in his gastronomical desires. His doctors seemed also powerless to help. In fact, all the efforts they put in place to impose a balanced diet on Arik never amounted to much, and as the years went by he gained more and more weight, easily breaking through the one hundred kilo barrier. His weight, his eating habits, and his stressful work all had an impact on his health, of course. He developed gastric and kidney problems, and needed surgery to dissolve many stones in the urinary passage. Another operation proved necessary to remove a benign tumor lodged in a cyst near his left temple. His left ear hearing was weak also. For years he had trouble understanding the words of his advisers, who often spoke softly close to his ear, and had developed the use of written notes instead, bypassing his infirmity. He kept these notes as souvenirs over the years, and was crushed when they all went up in smoke, along with his little notebooks, in the 1999 fire at the Sycamores Ranch.

Still, he got over the minor health problems as the years went by, In spite of his advanced age (he was seventy-seven at this time) and the frequent colds, nervous tics, "senior moments" and war wounds on his forehead and in his stomach, Ariel was, according to his doctors, in perfect health. There were good genes at work: his Paris uncle Joseph had lived to be one hundred and one, and his aunt Fania was ninety-nine when she passed away. Both had remained lucid to the last. If there was one nagging problem, it was that even minor physical effort resulted in a shortness of breath, which was indeed bothersome to a man who was both a bon vivant and a workaholic.

In truth, Arik Sharon's responsibilities were heavy, the tasks he needed to accomplish difficult. He had to rise early and retire late at night. Aides were authorized to wake him at any hour to impart important news, and commonly did. The P.M.'s daily agenda was always chock-full, with meetings, conferences, official visits, travel, Knesset debates, and reading of current briefings and confidential security reports. The time constraints made it impossible to indulge in the relaxation of a tasty restaurant meal, a classical music concert, or a good movie or live show, all activities he relished and had previously been able to enjoy. Instead, he often found himself stapled to his Knesset seat listening to endless, boring debates or participating in interminable ministerial meetings. In public, he always appeared dressed in suit and matching tie. After his wife Lily passed away, his thirty-eight year-old assistant Merav Levy had taken over the job of choosing his clothes – from the Big and Tall racks –, putting on his television make-up, and trying to ride herd on his eating habits.

At this point in his life, there was a single idea that obsessed Arik Sharon, and that was to be able to write into the glorious pages of the history of Israel that he had been successful in evacuating Israeli forces from Gaza without suffering significant losses. A trial balloon was sent up during meetings with newspaper editorial boards. Sharon followed this up by sending Dov Weissglass to sound out the Americans, Secretary of State Condoleezza Rice in particular, about the plan. Weissglass also gave a lengthy interview to the daily *Haaretz* on October 8, 2004, in which he set out the reasons for and the advantages of unilateral disengagement from Gaza. Ehud Olmert, Sharon's faithful ally and later on Prime Minister of Israel himself, went further. In an December 3, 2004 interview in the *Yediot Aharonot* daily he stated that there was reason to be concerned about the Palestinian population growth, and that he would be ready to dismantle many of the settlements and evacuate Gaza.

Sharon himself neither confirmed nor denied these statements, contenting himself with his usual practice of manipulating public opinion by leaving doubts about his true intentions, even among members of his own government. Shimon Peres declared that he would be astonished if Sharon dismantled the established settlements in Gaza. If the back-and-forth rumors worried the hawks of the Likud Party, with

Benjamin Netanyahu at their head, they alarmed the Gaza settlers who were more and more wary of Sharon's real plans for them.

As for George Bush, he wanted to know more about what the Israeli Prime Minister had in mind. Bush had no desire to abandon the Roadmap plan, and feared an inopportune manoeuvre on the part of his ally. In a smooth political move, Sharon sent messages meant to calm the president's concerns, while insisting on the fact that the Palestinian leaders were obviously not serious about sitting down at the negotiating table, and were in fact incapable of even taking care of their responsibilities as set out in Phase One of the plan. Consequently, he told Bush, a viable alternative had to be found to arrive at an equitable solution. He went further, stating that Israel "was prepared to make painful and unilateral concessions to advance the cause of peace."

Both George Bush and Condoleeza Rice were initially skeptical, but they finally signed off on the Israeli plan, without quite believing it could actually occur.

But two weeks after the Ehud Olmert interview, in the salons of the beachfront Acadia Hotel at Herzlia Pituah, Ariel Sharon was awaited to give the closing speech at the Institute of Political and Strategic Studies workshops. It was a chilly December evening, the eighteenth of the month, and inside the hotel there was a tangible effervescence among participants under the watchful eyes of the Prime Minister's security force. At nightfall, local police had blocked all access roads into the area to ensure the safety of the keynote speaker. It was obvious that whatever he was going to say, it was to be an important speech.

Sharon had spent the previous evening at his ranch, writing his speech on his own in the second-floor office that looked out over the fields of poppies. After lengthy meditation, he would put down his pen, rise from the desk, go over to the window and stare at the peaceful green hills, then return to his speech. Each sentence, every word, was composed and chosen with care. There was no room for mistakes about the contents of the speech, and no room for errors of formulation. Everyone was waiting for him to reveal his true intentions on Gaza. By habit not loose with his words, Sharon rarely made spontaneous declarations to the media. Especially since the reinforced security measures were imposed, he was surrounded by a detachment of twelve heavily-armed bodyguards who accompanied him even to the washroom; it was simply impossible for reporters to approach him. There was no more of the things he had loved so much about political life: the warm contact with admirers, the handshakes given and received with passers-by, and the walkabouts. He missed this primordial part of life tremendously – it was, for a man of his political rank, a much-needed breath of fresh air.

At eight o'clock on the dot, just when the national television news began, Ariel Sharon strode to the speaker's podium, surrounded by his security guards. He was dressed in a dark suit and sported a red tie, and all the room went hush as the camera "on" lights lit red. The speech was carried live on all three Israeli networks and CNN (with simultaneous translation).

Sharon began by highlighting the advantages of the Roadmap and calling it a clear and reasonable plan. He then launched into a criticism of the Palestinian Authority's laxism in carrying out their duties as prescribed by the Roadmap, especially as regards the duty to combat terrorism. He cleared his throat, took a breath and wiped the beads of sweat that had been building up on his forehead. The powerful lights had made the room warm, and the crowd attentive to his every word, as he returned to his speech and gave a severe warning to the Palestinians:

> "If, over the coming months, we see that the Palestinians are still not carrying out their duties under the agreement, then Israel will itself take the initiative and unilaterally disengage!"

The room was now silent. After a long moment, Sharon, calm and sure of himself, went on:

> "The purpose of the disengagement plan is to drastically

reduce our exposure to terrorist acts and to offer a maximum of security to the citizens of Israel. This is a plan that will improve our standard of living and reinforce the Israeli economy."

He underscored how this plan would be fully and closely coordinated with the Americans, and would come with a redeployment of Tsahal forces along new security lines. There would also be, of necessity, changes in the configuration of some Israeli towns and villages. This plan, he told the nation, was a security measure and not a political undertaking, "The decisions taken in this respect will in no way change the Israeli-Palestinian political reality. There is no reason why the Roadmap implementation could not be restarted with a view to signing a definitive peace accord."

Sharon was persuaded that in times of peace as in times of war, decisions like this one could only succeed if based on a vast national consensus. Even if the Israeli people was plunged into a complex and delicate, probably wrenching debate, the unity if Israeli society had to be preserved.

"I am convinced," he said in concluding his remarks, "of the resistance capacity of our small and courageous nation which has endured so many trials and tribulations. I remain confident that as long as we remain united in our convictions, we will succeed, whatever path we may choose to follow."

In a thunderous wave of applause, Arik Sharon left the podium, radiant. For the first time he had clearly outlined his courageous plan to disengage from the Palestinians, abandon at least part of the territories and dismantle the settlements the construction of which he had himself encouraged with such determination.

But if his speech was long on principles, it was somewhat short on details. What exactly was he referring to when he spoke of settlements to be evacuated, Gaza or the West Bank? And naturally, he offered no timetable for the plan, leaving, as usual, doubts in the minds of Israelis as to what he really meant. A majority of Israeli commentators and a good part of public opinion remained sceptical. Labor Party leaders readily discounted the speech's importance. Shimon Peres was indifferent in public; privately, he would say that Ariel Sharon was a "skilled manipulator and that he would be judged on his acts, not his words." Arik had been in power for three years and constantly talked about "painful concessions," words with a magical air to them, but still, only words. The land had not seen the least concrete act in this respect, and it was only legitimate that an informed public be concerned about Sharon's sincerity regarding disengagement. The nation was about to celebrate Hannuka, the Festival of Lights. What better moment for Israelis to hope for some clarification from their leader?

Sharon's plan was also discounted by Western governments and the Arab capitals, which regarded the former general as an unreconstructed hawk, a man who would never voluntarily take Israel out of the territories. They were wrong: He was no longer the introvert of past years. He had become more open, and consequently, tougher, and his face had taken on the lines imparted by life experience. The death of his wife and the police investigations of his sons had really shaken him, and in order to save face he tried to keep his emotions under wraps. In his immediate entourage, true friends were becoming scarcer. Some had passed away, others become distanced. As for real confidants, he needed less than five fingers to count them.

He could now face issues with a greater serenity. His tone and style had evolved also. If he was as determined and persevering as before, he had lost some of his former arrogance and gained in calmness. But he remained a man of action, ready for the struggle, primed to strike, always at the top of the wave. A pioneer of his tribe. Ariel Sharon had always aspired to set himself apart from his peers, be original in his actions, and merit his place in History.

He prepared to implement his undertakings to the letter and as one could expect of an old soldier, prepared a detailed plan. First on his list was a working committee restricted to his close collaborators and the Defense Minister. His was naturally of a suspicious nature and had been "burned" more than once before, and so, fearful of leaks, he preferred not to discuss his plans in Cabinet, nor, especially, with the representatives of the settlers. At first, even the Army Chief of Staff was not in the know. The downside of acting this way was to create needless tension and let the rumor-mongers freely ply their trade. Nor did the Prime Minister wish to present his plan to the Knesset or the Likud Party caucus. Fearing any organized opposition would paralyze the plan's preparations, he categorically refused to meet with anyone to discuss what was being done.

It was said that his behavior was undemocratic. It was said he displayed a lack of logic and that any such audacious plan could not be implemented without consulting his Cabinet, the army, the police, and all the families that would be affected by his decisions. There were calls for a national referendum, which he stubbornly resisted. He met any and all demands with a wall of silence. Of course, he had his reasons for acting this way, but he preferred to keep them secret for the time being.

As the weeks passed, though, his position became more and more precarious. First there were doubts about whether or not the State Prosecutor was going to in fact charge the Prime Minister in the cases concerning his sons. There was daily chattering in the press about this, with so-called authoritative leaks claiming a writ was imminent. The disengagement plan was relegated to the back pages, and seemed to no longer be a subject for daily speculation. Sharon's smug opponents - and they were more and more numerous now - seemed convinced that the government would quickly fall, leading to early elections. How poorly they misjudged him. They were quick to bury his unilateral disengagement plan, but their ephemeral joy turned to rage when they discovered that he had never abandoned his goal, nor could he ever conceive of giving up. They had failed to remember, to their dismay, the Sharon of old.

On February 2, 2003, Sharon invited the political commentator of *Haaretz*, Yoel Marcus, to breakfast. Marcus was a celebrated Israeli journalist who, like his paper, had never been on the Ariel Sharon bandwagon. Sharon had even sued the daily for libel – and won – over its comments about his conduct during the Lebanese War. In the years that followed, he had come to see *Haaretz* as a newspaper for "thinking people," as the paper's own masthead proclaimed. It was an independent publication, with a leftist bent. The political class, intellectuals and businessmen all read *Haaretz* every day. In that respect Yoel Marcus and his paper were the ideal choice for Sharon to use as a tribune to get his ideas out, win the confidence of those opinion-making classes, and polish up his image.

The breakfast was lavish, with cold cuts vying for attention with the P.M.'s favorite, sardines in olive oil. Once the plates were full, the interview began, and Sharon gave the reporter a scoop: all the long-awaited details of his disengagement plan were revealed. Marcus returned to his newspaper with a real "catch." It was of such importance that rather than wait for the next day's paper to be printed, he immediately put the main points up on the *Haaretz* website. It was there that Israelis discovered their Prime Minister had decided to evacuate seventeen settlements in Gaza and three more in the north of the West Bank.

The detailed plans for transferring the eight thousand inhabitants of the settlements back to Israel were soon spelled out. Sharon was convinced that despite difficulties that he could well imagine, it would be an evacuation accomplished with dignity. He considered reasonable that it would take eighteen months to accomplish this, and confirmed already having given the orders to begin preparations. In the print interview, published the next day, Marcus described the Prime Minister as serene throughout their meeting, obviously persuaded that his plan was the best way to advance the peace process and to improve the security conditions within Israel.

Sharon's *Haaretz* interview had the effect of a bomb going off among the members of the political class. It had enormous repercussions. Firstly, few of his own immediate entourage had been aware of all the key elements of the plan. Various Ministers, an overwhelming majority of elected Knesset representatives and even Army Headquarters were quite surprised to read about the project first on the Internet, then, in full, in the pages of *Haaretz*. They were all furious with Sharon, and justifiably so. There was no justification for the Prime Minister having first revealed his plans to a journalist, even one as respectable as Yoel Marcus. What should have been done, instead of taking such important decisions by himself in a manner incompatible with the democratic process and the normal methodology of government decision-making, was to consult before releasing information to the press.

But what a coup! Ariel had attained with this everything he had wanted. The media tipped their hats and congratulated him on his courage and his determination. The police investigations that had poisoned the political climate were now forgotten. The media got behind Sharon's disengagement plan and condemned Israel's presence in Gaza. The battle for Israeli public opinion had been won. But the way things would play out on the ground in Gaza was to be more complex. Still, it was said, who could stop Israel's "bulldozer" in full power glide?

Chapter 13

The Political Battle

Political life is a constant battle, with no truce offered and no mercy given.
Winston Churchill

Sharon's decision to evacuate some twenty settlements - several dating back three decades or more - shook the Likud Party to its core. The party "hawks " were in a state of shock and in open revolt against their leader. Some Likud members in the Knesset voted in favor of motions of censure moved by the opposition parties. The forces ranged against the Prime Minister rose up on many fronts, relationships based on trust collapsed, and at any moment it seemed the government would fall, putting an end to the disengagement plan. But Arik remained confident and unshakeable in his determination to carry the plan forward. There would be no caving in to the maneuverings going on around him, but yet, the agitation was obviously of a more serious nature, and he needed to use force to calm things down. He did use force...against the Palestinians.

He ordered the elimination of the spiritual head of Hamas, Sheik

Ahmed Ismail Yassin. On March 22, 2004, this wheelchair-bound man, directly responsible for a long list of terrorist attacks inside Israel, was killed by helicopter-launched ground-to-air missiles. But the assassination provoked a wave of ire throughout the Arab world and open disavowal in the West. The United Nations Security Council condemned the attack: only the American veto forestalled a more severe resolution, since George Bush was still, and practically alone, publicly defending Israel's right to defend itself against terrorism in this way. When, three weeks later, Abdel Aziz Rantisi, who had taken the Hamas reins after Yassin's death, met an identical fate when his car was blown up, panic followed among the surviving leaders of Hamas, and they all went underground.

It was a plus for Sharon and his plan. He was now back up in the polls, his popularity on the rise again, and all of a sudden, the shrieking criticism that had followed upon his revealing the disengagement plan had become a whisper. In fact, many of his opponents were convinced he had all but abandoned the disengagement from Gaza. At the Likud Party convention, he was acclaimed as the *Hatikvah* – hope – Israeli National Anthem, resounded throughout the assembly through loud speakers joined by a stirring vocal chorus.

No one could say of Sharon that he was ignorant of the delicate ways to mold the Likud, nor that he was any less adroit in manipulating public opinion. He basked in the show of support and quite naturally declared that he accepted a motion that he submit any final disengagement plan for approval by the Likud members before any action would be taken. In his mind the risk of defeat was minimal and he had little to lose by being accommodating in public; a confidential internal party poll assured him of greater than sixty per cent support within the party, more than enough of a margin to guarantee passage of whatever detailed plan he eventually brought for approval.

To shore up his position, he met with President George Bush at the White House on April 14, 2004. The president was in the middle of his re-election campaign; a diplomatic success in the Middle East could have a tonic effect on his plummeting poll ratings and mollify the growing rumblings over the Iraqi War - which was looking more and more like a fiasco with each passing day. The meeting was really a crucial one for both men. As far as Sharon was concerned, it turned out to be a major success: President Bush handed the Israeli Prime Minister a document (see Appendix, Document 7) underscoring the U.S. commitment to the peace process.

Bush welcomed Sharon's disengagement plan warmly and, conscious of the fact that the plan was compatible with the Roadmap, congratulated his guest for his real contribution to a peaceful resolution of the conflict. The President stated that Israel must retain the right to defend itself against terror, and admonished the Palestinians to take determined, productive and continuing steps towards democratic reforms. Sharon was pleasantly surprised when Bush clearly stated:

"Given the new facts on the ground, including the sizeable, already-existing Israeli population centers in the West Bank, it would be unrealistic to believe that the negotiations on a final peace agreement will lead to a return to the 1949 truce lines. The agreement on a definitive status must include the establishment of a Palestinian state and the reintegration of refugees in this new state, not within Israel itself."

This was the first time a sitting United States President undertook to guarantee the Jewish state "defendable borders," and reject both a return to the 1949 armistice lines and an eventual right of return of Palestinians to their former lands.

Arik Sharon could not have been more pleased at this unprecedented, historic diplomatic triumph. His vision, which had developed slowly over the years, of creating facts on the ground to modify the basis for a negotiated settlement with the Palestinians, had been proven right, and as of now, the existence of major West Bank settlements could no longer be termed an obstacle to peace. Jewish colonies would be a part of the Israeli-Palestinian final accord. He was overjoyed at what he had achieved. This was a fundamental and a great victory, but with it came the understanding of the heavy responsibilities of the measures that were to come.

Sharon's success apparently played better in the U.S.A. than in his own country though, for when he returned to Jerusalem, he was bitterly surprised at the extent of the opposition to his plan. Three government ministers, including Foreign Minister Silvan Shalom and Finance Minister Bibi Netanyahu led a broad popular movement aimed at preventing the disengagement plan from ever taking place. Realizing that Sharon could probably push his proposal through the Likud, his opponents were now calling for a national referendum on the matter. The streets of Tel-Aviv and Jerusalem were filled with demonstrations, and successive polls clearly showed the Prime Minister's support in his own conservative constituency was ebbing. The Prime Minister realized that his diplomatic achievement was in danger of shattering, which would have as a consequence aggravating the Americans and isolating Israel. Something needed to be done to overcome the opposition to disengagement and move forward with his plans, but the road was a rocky one, covered with several thousand settlers who were understandably up in arms, but whose ire could not be allowed to dictate the policy of the entire country. The task at hand was enormous. The first step was to reign in the rebel ministers and with them, the rank-and-file of the Likud Party. Sharon decided to employ a high-risk, high-gain strategy. After all, they had elected him their leader, and it was now time for them all to get behind him.

In no way was he about to permit his adversaries to influence his stance. He knew each and every one of them, militant, Knesset member and minister alike, knew their character, and their weaknesses; for the majority a Knesset seat and being in power was what they wanted most. Some of his adversaries he particularly disdained, calling them "lazy mediocrities." Taking his distance from the rebels, he called their bluff in no uncertain terms:

> "You chose me to govern Israel. I choose to exercise that power, and believe me, I have no intention of resigning or resigning myself to let you decide in my place. If you don't like it, I'm ready to let the people decide whom they want to follow. I'm ready for new elections, and I'll win, because the people will stand with me!"

Sure of himself – perhaps over-confident – Sharon agreed to put the plan to a Likud Party vote. It was a mini-referendum, and it took place at the close of a loud and chaotic debate. The climate inside the meeting hall was tense, probably influenced by a heavy sadness throughout Israel following a bloody attack in Gush Katif, a settlement in southern Gaza in which a pregnant woman and her four young children were murdered.

The results of the vote were astonishing: the disengagement plan was defeated by a sixty to forty margin. It was a ringing disavowal of the party leader by the rank-and-file, and in the circumstances could not be interpreted as anything but a humiliating defeat, a slap in the face for Arik. His sons and his friends tried to console and encourage him, but he could easily see the anxiety on their faces as he smiled in the face of what was obviously the beginning of a serious crisis. He had been duped by his own comrades and fallen into a trap laid by the militants of his own party. But if the crisis had begun, Ariel Sharon had only just begun to fight. Despite having lost the vote on disengagement, he announced that very evening that he had no intention of resigning as Prime Minister. He would be accountable to the people of Israel, and to them alone, and would pursue at all costs his policy of disengagement in the territories. With considerable courage he reiterated his stance before the grieving family survivors of the Gush Katif terror attack, not fearing to look them straight in the eyes and pronounce difficult words at a heartbreaking occasion. He shared their pain and their loss, but avowed that despite the pain and the suffering, he was determined to follow through on the disengagement plan, which was in the interests of the People of Israel.

Several days later, the country was again plunged into grieving when eleven soldiers were killed near Rafah by a powerful explosion that literally tore them apart. A contingent of IDF soldiers was forced to spend hours on hands and knees, recovering the body parts in a moving scene that would long affect the nation. Two days later, 150,000 people marched in Tel-Aviv in a show of left-wing support for the Prime Minister. The irony was rich, as the crowds chanted, "Arik, we stand with you, you will save the nation," for these were people of the same stripe as those who had called him an assassin twenty-three years earlier, and called for his resignation: "Go home to your ranch," they had screamed then.

Tsahal launched a broad-based offensive against terrorist bases in Rafah within forty-eight hours in retaliation for the loss of its eleven men. If in the field of action, the escalation was evident, within the Likud and the government itself things were getting completely out of hand. The ministers from the right-wing extremist and religious parties loudly resigned. Tomy Lapid's Shinnui Party quickly followed suit, and an overwhelming majority of Likud members signed a petition disavowing Sharon, calling on ministers not to approve his disengagement plan. The hard-core rebels held the balance of power and were quite prepared to use something akin to blackmail to achieve their ends. The government was being torn apart, ministers cowering in fear of what the rebels might reveal, and the coalition slipping away. The Prime Minister was now running every risk of finding himself in the minority in the Knesset.

With his back against the wall, as he had done so often in other forms of combat, Arik Sharon pulled himself together and counterattacked his adversaries. He convened an extraordinary session of the Cabinet and played his hole card. Prior to the meeting, he accepted Bibi Netanyahu's proposal to modify the disengagement resolution by removing any explicit mention of dates for withdrawal from the territories and the names of the settlements to be abandoned. As modified, the resolution passed by a vote of fourteen to seven. It was, coincidentally, June 4, the anniversary of the Six Day War, and Sharon had deftly crossed another important bridge on the way to implementing his audacious plan. The vote gave him some breathing room, and he felt a real sense of relief.

The departure of his Shinnui and extremist ministers reduced Sharon's room to maneuver though, so in response he made an opening to the left, inviting Labor to join his coalition with no preconditions. The offer was first submitted for approval to the Likud, where it was rejected by the slimmest of margins. But Arik decided to let things ripen for a while, and await a more propitious moment to move officially to a more comfortable coalition. In any case he enjoyed the support of the centrist and left-wing parties in the Knesset; the current confrontation was essentially with his own Likud, where a large segment of the party now considered him an undesirable. It was like being in the eye of the hurricane, calm in the political center, but facing the difficult-to-resolve conundrum of how to be certain of his support in parliament.

Rabbis were now openly calling on religious-minded soldiers to disobey orders if called on to evacuate the settlements. Anti-Sharon demonstrations were organized throughout Israel. A human chain of 125,000 persons opposed to disengagement stretched from the streets of Gush Katif to the Wailing Wall in Jerusalem. The country had never before seen such strong protest against a man who had been long perceived as the right-wing icon that personified the policy of settlement construction. Disorder, and the threat of worse, seemed omnipresent.

On October 25, the Knesset met in plenary session to take the disengagement plan to a vote. Back-room arm-twisting was ferocious, and the debates were broadcast live to the nation, as was the final vote. In a huge victory for Sharon, sixty-seven Knesset members – including the entire Left – voted for the plan, with forty-four against. Another momentous step had been taken. But within two days, the eyes of the world were suddenly turned to Sharon's old enemy Yasser Arafat. The wily Palestinian who had put his stamp on three decades of Middle Eastern history was gravely ill, and with this development, the future of his people and perhaps the entire region was uncertain.

Sharon had known of Arafat's deteriorating state of health for some time, as Shin Beth had succeeded in getting its hands on the PLO leader's medical reports. Wanting to avoid at all costs being accused of having Arafat's imminent death on his hands, the Prime Minister gave strict instructions to authorize any request for hospitalization or evacuation to a foreign country made by Palestinian authorities. Sharon had long wanted Arafat gone to meet his maker, and now, it seemed, events were following a path of their own to just that end. On October

24, 2004, Yasser Arafat was taken by air ambulance to a Paris hospital where he passed away three weeks later. Of course, there were accusations of poison from the Palestinian side, which tried to hold Israel responsible for Arafat's death. The truth was, according to some reports, that the PLO leader in fact died of complications from AIDS and cirrhosis of the liver. Destiny and the will of the Lord had carried Arafat off; Arik Sharon had finally outlasted the man he had wanted eliminated for so many years.

He declined a request from the PLO to hold the funeral in Jerusalem but authorized burial in Ramallah which was carried live on television, prompting a disgusted and angry Sharon to comment cynically to his son Gilad,

> "Look at this, look how abased human beings have become. Normal people would not devote an entire day's news to the burial of that 'dog.' What a fraud! How can the leaders of the countries of the world pay their respects to this killer of women and children who was even given the Nobel Peace Prize? This is more than just a grotesque act, it's flagrant hypocrisy, unnerving."

On the day of Arafat's burial, stupefying news emerged concerning large amounts of money belonging to the Palestinian Authority – which had been received from foreign donor states – that had been transferred to the leader's personal accounts and subsequently invested, not only in Arab countries but also in the United States.

Sharon especially resented French president Jacques Chirac, whose final eulogy he found profoundly irritating. Giving the full honors of the French Republic to a Palestinian terrorist leader went far beyond what was acceptable.

In any case, Arafat's demise put an end to the duel that began when Sharon, in a red beret uniform had had the keffiya-clad terrorist firmly in his sights. He was relieved at the turn of events, but not convinced that Arafat's successor would have the will or the capacity to control Palestinian militants, put an end to the Intifada and open a frank and constructive dialogue with Israel. There was still every reason to be concerned.

The settlers, however, saw Arafat's death as an expression of God's will, a miracle from the Master of the Universe destined to cure Sharon's bout of insanity and stop him from implementing his disengagement plan. Sharon, a convinced agnostic, laughed off this mystical interpretation of events and moved forward with preparations by first voting a budget setting aside funds for indemnifying Gaza evacuees for their material losses. On January 10, 2005, the Knesset approved the Labor Party entering the governing coalition: they were given seven portfolios in the new government. The portfolio to be given to Shimon Peres was certainly the most difficult nut to crack, but after many discussions and bargaining, a successful formula was found. In Sharon's own words:

> "I have known my old friend Shimon for more than half a century. Over the course of his long career he has occupied many important positions in our government, including that of Prime Minister, and is completely qualified to assume any responsibilities and missions I may offer him."

Peres, a power-hungry and proud man, accepted a portfolio that had been made to measure for him: Deputy Prime Minister, charged with the implementation of economic infrastructure after the Gaza disengagement and responsible for the development of the Galilee and Negev Desert regions. Sharon was now satisfied that events would move quickly. On January 30, while George Bush was swearing the Oath of Office for his second term as President of the United States, the Government of Israel approved the final disengagement plan by an overwhelming majority - seventeen to five - as Sharon beamed at his victory. Still, later that day, at an evening event with a large contingent of American Jews, he confided with a mixture of satisfaction and bitterness that he had just taken the most difficult decision of his life.

Chapter 14

Lost Illusions

This is no illusion, nor just chatter: it's the truth.
The Marquise de Sévigné

Sixty years had passed since the day young corporal Ariel Sharon entered the service of his country in the Alexandroni division of the Israeli Defense Forces, and four years since the "little corporal" then legendary General had become Prime Minister of his country. Over the course of those many years Ariel Sharon had taken hundreds of important decisions, some of a delicate nature, some grave, some a matter of life and death. His choices had been crucial to the army, to the survival of his soldiers, and for the future of Israel. But deciding to evacuate the Jewish inhabitants of the Gaza strip had been the most difficult and wrenching decision of them all.

During his time as head of Southern Command, and then as Minister of Agriculture, he had crisscrossed the region ensuring the security of the very settlements he now proposed to evacuate. He had mixed with the settlers, accompanying them on their path and witnessing the miracle created by these hard-working pioneers who had turned the sand dunes into gardens of green. These people had planted trees, built residences and greenhouses, schools and synagogues and raised large families. An unshakeable belief in the righteousness of their cause and in a blessed future coursed proudly through their veins.

Arik Sharon had encouraged them to enlarge and improve their settlements, and to never despair despite the terrorist attacks they suffered. After all, he was practically their neighbor - his Sycamores Ranch was not that far away - and he brought them support and pled their cause with the government. Always on their side, his solidarity was never in question through the good times and bad, in happiness and anguish: he was their attentive tutor, their lawyer, their friend, and never once did he ever dream it would all have to be one day thrown away. But after three decades, in the driver's seat as Prime Minister, he would abruptly change his mind, enraging the settlers. Their sense of broken-hearted betrayal was all the more acute since he had been so deeply rooted in their history in Gaza.

For his part, Sharon had come to the unhappy conclusion that he had long fooled himself - and others - with the dream of holding on to the occupied land forever. Now, he realized, affairs of state had their own logic, and the interests of the country at large had to take precedence over those of the settlers. The Palestinian problem needed to be resolved so that the country could concentrate its energy on building the strength of the democratic Jewish state and maintaining its spiritual base and economic health. New Jewish immigrants were needed - and they needed to be properly integrated into Israeli society. The nation was still facing a hostile environment and needed to remain in a dominant position in order to reach a long-lasting peace with all of its neighbours. It was an enormous task to confront and a heavy burden to shoulder. Succeeding - and it was vital that Israel succeed - required taking decisive action to rid the land of the problem that was sucking it dry. Debate time was over; it was time to disengage from the Palestinians.

Arik set the date. August 15, 2005 would be his deadline for evacuating twenty settlements and eight thousand settlers from Gaza. That gave him twenty-three weeks to find these people new homes within Israel and organize a massive population move under the threat of terrorist action and faced with the absolute refusal of some of the settlers to cooperate. Violence from without and from within were definite possibilities, so the question was, how could the settlers be evacuated without recourse to force? How could he ensure that women and children would be moved without people being hurt or damage being done? The answer, for an old soldier, lay in a highly-detailed plan that was to be conceived as a plan of battle – only there were to be no casualties. Every possibility was considered in the most minute detail, every initiative and reaction on the part of the settlers taken into account, step by step plans made and examined with a fine-tooth comb.

Sharon had a lot of experience in dealing with this kind of situation. He had already evacuated the residents of the towns in the northern part of the Sinai in April, 1982, while he was Defense Minister, but he had no intention of making the same mistakes in Gaza. The context of the evacuation was entirely different, in any case: as regards the Sinai, Israel had signed a peace treaty with Egypt. With Gaza, the retreat was unilateral, without the agreement of – or even discussions with – the Palestinians. And there was no peace treaty, nor any likelihood of obtaining one in the near future.

A bureau tasked with handling all aspects of the evacuation was set up under the aegis of the Prime Minister's office. Adequate compensation and assistance in relocating were offered to each family that left Gaza of its own accord. The amount proposed was about 400,000 U.S. dollars. But the offer, for the most part, fell on deaf ears. Only a small number of settlers took Sharon up on his offer. The vast majority of settlers were convinced that the Prime Minister would renounce his project before evacuation day. They were waiting for a miracle, an event big enough to derail the disengagement plan and put off forever the abandonment of their homes and communities. The slogans "No Jew will ever 'transport' another Jew," and "A Jew will never pull his brother out of his land" encouraged the settlers to hang on. Everyone knew to what the expression "transport another Jew" made reference.

The size of the undertaking made it necessary to put Tsahal, working in a coordinated effort with the police, in charge of logistics on the ground. The army Chief of Staff, Moshe Bougy-Yahalon, gave a glacial reception to this order, as he was personally not enthusiastic, to say the least, about undertaking the evacuation. He clearly indicated the reasons behind his reticence and proposed different – and according to him, better – solutions to the problem at hand. Yahalon was a modest and righteous soldier who had rejoined the armed forces at the start of the October War, leaving behind his kibbutz in the Negev Desert. An apolitical man who saw things from a purely professional and military point of view, Yahalon in fundamental disagreement over the disengagement plan with his boss, Defense Minister Shaul Mofaz, as well as with Ariel Sharon.

According to Yahalon, the disengagement plan as set out would neither stop terrorist attacks nor restore peace in the region. Sharon's plan would be doomed to failure because Israel was proposing to evacuate the territories without having beforehand struck a peace and security accord with the Palestinians. The Intifada, he was certain, would continue in the West Bank. Still, he was a disciplined military man and as such implemented the orders of the executive branch of government and began to prepare the army for pulling out of Gaza.

Yahalon's declarations and opinions about the evacuation were public knowledge and as such, encouraged the settlers to pursue their attempts to block the disengagement plan. The Likud hawks used his words as fodder in their own conflict with Mofaz and Sharon. As Army Chief of Staff. Yahalon wanted to avoid becoming involved in the politics of the matter, especially as this particular matter was of so delicate a nature. But his views turned him into a political football and he was thrust into the limelight, then summarily relieved of his post.

Shaul Mofaz, Yahalon's direct superior and predecessor as Army Chief of Staff decided to cut off all contact with Yahalon and refused to renew his employment contract, counseling Sharon instead to replace Yahalon with General Dan Halutz, Yahalon's second-in-command. Mofaz enjoyed a strong friendship with Halutz: the fact that they were both originally from Iran certainly didn't hurt! Sharon, who knew the arcana of the army bureaucracy like the back of his hand, and who still recalled the time when he had been turned down for the top rank position for hidden political reasons, decided to act fast. The application of the disengagement plan had to be implemented quickly, authoritatively, and with no room for agitation or milling about.

Yahalon was in fact fired with little discussion and in a brutal manner, causing the general considerable humiliation. Angry at what he considered to be an unjust and unjustified act, he decided to counterattack, telling the media that he was now obliged to wear his boots at all times in his office, since he had recently discovered the presence of vipers in the building – a thinly-veiled allusion to Mofaz and his staff, who worked less than a hundred feet away. In the end, Yahalon, a man who had led an exemplary war on the Intifada during his three years in office, and who had successfully reduced terror attacks and pushed through important reforms within the army, was done in by politics. Israel owed him a great deal, and his professional conduct was lauded in the newspapers and on television. But in the corridors of power, in the maneuvering among the top staff and the incessant political intrigue, he lost out on points, paying a heavy price for his forthrightness and integrity.

Dan Halutz, the man who replaced him on the fourteenth floor of the modern and fortified tower situated in the heart of Tel-Aviv, was an Air Force man, an F-16 pilot who had risen in the ranks to the top spot. His nomination was something of an anomaly since his predecessors had all been Red Berets, like Ariel Sharon.

At fifty-seven, Halutz was a little older than the men he succeeded, and symbolized the second-generation "Oriental" success story of Sephardic Jewish families who had immigrated during the 1950s. Trim and fit, head shaven and sporting pilots' Ray-Bans, Halutz was a young and happy grandfather who wore the royal blue beret of the Israeli Air Force. His peers were to be found at the highest levels of the government of Israel: Moshe Katsav, the Israeli president, was like Halutz of Iranian origin. There was also Defense Minister Shaul

Mofaz, also from Iran, while Foreign Minister Silvan Shalom and Labor Party leader Amir Peretz were from the North African Maghreb region. Halutz, in fact, had an Iranian father and an Iraqi mother, both Jews of course, but when the Iran-Iraq War broke out in the 1980s, there was lingering unease in the family; national feelings proved to have a life of their own.

Halutz threw himself into his new job and used his native energy to brush away the morosity that had taken root since the departure of Yahalon. The supremacy of aviation formed the backbone of his approach, and under his direction, targeted attacks on terrorists would be carried out more and more frequently using drones and Apache helicopters.

Meanwhile there was a disengagement plan to put into place. Halutz, warm by nature, was a "people person," and he decided to first tackle the public relations profile of the army and improve its image by fitting in to the needs of the media and the operational requirements created by the more and more frequent live television shows. The army spokesman was replaced by a dynamic and gregarious woman who already enjoyed an excellent relationship with both the Israeli and international press.

Halutz knew that the evacuation had to be a calm, dignified and respectable process, which meant he had to try and reach an understanding with the bulk of Gaza settlers to avoid a physical confrontation. Giving the media – with which Halutz was much more at ease than Yahalon had been – the impression of watching a military conflict would be a public relations disaster. The settlers were not enemies of Israel and Tsahal had certainly not declared war on its own people. The "rebels within the army," a relatively small number of activists composed of religious zealots and dissidents influenced by the more messianic rabbis, and who refused to obey direct orders, had also to be dealt with. The mission was a delicate one since some of these soldiers lived in the territories with their families, and had close friends and relatives in the settlements. Many of them were officers and part of the army elite.

Sharon had issued precise orders that the evacuation be carried out peacefully, and with sensitivity to the feelings of the evacuees. A special unit of former elite commandos was held in readiness for cases requiring drastic action, but for the most part, soldier-psychologists and specialists in hostage negotiations were to play a central role, and no soldier or police officer was to be armed. There was understanding from the top down that everyone was sitting on a tinder-box that could ignite with a single incident. Most of the settlers had handed in their weapons, but there were still many walking around with Uzis and ammunition bandoliers around their shoulders. The recalcitrant groups had to be coaxed – almost "loved" – into leaving their homes and neighborhoods. Faced with an explosive situation, the best recourse was to thoughtfulness, not force, so as to avoid what could look to the country and the rest of the world as a "civil war."

Shin Beth provided a lot of intelligence, as did the police, whose informers helped to identify secret weapons caches and the identities of agitators, known as "the young men on the hills." Knowing their intentions became a priority, as did separating them form the main body of settler evacuees. In this case, it was decided, some sort of force could be employed.

Gaza was then declared a closed military zone, with the plan calling for complete evacuation to take place over a period of four to five weeks and ending before the celebration of the Hebrew New Year that fell in October. More than 2.5 billion dollars were expected to be spent during the process, including relocation and compensation expenditures; the United States promised to pay a share of the cost. Israel's Finance minister opined that the Gaza retreat would open new economic opportunities for the country, creating new jobs and encouraging new foreign investment. A good business proposition for the State of Israel, in sum...

Meanwhile, Abu Mazen, Arafat's successor as president of the Palestinian Authority, was trying to keep his own troops under control, conscious of the fact that Sharon would not proceed with the Gaza plan under fire. There had to be no terrorist attacks and no shelling as things proceeded. Concerned at the ongoing developments – Gaza was after all on its borders – Egypt offered to serve as an honest broker and sent Omar Suleiman, the country's head of Intelligence, to meet with the Israelis and the Palestinians to help with surveillance of the most dangerous saboteurs of the peace process, in particular the Hamas militants. Suleiman would coordinate with Ariel Sharon directly as matters proceeded, while Egyptian president Hosni Mubarak, about to hold "democratic" elections under intense U.S. pressure, invited Mazen, King Abdullah and Ariel Sharon to a summit conference at the resort town of Sharm-el-Sheikh.

On February 8, 2005, after 1558 days of the Intifada with 1036 Israelis and 3592 Palestinians killed, a new page in the history of the Middle East seemed to be turning. In the first real meeting of the region's leaders since the death of Yasser Arafat, the antagonists publicly talked of peace and coexistence. Abu Mazen proclaimed that armed revolt was over, and Sharon promised an end to the Tsahal raids and moved to lighten the harsh conditions of Palestinian daily life. It seemed there was real hope in the air, and the Sharon-Mazen meeting took place in a friendly atmosphere, helped by the relaxed climate of the resort that had stunning views of the Red Sea. The leaders knew each other for a long time and there was mutual respect between them. Abu Mazen, adjusting his glasses, told the world that they were embarking as of today on a new path. And if they failed, the world would hold both Sharon and himself responsible.

"I know that there are those who would sabotage our efforts to reach a peace," he said. "We will fight them without mercy, but you must understand that the combat will be a difficult and long one. Please be patient, we will persevere." Sharon replied, stressing the fact that security problems demanded more determination than ever in the struggle against the terrorists, and Mazen, with a smile on his lips, spoke in Hebrew, asking for "Regaa, regaa sablanut." *Wait a while, please be patient.*

Abu Mazen then turned to the interpreter and went on in Arabic, telling Sharon that he was asking for too much, too soon: "I have only been in office for three weeks, and have not even had the time to form a government."

The Israeli Prime Minister laughed and replied, "You may well have difficulties in forming a government, but as for myself, I have a great deal of difficulty just saving my coalition!"

Sharon suggested that Abu Mazen set up their next meeting at Yasser Arafat's former headquarters in Ramallah, the Mukhata. "I can promise you there will be many more reporters and photographers present than there are here today," he bantered, to which Abu Mazen replied, "And how are your sheep doing on the ranch?"

"The sheep are in good shape, as you will see if you accept my invitation to visit. And now that you have promised me that there is no chance of any stray Qassam rockets falling on their heads, I feel assured about their future." The overt sarcasm and reference to the home-made and notoriously inaccurate Qassam missiles that Islamic Jihad and Hamas militants regularly fired at Israeli border towns did not hide the menace behind the words. Successive generations of these simple missiles have increased their range from less than three kilometers to more than eight and they have become weapons of major concern to Tsahal.

Sharon then turned to the disengagement plan, telling Abu Mazen that Israel was prepared to coordinate the evacuation with him, but warned that Israel would not tolerate any firing upon its forces or the convoys evacuating settlers and their possessions. "Should such any incidents take place, our response will be overwhelming."

"Mister Prime Minister," Mazen responded calmly, "I promise we will take all necessary steps to ensure that the evacuation does not take place under a rain of fire."

"Mister President," Sharon went on, "I am ready to walk with you on this long road we have begun today, but I must tell you that there is one thing I will never accept, and will fight mercilessly, and that is terrorism. Everyone, from the Americans and the Europeans to my own ministers, advise me to assist you in managing your affairs. I have told them that I will help you as long as Israeli citizens can live in peace and security. I could not be clearer on this point."

The Sharm el-Sheikh meeting was important since it meant a renewal of dialogue after so many years of the Intifada, and with the old, tainted Arafat leadership gone. There was real anticipation of moving forward in both camps, and as a concrete and significant signal, both the Jordanian and Egyptian Ambassadors returned to Tel-Aviv for the first time since the second Intifada began. In another positive development, a *Yediot Aharonot* public opinion poll revealed that sixty per cent of Israelis trusted Abu Mazen and were optimistic about the chances for peace.

Ariel Sharon was somewhat more prudent, and as always, pragmatic in his approach, saying he was ready to engage in a serious dialogue with the new Palestinian president, but he would form his opinion based on events, waiting for concrete results on the ground. Abu Mazen, he vowed, would be judged on the basis of acts, not words.

Washington welcomed developments at Sharm el-Sheikh. Enthusiasm from the Americans was matched by a new attitude in Europe, and a single week after the meeting, Israeli Foreign Minister Silvan Shalom was welcomed in Paris at the Elysée Presidential Palace by Jacques Chirac, who had long refused to meet with the envoy from Tel-Aviv. The meeting, which took place in a "very positive climate," according to both sides, was marked by some very troubling news from Beirut: former Lebanese Prime Minister – and close friend of Chirac – Rafik Hariri, had been killed along with many of his close collaborators and bodyguards in a massive car bomb attack. Chirac was ashen. The multi-billionaire Hariri had been a frequent week-end guest at Jacques Chirac's residence. The men had often met to discuss problems in the Middle East, and Chirac had named his friend to the Legion of Honor in 1996. And now he had been brutally murdered.

The hand of Syria in the attack was obvious, as Hariri had been personally warned by Syrian dictator Bashar al-Assad to cease interfering with that country's imperial ambitions over Lebanon. Hariri apparently believed, wrongly, as it turned out, that his wealth and prestige would protect him from assassination. The killing turned France's foreign policy in the region on its head, and Chirac, whose Prime Minister and friend Dominique de Villepin had enraged the Americans in the run-up to the invasion of Iraq, now joined with the United States in leading an unprecedented diplomatic initiative aimed at discovering the truth surrounding his friend's death, and, more importantly, evicting Syria from Lebanon. The new turn of events was greatly appreciated in Jerusalem. Sharon immediately accepted Jacques Chirac's invitation to officially visit Paris at the earliest occasion.

Chapter 15

The French Connection

"Passion, not reason, rules the world."
French philosopher Alain (Émile Chartier)

Karol Wojtyla – Pope John Paul II – passed away on Saturday, April 2, 2005, and the world cried. Catholics were plunged into a profound sadness. More than one hundred heads of state, government leaders and monarchs attended the Vatican funeral of the man the Israelis had called "The Pope of the Jews." John Paul II was without a doubt the most prestigious personality of the twentieth century to have worked for reconciliation between Christianity and Judaism. He denounced the Inquisition of "our older brothers" and worked tirelessly to combat the falsification of the history of the Chosen People. It was during his reign that diplomatic relations were opened between Israel and the Vatican, explicit recognition of the existence of a Jewish state in the Holy Land. He was also the first pope to walk through the ruins of the Nazi extermination camp at Auschwitz, in Poland, and the first to come to pray at the Wailing Wall in Jerusalem and beg forgiveness of those who escaped the death camps, in the name of the Roman Catholic Church.

The President and the Grand Rabbis of Israel were among the mourners, come to Rome to pay their last respects. Ariel Sharon described the man who rose from humble Polish beginning to the heights of church power as "a man of peace and a friend of the Jews." During his last visit to the Vatican, Pope John Paul had confided that for him, the Land of Israel was sacred to Jews, Christians and Muslims alike, but the land had only been promised to the Jews.

Several weeks later, Ariel Sharon participated in the March of the Living at Auschwitz, where the past is never gone. Along with twenty thousand young Jews from around the world and Holocaust survivors, in this cursed place in the heart of the Polish countryside where humanity had sunk to indescribable acts of horror, Sharon denounced the silence of the world while millions of Jews had been slaughtered like cattle.

"Remember the victims," he said, "but remember the murderers as well. Bear witness to the Shoah, when the last survivors of the camps are no longer among us."

As the strident sound of the ram's horn – the traditional Shofar – carried across the memorial and through the souls of those present, the Prime Minister reminded the crowd that Israel was the only place in the world where Jews had the right and the power to defend themselves on their own. Then Hatikva, the Israeli national anthem, was sung by voices young and old, in a powerful and stirring symbol linking the generations of Jews. The solemn ceremony ended as the gathering quietly dispersed. Never forget! Never forgive!

Sharon may have been thinking about the past on his way home, but once back in Israel itself, the present reality with all its chaotic moving parts was inescapable. Tens of thousands of activists had descended upon the Gush Katif settlement in Southern Gaza. They came by car and by bus, intent on manifesting their solidarity with the settlers and declared their intention to remain as long as it took to stop the evacuation. The orange color of the Ukrainian dissidents – that had succeeded in overturning a fraudulent election – had been appropriated by the demonstrators, who were evidently intent on pursuing a policy of civil disobedience. Encouraged by Yesha, the elected council representing the West Bank settlers, the demonstrators also took comfort in the religious support that came from some rabbis, including Ovadia Yossef, the spiritual leader of Orthodox Sephardic Jews. Employing biblical metaphors and speaking in the language of the common people, he went so far as to declare that Ariel Sharon was a wicked, cruel, and pitiless man. "Let God strike him down," Yossef told his followers, "so that he may perish and never recover."

The rabbi, well versed in the Talmud and a follower of the Kabbalah, was often in the news. His weekly admonishments were avidly followed by his congregation, and widely reported in the press. But this time he went too far, and was soon forced to excuse himself, declaring that he had been misunderstood, and adding, "Long life to Ariel Sharon." The damage had been done, though. Demagogic insults and needless words are the fodder of fanatics. They can strike as surely as the sharp steel blade. As respectable as some rabbis may be, they ignore at their risk the anarchy that can result from ill-considered sermons. In the jungle of violence and hatred that is the Middle East world of today, quoting the bible out of context can easily touch off explosive acts, and those who have the pulpit also need to use it responsibly.

Sharon of course, known publicly for his agnosticism, brushed off these blasphemous declarations with a smile. After all, Ovadia Yossef's religious party – Shas – might one day come back into Sharon's governing coalition. In political life, there was no room for sentiment. Better to put up with the insults, swallow the serpents, and turn the page. So once he had digested the incendiary oratory, it was time to move forward, successfully crossing another step on the road to the realization of his plan. The Knesset was seized with – and rejected, by a fifty-nine to forty majority – a motion to submit the Gaza disengagement plan to a national referendum. With this comfortable majority in hand, Sharon easily got parliamentary approval for the new budget that included supplementary funding for the evacuation.

Now that the way was in all respects clear to proceed, it seemed the right time to accept French President Jacques Chirac's recently-proffered invitation to officially visit Paris. A few days away from the office wouldn't hurt, either, and in this case, would provide a good opportunity to repair some bridges with the French. Jacques Chirac had issued strict guidelines to the Quai d'Orsay, France's Foreign Ministry: Ariel Sharon was to be given a smoothly prepared, royal welcome, with no constraints. Political demands were to be avoided, as were lessons of morality, and only issues on which the two governments were in agreement were to be brought up. All attending staff were well briefed on the necessity of keeping their lips buttoned and their minds centered on "approved" subjects of conversation. As Chirac said, "It would be neither desirable nor intelligent to make Sharon's life more complicated. He has enough on his plate as it is."

Chirac's instructions were followed to the letter. Both he and Sharon gave lengthy interviews to the press, evoking, each in his own style and from his own perspective, the future of French-Israeli relations. Obviously, topic one was the disengagement from Gaza, presently under way. Chirac saluted the Israeli P.M. for his courage and determination, while Sharon applauded the French President's open war on anti-Semitism and the measures he had adopted to eradicate this evil from France. On the day of his departure for Paris, the European Jewish Congress, in an unprecedented move, took a large front page ad in *Haaretz*, in which Pierre Besnainou, the Congress President, offered words of encouragement: "Thank you, Ariel Sharon! Welcome to Europe. Welcome to France. We salute your vision for a viable peace in the Middle East, and applaud your courage in applying the disengagement plan."

Besnainou had two goals in mind with this ad, taken by European Jews in Hebrew, in one of the major papers. First, he wanted to show support for Sharon. But he also wanted to make it clear that his dynamic leadership and style were willing to take on and stop the erosion of Israel's image in the countries of the European Union.

Of course, it was hardly the first time in Paris for Ariel Sharon.

Since his first discovery of the charms of the City of Light in 1951 he had often returned to visit the impressive Châteaux and museums, and to partake of the wonderful cuisine served in some of the best restaurants of the world. Contrary to Shimon Peres who was an exuberant Francophile, Sharon was less passionate in his public declarations of love for the country and more reserved, even as Jacques Chirac received him with all the pomp and circumstance of the French Presidency. There were good reasons for this: while he respected French history and civilization, and admired the French military and the country's advanced technology, he was overtly critical – sometimes bluntly so – of France's Middle East policy. In truth he was no Francophile, and his interests and bent lay elsewhere, on the other side of the Atlantic Ocean, in America.

French media had returned the favor, and had been critical for the most part of his policies. For a long while he had been officially unwelcome in France, and during the Intifada, the Israeli Prime Minister refused to receive the official representatives of the French State or even personal emissaries of the French President. He had virulently condemned Chirac's moralistic and partisan policies, and France's "pathetic" support of Yasser Arafat. Commenting on recent acts of anti-Semitism in France, Sharon had accused Chirac of laxism and encouraged French Jews to leave the country *en masse* and emigrate to Israel, making *Aliya,* for their own safety. His blunt comments had profoundly irritated the French governing class, and worried the leaders of that nation's Jewish community.

But that was then. He had since softened his stance and even congratulated France on its efforts to stamp out anti-Semitism, calling it a model for other European governments to follow. Bilateral relations had vastly improved from then on, and Sharon had every intention of moving things forward. Commercial exchanges totaled more than two billion dollars and covered a wide range of products, services, and commodities, despite a polemic that broke out in October, 2005, when Palestinians protested a contract given by Israel to French industrial giants Alsthom and Connex. The four hundred million euro contract called for a new, thirteen-kilometer urban transport system linking downtown Jerusalem with the northern Pisgat Zeev and Haguiva Hatsarfatit quarters. The later was commonly known as "The French Hill," since that was the name of British General Allenby's Chief of Staff. When Allenby took Jerusalem from the Ottoman Empire in 1917, French's residence dominated the city from this hill. The problem was, according to the Palestinians, that these lands had been confiscated from them during the Six Day War. Chirac had been forced to intervene and the matter was still tied up in bureaucratic wrangling.

The agenda for the meeting was replete with files on a wide range of subjects. Regarding vital strategic matters such as the Iranian nuclear question and Syria's meddling in Lebanon and support of terrorism, there was a convergence of views and the talks' success was widely expected.

Sharon and his party had taken up residence at the Raphael Hotel, on Avenue Kleber, near the International Conference Center and close by the Arc de Triomphe. An impressive security force protected the Prime Minister himself - ensconced in a magnificent suite in the Louis XVI style - as everyone knew he would be a prime target for terrorists. Israeli and French agents kept a close watch.

On Wednesday, July 27, 2005, at half-past noon, the Elysee Palace was abuzz, with the Republican Guard standing at attention, cavalry sabers raised, staff briefed and attentive, and Jacques Chirac himself impatiently waiting at the palace door for his guest's convoy to turn into the courtyard. Promptly at the appointed hour, Sharon's official limousine with the Star of David flag fluttering in the breeze rolled onto the crushed stone of the yard, surrounded by the usual complement of motorcycle police. Dressed in a well-cut dark grey suit and wearing a striped red tie, the Israeli P.M. emerged and, smiling broadly, shook his host's hand with evident pleasure. The French President, manifestly jubilant in his dark suit and matching tie, was every inch the perfect host, his warm welcome underscoring the esteem in which France held its important guest. Chirac was a stickler for questions of honor and protocol and made certain everyone paid attention to every detail of the welcoming ceremony. A small army of photographers surrounded the leaders, snapping countless pictures: each smile, each gesture, was immortalized for the generations to come. The cool relations of years past were relegated to the trashbin: friendship between the two sovereign peoples and their states was now *l'ordre du jour*.

The ceremony quickly led to the first order of business, a working lunch of flatfish, caviar and sardines served with chilled kosher white wine. Sharon, whose *gourmandise* was widely known, raised a smile and opened his eyes wide in evident satisfaction. He told the Frenchman that he considered this visit of capital importance and held Chirac to be one of the great leaders of the world. Thanking the President for his firm struggle against anti-Semitism, Sharon underlined how appreciative he was for Chirac's commitment to the reinforcement of bilateral relations between Israel and France. The bilateral relationship, he went on, had become very intense.

Regarding the Middle East, the two leaders had seen their positions moving closer, but in spite of each having been personally involved in hand to hand combat with Arabs (the young lieutenant Chirac having fought Algerian fellaghas during France's last attempt to hold it's colonial fiefdom in North Africa, and Sharon of course had led raids against the West Bank and Gaza fedayin) they still had different views on the means to achieve their common goals.

Lebanon and Syria were of major concern to both leaders. Following the car bomb assassination of Rafik Hariri, the United Nations Security Council had, instigated by France and with urging from the United States, Great Britain and Germany, passed Resolution 1159 calling for a return to national sovereignty and democracy in Lebanon. A decisive step had been taken when the Syrians had been compelled to evacuate their army back across the border and free elections, with no foreign meddling, had been called. The call for disarming of militias was also a positive step forward. With this in mind, Sharon felt the time was right to insist that France, its influence in Lebanon on the rise now, use it to discourage any escalation of violence on Lebanon's border with Northern Israel:

"I am convinced, mister President," Sharon said, "that you can demand that the Lebanese government warn Hezbollah against any attacks on us during the Gaza disengagement."

Chirac replied, with some obvious gravity, "I am concerned about this also, but as you well know, mister Sharon, the Lebanese government does not control Hezbollah. Quite frankly, I can't see Iran encouraging any escalation, not while it is in the midst of the crisis of its nuclear aims. However, Syria is another story. France has strong historical ties with it and the Syrians must learn to evolve and take into account the changed environment. The Hariri assassination has isolated Syria and focused world attention on it. We are putting strong pressure on Damascus to ensure the truth in this matter comes out. Their incomprehensible stonewalling carries the risk of destabilizing the entire region. There is obviously the possibility of the government being tempted by a military adventure as a means of ending its isolation. I am quite concerned by its behavior, and in truth, I don't really understand the Syrian way of thinking."

"But we should apply Security Council Resolution 1559 that demands all armed militias in Lebanon be dismantled. It is unthinkable for a democratic state to permit political parties to arm themselves. Hezbollah's forces are in place in southern Lebanon, right along the border with us. The Lebanese army is well back of them," Sharon, who knew the details of their deployment, countered.

"Of course I am for the application of this resolution, but we also need to understand the stabilizing role Hezbollah has on the Lebanese regime. If we push it aside, quarantine it if you will, it will react with force and the whole country will suffer." Quite obviously, Chirac was satisfied that in intervening in favor of democratic elections in Lebanon, France had done enough.

Sharon was not satisfied with the French President's response, but the question was a highly sensitive one and he did not want to openly contradict Chirac. The men went on to discuss at length the growing Iranian nuclear crisis. France, Chirac proclaimed, would be very firm on this issue. Only a few days earlier, the Israeli Atomic Energy Commission chief, Gideon Frank, came to Paris for discrete talks on the problem. Iran's nuclear weapons ambitions were a menace not only for Israel but also for Europe. The French President made it clear that it was unacceptable to France for Iran to possess a nuclear military arsenal:

> "We will demand objective guarantees from Tehran concerning the peaceful and civilian nature of its nuclear program – and that it renounce all activity that could produce enriched fissile material. What is vital, is maintaining the unity of the international community on this issue. This has so far been maintained. I am not able to tell you what result will come from this joint effort. I do hope it will end favorably and that the danger will be eliminated. We should first and foremost use diplomacy here."

Jacques Chirac ended on a somewhat optimistic note. Sharon nodded, showing appreciation for France's diplomatic efforts. He was also convinced that the Security Council must move forward on the question. The Israeli government had also by now changed its view of the role the United Nations could play, and no longer considered the organization "a gadget," as former French leader Charles de Gaulle had once disdainfully called it.

Concerning the resolution of the Palestinian problem, there had been prior agreement to not evoke, in the talks between Chirac and Sharon, subjects on which there was disagreement; these were to be put off until a later date. The question of West Bank settlements was thus off the table, as was the thorny issue of the protective wall the Israelis were building along the old West Bank demarcation line. Regarding the essential question, i.e., what was Sharon intending to do after the Gaza evacuation? There was silence. Would the Israeli Prime Minister take advantage of the momentum and proceed to disengage in the West Bank? Despite Chirac's great curiosity and the legitimate desire of the Quai d'Orsay – France's Foreign Office – to know more, on this matter nothing was said.

Chirac did salute Sharon's courage, and was sympathetic to the difficulties he faced in carrying off the disengagement plan in Gaza:

> "I am closely following the evolution of this situation in your country. Actually, I listen to your ambassador on the radio practically every morning while shaving, and I faithfully read my briefings. I am quite aware of the great difficulties you face within your party, and must say I greatly appreciate your determination."

Sharon responded, "I have arrived at the conclusion that this disengagement is in Israel's interests, and I intend to implement it on August 15, But I would like you to know that should our people come under Palestinian fire during the evacuation, our response will be overwhelming."

Chirac insisted on the necessity of reinforcing Abu Mazen's position which was endangered by Hamas:

> "The American administration has asked me to bring up with you the subject of providing munitions to the Palestinian security forces, without which they cannot defend themselves."

Sharon quickly replied, "The United States has recently spoken to me about this. But last Saturday, an Israeli couple was killed and one of the assassins was a Palestinian policeman in uniform. Do you understand our position? Why should I give these people cartridges? They already have munitions, perhaps not enough, but they could acquire more by disarming the many armed factions that abound in Gaza and the West Bank. There are more than sixty thousand armed men within the Palestinian Authority's reach. No more than ten thousand loyal soldiers would amply suffice for Abu Mazen. You don't think that this number would be enough to restore order?"

"I agree on the numbers," Chirac concurred. "But still, we must not lose the opportunity to shore up Abu Mazen's power. As a new president, he does need our help."

Sharon diplomatically remained silent on the "help" the French had long given Yasser Arafat. Chirac had in fact been the last Chief of State to see Arafat before his demise in a Paris hospital.

After the main course of the meal, during which the more "meaty" issues had been broached, came dessert, a frothy chilled sorbet, and with it, the conversation took a lighter turn. Both men had been, in their past, Ministers of Agriculture in their respective countries; the Israeli recounted amusing stories about life on his ranch, and made several cynical allusions to his political adversaries and the Rabelaisian story about Panurge and his sheep, who mindlessly followed one another off a cliff. Chirac, carried by his traditional Correzian machismo, reminded Sharon that he had once offered him a powerful French bull, potent and ready to reproduce. Laughing, Sharon replied:

> "The King of Jordan once gave me a thoroughbred stallion, but alas! I was unable to accept the gift. Under Israeli law, all gifts worth more than three shekels, just about nothing really, must be warehoused at the Prime Minister's Office. We concluded that the building was not set up to stable an Arabian steed in an uncomplicated manner..."

At the end of the meeting, Chirac offered his guest an attractive sculptured portrait of Marianne, the symbol of the French Republic, perhaps an easier gift to showcase in the halls of government.

Chapter 16

The Massive Retreat

The weakness of those that employ force,
is that they come to only believe in force.
Paul Valery

Several days before Sharon's successful trip to Paris in the last days of July, 2005, Condoleeza Rice had come to meet with him at his desert ranch. The U.S. Secretary of State was a seductive woman, and the Israeli Prime Minister had always been appreciative of her dynamism and her charms, going so far as to confide with a smile to one of his aides, "This woman, Condoleeza, has such beautiful long legs..." It was meant as a sincere compliment.

The Secretary and her delegation arrived at the Sycamores ranch in an Israeli Army helicopter. Dressed casually in a sky-blue open collar shirt and khaki pants, a jubilant Ariel Sharon warmly welcomed his important guest, showing her considerable deference. A quick tour of the property was the first order of business. Standing with Ms. Rice in front of the sheep pen, Sharon the old shepherd exclaimed with pride as he caressed the wool of a little lamb, "As you can see, Madame Secretary, the farm is bustling. When I awake each morning I never fail to be amazed by the warmth emanating from these magnificent creatures. Just look at them all, they're fantastic."

The American warmly responded in kind:

> "Each time I visit a farm I feel touched. You know, I spent my entire childhood in an urban setting."

Sharon went on, with a touch of his traditional sardonism:

> "As for myself, I have confidence in the future. Like my late mother, I am a peasant. I was born in an agricultural village, and my father was an agronomist. This is my secret home; here on the land I'm in my true element. If I leave office tomorrow, I would still have in me a great passion, the will to raise my sheep, and mount up on a horse and gallop alone through the prairie. It's a magnificent feeling, and it is the reason I do not fear political battles. My place in the sun will forever be here, at the Sycamores."

Condaleeza Rice broke out in laughter. She truly admired Sharon's courage and perseverance. The tour over, they went inside to discuss more serious matters at a working breakfast prepared by Arik's daughter-in-law, Inbal. It was a typical Israeli meal to which had been added Sharon's favorite dish, roast lamb. Inbal – Gilad's wife – had become the soul of the ranch since Sharon's wife Lily had passed away. She was an artist who worked in ceramics when she was not managing the farm and taking care of her father-in-law. Inbal had in fact lived at the Sycamores since finishing high school, and knew the epicurean caprices of the family patriarch by heart; she always spoiled him with the succulent treats he so enjoyed. The conversation at the table was relaxed and friendly. Rice told the Israeli P.M. that President Bush was closely following events in Israel:

> "We have seen the television images of the demonstrations against the disengagement plan and greatly admire your determination. We are strongly committed to seeing you suc-

ceed. This is an important step in the peace process that you have undertaken."

Sharon thanked Rice for her kind words:

"You know, Madame Secretary, I first met President Bush in 1998, when he was still only Governor of Texas and I was Foreign Minister in the Netanyahu government. I accompanied your president by helicopter to see Samaria and the Jordan Valley and from above he saw the hills and the mountains, the historical sites such as Herod and Masada. He was a good listener and tried to understand my explanations of our problems of defense and security. He was moved by the Jewish people's strong links to its past, and by our unshakeable attachment to our ancestral lands. Since that time we have deepened our friendship and strengthened the ties that bind us. In fact, George Bush was the first to call and congratulate me on my February, 2001 election victory."

Taking advantage of the warm ambiance, Sharon asked the Secretary to put pressure on Palestinian president Abu Mazen to keep his forces on a tight leash and control the activities of Hamas. She promised to do just that and to speak of the matter with the President.

"As far as we are concerned," she said with firmness, "Hamas is a terrorist organization, and that must change."

Sharon added with considerable force to that statement: "Not only must this abject organization put down its weapons, and cease its violent activities, it must also bury its ideology, which still calls for the destruction of Israel."

"We will act closely and in concert with the Europeans to put pressure on Hamas and Hezbollah. I remain confident. By the way, how do you see the post-Gaza disengagement situation?"

This was a question the Israeli P.M. knew was coming, but he had decided to not give a direct answer, and especially, to abstain from making any new commitments on further retreats. He did say that once out of Gaza, Israel had no intention of remaining on the so-called "Philadelphia line" linking Rafah to the Egyptian border. The message was clear, and the Secretary of State had no desire to pose any other embarrassing questions, conscious as she was of the many current difficulties Ariel Sharon had to resolve. It was manifestly impossible for him to give any precise guidance as to the near-term future.

After lunch the two leaders walked up the hill that looked out onto the expanse of plain running right to Gaza. From an observation post, Sharon pointed out the area from which Palestinian militants fired their home-made Qassam missiles on the border town of Sderot. He also revealed that a missile had recently landed not far from his farm, but that, luckily, there had been no damage and no injuries. The visit ended in a meeting of the minds, and the Secretary's helicopter then whisked her back to Jerusalem. That was the day before the Sabbath, and after a fine family dinner, there was, as customary, a time reserved for playing with the grandchildren. After the kids went to bed, Sharon put on a good Western, and fell asleep watching the cowboys and Indians slug it out in the wild west.

On Saturday, August 7, only a week before the Gaza evacuation was to begin, there was another dramatic move by Sharon's adversaries. Benjamin Netanyahu resigned as Finance Minister. It was a calculated move on the part of the Prime Minister's main Likud opponent and the timing was meant to shake up the Israeli political and economic chess board. During a press conference carried live on Israeli television, "Bibi" violently criticized Sharon's disengagement policy and affirmed with conviction that he was acting according to his conscience. He could not, he went on, "accept a disengagement plan that would divide the people, bring us back to 1967 borders and imperil the unification of Jerusalem."

The former Prime Minister added, somewhat pretentiously, that as the son of an historian, he was concerned about what would be said of him ten, fifty, or a hundred years down the line:

> "In the glorious pages of the history of Israel, would it be written that Bibi Netanyahu had bowed to pressure and endorsed a unilateral retreat that would allow terrorism to be unleashed, endorsed the policies of confusion, national division and in the end, of the tearing apart of our nation? Never! I will never allow that. I will always act according to my conscience and in the best interests of Israel, shoring up our ranks and promoting the cohesion of the Jewish people."

Netanyahu's resignation had been expected for some time, though no one actually thought he would stab Sharon in the back by leaving a week before the evacuation was to begin. The situation was in fact quite complex, and worrisome. Netanyahu had, despite public reservations, supported Sharon and voted for the disengagement, even authorizing a two billion dollar budget for the operation. He had performed well as Minister of Finance and was highly regarded in the Israeli industrial and stock market milieus. The country had rebounded from economic disaster on his watch. He had the confidence of the business community: his departure was thus a source of some considerable concern. Among his successes could be counted a series of much-needed reforms in the way the economy worked, including the privatization of many state enterprises, including banks. He had also succeeded in naming an American economist – Stanley Fisher, a man who spoke little Hebrew – as Governor of the Bank of Israel. Fisher, even if he could not at first read the Hebrew files he had to deal with, was an expert at a more important language: the language of numbers. He subsequently made remarkable linguistic progress.

Netanyahu's reforms were not universally acclaimed however, since they did exacerbate the difficulties of the Israeli poor, and widen the economic rift between socio-economic classes within the country. Whatever the case, his departure was a bitter blow to the new direction of the state treasury. Sharon was not a great expert in economics and had given Netanyahu an absolute free hand. Now, the intentions of the brilliant ex-Finance Minister were abundantly clear. The political storm his resignation brought about was a slap in Sharon's face meant to force the Prime Minister to resign, which would give Bibi the presidency of the Likud Party, and as a consequence, the Prime Minister's chair once again. Likud Party militants believed that the move could force a postponement of the Gaza retreat, and hasten Sharon's own resignation. Poll after party poll showed Netanyahu to be the Likud favorite now, and his position within the party central committee was becoming stronger by the day.

Ariel Sharon was revolted at this overt maneuvering. He responded rapidly and forcefully, declaring Netanyahu to be "a strange man endowed with a highly flexible spinal cord that allowed him to bend at will under the slightest pressure. No political leader worth his salt can abandon an important mission in midstream. Bibi needs to take his responsibilities seriously and go right to the logical end of his decision."

Within hours of Netanyahu's departure, Sharon named Ehud Olmert to replace him. Olmert was the former Mayor of Jerusalem, and if he did not possess the charisma and media savvy of his predecessor, he had become the Prime Minister's principal confidant within the government, and his loyalty could not be questioned. The markets, which had been shaken by Bibi's resignation, quickly calmed down. There was to be no major change in policy, but there would be a major effort made to reduce poverty in Israel. More than one sixth of the population - one million Israelis - lived close to or beneath the poverty line, earning between six and eight hundred euros a month. There was also a social component at work, with the Ashkenazy population earning an average of 36% more than their Sephardic brethren. It was a shocking phenomenon in a modern country that prided itself on being at the leading edge of technological innovation.

Once the financial markets had quietened, Ariel Sharon could turn his attention to the roiling - and majority - opposition he faced within the Likud Party. His policies were not only called into question, he was faced with demands that he resign at once. The nadir was reached at an August 10 party meeting when someone poured boiling water on the audio system console, sabotaging the microphone and making it impossible for Sharon to address the crowd. It was a foolish and undignified act, but it was also accompanied by whistling and booing. Sharon, the old veteran of so many combats, walked silently off the stage, hardly containing his wrath. Later that evening, still disgusted by the behavior of party activists, he took a momentous decision: he would never again set foot in the Likud Central Committee. It was a decision destined to have a fateful impact on the fortunes of the governing party, but Sharon saw the writing on the wall: Likud was no longer what it had once been. Netanyahu had thrown the party into disarray with his resignation and provocation of unfounded, needless conflict. There was no more coherent ideology in the party; whatever was left was a mish-mash of internal quarrelling and personal settling of accounts. Opportunistic populism had now taken over, and there was no going back.

The next day, 150,000 demonstrated in Rabin Square in Tel-Aviv, calling for the Prime Minister to resign. The wave of orange banners – the color chosen by the settlers and opposition activists – rose and fell in a human tide watched by thousands of policemen and security agents. It was quite a show of force by the diehard Right, but in spite of it, or perhaps because of it, Ariel Sharon went on with determination to implement the disengagement. He was obstinate, he was crafty, and he was apparently unaffected by the political storm that raged around him. Like a man driving one of Israel's giant bulldozers, he drove the machine of state forward, overturning one obstacle after another that had been placed in his path by his adversaries.

In Gaza, preparations for the evacuation had by now been completed. A large-scale simulation had been successfully carried off, and all indicators were green, when news suddenly came of a fanatic Jew who had been expelled from the military deciding to take matters into his own hands. He boarded a bus in Galilee and began firing at close range at the Israeli Arab passengers. Three died before he was overcome by others on board and killed. The act was shocking to the point that no cemetery could be found willing to accept the extremist's remains. In the end, the man's lunatic act was self-defeating: Sharon succeeded in calming the Palestinians, and no one or nothing would be allowed to stop events from proceeding as planned.

Fifty thousand Israeli police and soldiers entered Gaza on August 15, exactly as it had been announced. They came in small groups to keep the lowest possible profile before taking on the task of evacuating more than fifteen thousand recalcitrant settlers and their supporters who had slipped in through the army checkpoints despite Gaza having been declared a closed zone. The core of the resistance was to be found among a small number of messianic hotheads, young men who blindly followed a number of fanatical rabbis who encouraged civil disobedience.

Sharon's directives to his forces had been crystal-clear. Force was only to be used as a last resort in cases where there was an absolute refusal to leave a property. Friendliness, moral persuasion, and solidarity between Jews was to be the order of battle. No firearms were to be employed except in case of self defense and threat of death. There must be no Jewish victims, no fratricidal war among the Israeli people.

No such directives were apparently in place among Palestinians. On September 7, a week before the last settlements were to be evacuated and destroyed, an armed group named after Salah el-Dine – Saladin the Magnificent who took back Jerusalem from the Crusaders in 1187 – decided to wreak vengeance on the old PLO guard they termed corrupt and incompetent. Yasser Arafat's cousin Moussa Arafat was assassinated by men armed with rifles and anti-tank grenades. The man was dragged from his home and beaten to death in front of his family. It was the first, but not the last, such incident. In fact, the Israeli retreat sparked a whole wave of Palestinian internecine violence and called into question Abu Mazen's capacity to maintain order among his troops. On the Israeli side, Tsahal was content to follow events without interfering and pursue the evacuation task it had been ordered to complete.

The plan was scrupulously followed, down to the last detail. Ariel Sharon personally supervised the implementation of disengagement, but his presence was a discrete and non-uniformed one. In his heart, he felt no small amount of solidarity with the settlers. He knew their villages, and knew many of the evacuees personally, making the events even more heartbreaking. But once the decision had been taken, the old soldier would follow the plan to its conclusion, and he was on the scene, watching his maps as his troops progressed, hearing the play-by-play reports of skirmishes and confrontations, issuing orders as necessary.

For three weeks – to some it must have seemed an eternity – the world watched live as Israeli police and soldiers evacuated Israeli men, women and children, taken from their homes, their day-care centers, their schools and their synagogues with kindness, encouragement, and often, with tears. There was also footage showing angry settlers, determined to use almost any means of resisting the evacuation, who had pinned yellow Stars of David to their clothes evoking the horror of the Nazi Holocaust. They screamed epithets at the men and women come to bring them back within Israel, calling them Nazis, or Gestapo, or even worse, Kapo – collaborator. To any reasonable observer this was a revolting and inadmissibly vulgar comparison, an insult to the memory of the six million Shoah victims, massacred simply because they were Jews. On the other side were the soldiers, quietly determined to carry out their mission, but often crying freely themselves, demonstrating human compassion for the feelings of their compatriots, and caring about the families whose lives were being turned upside down.

Watching the television images, Ariel Sharon felt admiration mixed with sadness. The scene that touched him the most involved Tsahal soldiers picking up a child's teddy bear, tenderly packing it away in a box to be opened in the family's new home:

> "I will always remember the young, athletic soldier carefully wrapping a little stuffed toy and placing it lovingly in a cardboard box. I'll never forget the faces of the soldiers, men and women alike, the tears running down their caring faces. They accomplished a difficult and delicate mission

calmly and with a serenity that was immune to the provocations, insults and vile calumny that were screamed out at them. I could not be more proud of the ethics of our armed forces; their deportment is unparalleled in the whole world."

But there were other images to be seen, harsh, revolting shots of young extremists acting like thugs, cowardly taking advantage of the courtesy being shown them, standing on the roof tops of synagogues and public building and confronting the police and the army. Nothing, it seemed was base enough not to be employed in their attempts to sow anarchy and discord; they fought, they screamed, they threw projectiles, stones and cans of paint and chemicals. In the end, the insolent hard core – most of whom were not even Gaza settlers, but troublemakers from other parts of Israel – was expelled. The main body of Gaza settlers left with their dignity intact, even if their hearts were broken. In the end, the difficult decision taken by their government was obeyed.

After thirty-eight years, the Israeli presence in Gaza was no more. Not a single shot was fired in the evacuation. Despite the diehards' threats, the synagogues – last religious bastions of the settlers – were left intact, in the somewhat naive hope that the Palestinians would put these sacred buildings to use. That hope was quickly extinguished by the hateful and ferocious mentality of the crowds that overran the settlements less than an hour after the soldiers of Tsahal left. Every last synagogue was ransacked, demolished and burned to the ground by enraged groups intent on leaving no trace standing of the "colonization of the Zionist enemy."

Reconciliation and peaceful coexistence would have to wait for another day...

Still, despite the difficulties encountered during the evacuation and the uncertain security future Israel faced, the disengagement was of real diplomatic benefit to the nation. The prestige of the Jewish state was enhanced all over the world. Prime Minister Sharon's personal reputation took a sharp turn for the better, and he received encouragement from many foreign heads of state. On September 17, for example, he was acclaimed by more than 150 world leaders at the United Nations building in New York City. The occasion was the ceremony celebrating the sixtieth anniversary of the creation of the U.N. Sharon, obviously moved by the applause, gave his speech in Hebrew, and began by declaring,

> "I have come here from Jerusalem, the capital of the Jewish people for more than three thousand years, and the united capital of Israel for all time to come. I am the proud representative of an ancient people, small in number but whose contribution to human culture and moral values, justice and religion has transcended the universe and embraced history. I was born in Eretz Israel – Palestine as it was called before the creation of Israel – in a family of pioneers who tilled the soil. They sought no quarrel with anyone. They had no wish to dispossess their neighbours. Had it not been for the obligations of circumstances I would have never become a soldier but remained a simple peasant and farmer. My first and enduring love was for the work of sowing and harvesting crops, of improving the farm, and raising my sheep."

Then came a solemn appeal to the Palestinians:

> "As a man whose life was spent in combat, a man who took part in all the wars our nation fought, I extend the hand of friendship to our Palestinian neighbors. I call upon them to accept the road of compromise and peace. Let us put an end to this bloody conflict and together follow the road to reconciliation between our two peoples. This is how I conceive my mission and my responsibilities for the years to come."

Ariel Sharon then announced that there would be future, painful territorial concessions made by Israel to achieve peace. The applause was overwhelming, and moving. Never before had an Israeli leader received such overt manifestations of empathy in this hall. It was a well-known fact of political life that the international arena was long hostile to Israel's leaders. Often, in the past, entire delegations would exit the assembly hall as a sign of protest, but today, the most controversial Israeli leader ever was being acclaimed, and the irony was lost on few present. This was the first time Sharon had ever received such an ovation: the thunderous public acclamation would have been unimaginable in prior years.

The Israeli Prime Minister was radiant with joy. Heads of state, ministers, bureaucrats and journalists all jostled with each other to be first in line to shake his hand or beg for an audience with the new hero of the hour. In the end, they waited their turn patiently for a few brief words with Sharon, and the opportunity of an historic photo. The moment was bittersweet for the old warrior; he was jubilant but reminded of earlier, sadder times. The ways of politics were indeed labyrinthine. But finally, on the eve of the Jewish New Year, he had emerged victorious. It was a wonderful gift.

On the eve of Rosh Hashonah, the third of October 2005, which was also the anniversary of the accident that killed his son Gury at the age of eleven, Sharon declared to Shimon Schiffer, the political correspondent of *Yediot Aharonot* and the man who had become his preferred journalist and confidant, that "We will take a giant step towards peace next year." It was a reassuring and optimistic declaration that the newspaper carried at the top of page one of its next edition. That very morning, both Abu Mazen and Hosni Mubarak telephoned Sharon with wishes for a Happy New Year, *Shana Tova*.

As of now Israel would be seen as a powerful and serious country that ardently desired peace. Now, Muslim countries like "father of the Islamic Bomb" Pakistan with its sixty million citizens, and Indonesia whose Muslim population was more than two hundred million, seemed ready to recognize Israel and exchange ambassadors. It was true that in their haste, both countries gave some credence to the old anti-Semitic fables about Israel's powerful Washington lobby that held sway in the U.S. capital. A flattering, if grossly exaggerated story, similar to those told throughout history about the secret Jewish plans to rule the world. Other countries, from North Africa to the Persian Gulf were now ready to open diplomatic relations or re-open relations that had been cut off in 2000 at the start of the Second Intifada. Tunisian President Ben Ali officially invited Ariel Sharon on a state visit, and Foreign Minister Silvan Shalom arrived in Tunis in November 2005, on a direct flight from Tel-Aviv, to prepare the future meeting between the two heads of state. Shalom brought with him a large contingent of negotiators and...his mother, a native of the Tunisian city of Gabès.

Tourism was now to be encouraged between Israel and both Tunisia and Morocco, with Libya thought to be not far behind. The year 2005 saw a sizable increase in tourists visiting Israel also, with more than two million foreigners coming to experience the soul-enriching joys of the Holy Land. This was good news, but Ariel Sharon also knew that how well these developments would continue depended to a large extent on the political evolution in the Middle East and the application of the Roadmap. Stability in the West Bank and improvements in the local economy were essential components of any future steps toward a lasting peace between Israel and the Palestinians.

But the Qassam missiles still flew into Israeli border towns and kibbutzes. New, more powerful versions of the rocket slammed into Sderot, the outskirts of Ashkelon and even reached military bases near the city. The factional infighting among Palestinian militant groups raged on in the streets of Gaza where Tsahal had formerly maintained at least a semblance of order. The "democratic" elections in the territories were approaching, and the battle between the Old Guard of the PLO – the men like Abu Mazen and Abu Alla, who had returned from Tunis with Yasser Arafat and were now his successors – and the Young Turks like Salam Fayad, Mohamed Dahlan and Marwan Bargouti who had known nothing but the years of Israeli occupation, was ongoing in a climate of violence. Hamas extremists had won municipal elections and this certainly gave Abu Mazen less room to maneuver. Israel saw the rise of Hamas as extremely disquieting, as did the Americans and even the Europeans. It was also common knowledge that thousands of rifles, automatic weapons and Katyusha multiple rocket launchers had been discretely brought across the border from Egypt through the Rafah crossing by Al-Qaeda partisans following the evacuation of Gaza.

Hamas demanded democratic elections to legitimize their power in Gaza and set up their own Hamas-Land there, a mirror of the Hezbollah-Land in Southern Lebanon. This would leave the Palestinian Authority to have their own Fatah-Land in the West Bank. The Hashemite Kingdom of Jordan worked as hard as it could to stop the growing efforts of the terrorists to turn that country into a revolving door for terror. Al-Qaeda militants from Iraq and Saudi Arabia were now entering Jordan and preparing to use it as a base of activities, as were other hard men from the West Bank. Hamas was preparing to set up huge hidden munitions depots in Amman, a plan which would only become public knowledge in May 2006 when Jordanian security forces found it. The Egyptians had problems of their own, as they tracked down the Al-Qaeda network responsible for massive, murderous bomb attacks in the Sinai resort cities of Sharm-el-Sheikh and Taba.

Egypt undertook to resolve the Rafah border crossing issue and in fact a new terminal opened in November 2005. For the first time, Palestinians would be in control of one of their borders. The agreement, brokered by the United States and Europe, allowed for Israel to supervise the movement of persons and goods through the presence of European observers and watch via a live video feed. It was a giant step, but it would not erase the mistrust that persisted between the Israelis and the Palestinians. Sharon himself would not yield as far as security issues were concerned and on this point would only rely on Tsahal and Israeli intelligence services. The facts concerning the possible return of Palestinian refugees to Gaza were as follows: according to the U.N., 1,718,00 lived in Jordan, 409,000 in Syria and 391,000 in Lebanon. Israel would refuse to recognize their right of return to lands now within Israeli borders, considering that to be a demographic menace to the Jewish state, but at least one hundred thousand currently residing in Jordan were expected to move to Gaza. As for the rest of the refugees, their future, as much as the future of Jerusalem, would have to await a final settlement between Israel and the eventual Palestinian state, yet to be born. It may have been considered the deal-breaker by many, but on these two issues Ariel Sharon would make no concessions.

Chapter 17

The Earthquake

Good things arrive slowly, a little at a time, but catastrophes and earthquakes come suddenly, like a powerful geyser.
Chinese proverb

On Thursday, November 10, 2005, dawn came to Tel-Aviv at five-forty am But Labor Party – Mapai – workers took little notice: they had been up all night in a state of effervescence awaiting the final count of the party elections, and the surprising results were historic. For the first time, a "Moroccan," Amir Peretz, was chosen to head the political formation whose former leaders – David Ben-Gurion, Levy Eshkol, Golda Meir, Moshe Dayan and Shimon Peres, among others – had all played such vital roles in the history of Israel. As for the eighty-two year-old Polish-born Knesset Member Shimon Peres, who had been the campaign favorite, he had been Defense Minister, Head of the Labor Party, Foreign Minister and Prime Minister...but he had never achieved those high positions by virtue of a general election victory. Now, this blow: it was a humiliation of unprecedented proportions. All of a sudden, everything seemed to be falling apart for the veteran politician, and he took it very badly indeed, angrily calling for a recount and an investigation into possible vote fraud and falsification of ballots. As a melodramatic act bordering on paranoia, Peres' gesture reflected poorly on himself. People saw him as a bad loser, unable to leave the arena with dignity. Apart from a summary handshake, Peres refused to even speak with the man who had pipped him at the post and then patiently waited fifty-four hours for the customary kind words of encouragement... that never came. The two were, after all, members of the same party. Peres remained at home, in isolation, considering his future and reflecting on his loss. If power was indeed a drug for politicians, Shimon Peres was now facing the unpleasant prospect of going "cold turkey."

But Ariel Sharon could not have been more of a gentleman. Placing a congratulatory call to Amir Peretz only minutes after the elections results were announced, he wished his new opponent in the Knesset well. After all, the pair were practically neighbors in the Negev Desert. Nonetheless, the strange behavior of Shimon Peres compared poorly to Sharon's magnanimity.

Peretz was small in stature, but at the age of fifty-three, a charismatic and larger-than-life orator whose trademark Stalinesque moustache made him a favorite of political cartoonists. In fact, in a gesture of political generosity tinged with realism, Peretz, a trade union leader born in the small Moroccan village of Boujade in the Atlas Mountains, had recently trimmed his moustache to accommodate hearing-impaired supporters who were unable to read his lips during his fiery speeches. His parents had emigrated to Israel during the early fifties, at the time of Moroccan independence. Like many other North African Jews at the time, the family took up residence in low-cost housing in Sderot, a bleak Negev desert community that some called "forgotten by God." Sderot was close to Gaza, and close to the Sharon Sycamores compound, and would become known in later years not for being far from the center of the country so much as being close to the fields from where Palestinian militants regularly fired their high trajectory Qassam rockets in an attempt to terrorize the population.

Peretz had been an Army engineer in a paratrooper division. Promoted to the rank of Captain, he left the military in 1974 following a serious injury received in a battle in the Sinai Desert, and because of which he spent two years convalescing in hospital, wheelchair-bound. Even now he retains foot problems and walks with a slight limp. Despite his injuries, he purchased a farm in the moshav community of Nir Akiba (unlike the kibbutz setup where property is communal, moshav arrangements call for private ownership of the land) and grew roses in an astonishing variety of colors and aromas. With children of an artistic nature (his daughter Shani studies cinematography in London, his son Ohad is a musician, while the younger boys Yftah and Matan are still in high school) Peretz might have seemed to be content to farm, but he had other ambitions. In 1983 he was elected Mayor of Sderot. He was also an active member of the executive of the Histadrut union movement and subsequently became its all-powerful leader; this exposure helped him to successfully run for parliament.

By 1999 he had become a dissident voice in the Labor Party and founded the Haam Ehad – one people – party under whose banner he was re-elected. By 2004 he had rejoined Labor and Ham Ehad was dissolved; a year later, Peretz stood for the presidency of Labor and became its candidate for the position of Prime Minister of Israel in the subsequent elections in March of 2006. It was, for a man of his humble background, a meteoric ascension.

Peretz had a set of priorities that was entirely different from those of his opponents. He considered the Defense budget ripe for significant cuts. The fear of war and terrorism had, for him, to cede pride of place to a policy of fighting unemployment and poverty. His platform called for the state of Israel to guarantee each worker an honorable job with a decent minimum wage – at least one thousand dollars a month. National budgets must aim at reducing social disparity, investing in education and health, not throwing colossal amounts of money into increasing settlements in the territories. As far as foreign policy was concerned, Peretz was a decided dove: he openly called for the creation of a Palestinian state by 2010. His economic and security brain trust included the former head of Shin Beth, General Ami Ayalon, and the former head of Mossad, Dany Yatom.

The surprising victory of Amir Peretz over Shimon Peres was more than just a symbolic statement of a new reality in the Labor Party, though: it sparked a series of events that led to the fall of the Sharon government. Like one of the automobile ads popular on television, the Peretz win was the first domino to topple over. It was quickly followed by the resignation of Labor Ministers, the resignation of the Prime Minister, the Knesset being dissolved and new, early elections called. And then the biggest domino of them all fell when Ariel Sharon left his Likud Party, founded Kadima – "forward" in Hebrew, and invited the dissidents from both Likud and Labor – among them Shimon Peres – to join him in a national unity party.

Israel had never before seen such political agitation. Some called the quick succession of rapid changes a kind of "big bang;" whatever metaphor you wanted to use, the events had the unquestionable effect of a gigantic earthquake on Israeli politics. Sharon's departure from Likud was predictable; he had been preparing for it for some time but wanted to go at a time of his own choosing, and if possible, of his own making. It was no longer feasible for him to run a government that had become undisciplined and lacked unity, just as it had become unthinkable to be president of a political party whose members he could not even be assured of addressing in public.

Sharon had had his fill of being humiliated by his own party in non-confidence Knesset motions where his supposed allies rallied public opinion against him. He had had enough of seeing Israel sink into parliamentary chaos at the mercy of a few extremists. He had had enough, and more, of having his hands tied and being unable to name new ministers or take crucial decisions. Patience had its limits, and Ariel Sharon was an old military man who refused to accept disobedience; besides, he could simply no longer put up with the political blackmail he was subject to, or abide the base mediocrity of the Likud militants.

There remained though, the thorny problem of finding a solution. Few Israeli politicians were more skilled at strategy or political manipulation than Ariel Sharon. Showing remarkable composure, like an expert poker player he kept his cards close to his chest and even hid an ace up his sleeve. When he finally showed his cards, everything changed in Israeli politics. A brutal and often spiteful tactician, Ariel Sharon was ready to bring down the house if necessary: the end, ridding himself of the noisy naysayers who rejected his well-thought through analysis and plan to bring peace to his country, justified the means. He considered the future of the Jewish state to trump party politics, and in this matter he had a spectacular, take-no-prisoners style that involved, like his famous military victory in the October War, striking deep into the hearts of his adversaries. He would be daring, and as always, never retreat in the face of counter-attack.

Sharon met with the new leader of the Labor Party on November 19. If Peretz was looking forward to fighting the next election campaign, Arik, as Prime Minister and still head of Likud, had not revealed his true intentions despite an abundance of rumors. The two agreed to hold new elections on March 28, 2006, and the countdown began. But the environment was one of total confusion: no one knew for sure if Ariel Sharon would still be leading Likud into the fray, and disinformation – the weapon of choice in psychological warfare – was in no short supply.

It was a time for Ariel Sharon to pull back and reflect. His advisers and close friends were bathed in a deep pool of uncertainty, unable to come to a decision as to the right thing to do. Omry and Gilad Sharon, always consulted by their father in times of turmoil, were not ready to give a determinative response but they were leaning towards the creation of a new political party. Ariel listened, of course, but the consequences of such a decision were serious, perhaps grave, and to carry so heavy a load he needed first to find the clarity his act would require in solitude. So alone with his cows, his horses and his sheep, he spent the Sabbath in quiet reflection, meditating on the best course of action as he walked his sheep-dog through the fields of the ranch.

By nightfall his mind was made up. The following morning he called a press conference. Seeing the firm and combative look on the old general's face, the journalists could pretty well anticipate what their Prime Minister was about to say:

"After giving the matter a great deal of thought, I have decided to leave the Likud Party and create a new political formation. I'm still a young man, only seventy-seven, and have a long life before me," he declared, his face conveying an alert and determined spirit.

The news stirred the entire country. It was an explosive decision that the political class may have been awaiting, but when it actually came, much changed in the course of a few sentences. Ariel Sharon was no longer the head of the Likud, and his former party was now – instantly – in deep trouble. It was one thing for the rebels to scream epithets at their leader, but their party was suddenly a ship with no helmsman, and that was an entirely different matter. He would no longer need to suffer the revolt, disobedience and waves of protest in silence. But now that Ariel Sharon was out, there was a sudden, no-holds-barred combat for the succession; cheap politicking and low blows became the order of the day. Seven candidates declared for the Likud vacancy. Raucous debates took place, accompanied by intriguing, vague electoral promises and open clan warfare.

Sharon watched closely from the sidelines. The self-destruction of Likud played to his strength and the early public opinion polls showed him the favorite, and by far, to win the March elections. For the average Israeli, Ariel Sharon was the charismatic leader whose quiet strength was admired, venerated even. He had the stuff of which great men were made, and the majority of the people were ready to follow him whether his party was called Likud, Kadima, or Shlom Tsion, or even if he led no political formation at all. The people were solidly behind a man, not a party.

In taking this momentous decision, Ariel Sharon realized that he had a lot going for him. There was the complete confidence of his supporters, for one, and the mediocrity of his adversaries, for another. He would undoubtedly get the vote of the people who saw his brilliant military career and political experience as vital components of the leadership Israel needed at this crucial time in its history. Sharon was an authoritative and pragmatic leader who symbolized the Jewish people's attachment to the Land of Israel, a great patriot who was ready to serve the national interest with humility and sincerity.

But if all this were true, he still had to fight an election with no organization on the ground, no volunteers to run the machine a political campaign requires, no infrastructure, no logistics...and little time to put all of these in place. He had only sixteen weeks to put it all together and let the people decide the course Israel was to take. It was a delicate and risky adventure of colossal proportions in the best of circumstances, and even if Sharon was a young seventy-seven, as he laughingly told the nation during his press conference, he still was a seventy-seven year-old man with health problems and the enormous weight of running the country would be on his shoulders throughout the campaign.

Sharon was still ready for the battle. He was quite capable of splitting the traditional party vote, always ready to take whatever risks were required in the interests of his people as he saw them. He even declared himself ready to plunge forward like a tightrope walker on a high wire act with no safety net below him.

On the day Kadima was created, fourteen Likud Knesset members, including many ministers, resigned from their party and announced they would join Sharon in his new formation. Their decision was quickly followed by a like move in the traditional Likud electoral constituency.

Sharon was satisfied by developments. Under Israeli election rules, Kadima was eligible to receive state funds to finance its campaign, and the party mechanics were quickly set up. Ten thousand Israelis joined the party in less than a week, and thousands of letters of support were received at Sharon's office. On the Likud side, things were not looking so good. The candidates for the party primary elections, in a state of concerned uncertainty, were fighting for votes inch by inch. They kept a confident public face, but in reality they feared the worst. Would their constituency move to Kadima and significantly reduce their Knesset presence? Would the numbers of elected Likud members – called traitors and stool pigeons by their former comrades – switching sides snowball, in spite of all the insults they were subjected to? All possibilities seemed to be on the table.

Labor was having problems also. Shimon Peres had gone to Spain to participate in the celebrations marking the tenth anniversary of the Euro-Mediterranean Peace Process. In truth, Peres rarely missed an occasion to take part in major international political events like this. He adored the magnificent receptions and the grand pomp with which the stars of the political and show business worlds were honored, and Barcelona was no different. As guest of honor at a soccer match between an Israeli-Palestinian team and a Spanish All-Star team, he was seated next to the legendary Scottish actor Sean Connery, known better as the incarnation of James Bond. When he returned to Israel, Peres decided to score a goal on his own team, publicly announcing his departure from the Labor Party. The 1994 Nobel Peace Prize laureate – he had won jointly with Arafat and Rabin – read from a prepared text in a voice dripping with melancholy:

> "I am resigning from the Labor Party as of today. My ability to work in this political formation has come to an end, and I have decided to support Ariel Sharon who is the only one able to lead a coalition for peace. He is best suited for this task and the most open to innovating ideas needed to finally achieve peace and security, and I hereby support his election and will cooperate with him in order to reach these goals."

His words were clear. Behind them, though, was the obvious fact that the Shimon Peres of old had not changed an iota. He enjoyed power and was ready for all sorts of contortions to remain in a position of power, especially after his humiliating defeat at the hands of Amir Peretz. This appearance spotlighted his lack of self-assurance, vacillating behavior, distress and embarrassment. Talleyrand once said that betrayal was, in politics, simply a question of dates. With regard to Peres, one could add, "dates in the Hebrew calendar."

Shimon Peres had been, right from the beginning of the State of Israel, at the heart of and behind – as opposed to in front of – many of the crucial decisions that marked its history. He was known as "the grey eminence" of the nation's politics, since sooner or later, most of his ideas were adopted and his policies implemented without giving him credit. In this case, the events of the Labor Party elections had made it once again impossible for him to initiate his own policy; supporting Ariel Sharon was thus the best way for Peres to see his vision, and the ideas he had developed over a long time, put into practice. Some said Peres was the elephant man: he certainly had a thick skin, and appeared always cool to the touch, emotionless, showing neither regrets nor remorse. As far as public life was concerned, though, Peres had no intention of leaving the scene. As his favorite poet, Nathan Alterman put it, "I will not stop staying up late, nor cease breathing, and when I die, I'll go on walking..."

No one in the world of Israeli politics doubted that the political animal that was Shimon Peres would be around forever, like an unfinished diplomatic symphony. He once commented to the author of this book, "My last wish is that they write on my tomb, "Gone too soon." Shimon Peres, what a guy!

There had been other cases in the history if the country where leaders of one party or another had left for greener pastures. Moshe Dayan was a case in point: he had resigned from the Mapai to join Menachem Begin – "the hawk" in his march to peace with Egypt. Of course, Dayan had been a military man who excelled at questions of security, not a career politician and master of inner party intrigue. There had also been the case of David Levy, former Likud militant who in 1999 had joined Ehud Barak and the Labor Party: that move lasted only a year, and Levy was soon back in Netanyahu's Likud, hoping to one day become President of the State of Israel. In this case, Peres did not leave alone: he took Haïm Ramon, who was Minister Without Portfolio, and Telecommunications Minister Dalia Itshik with him. While their departure was a serious blow to the Labor Party, it was a blessing for Kadima, who warmly welcomed the trio to the new formation. All three had come with no existential baggage: in exchange for a guaranteed seat in the Knesset they freely abandoned their former party and its ideology.

All of these developments had a tonic effect on Ariel Sharon. His plurality – the margin for governing serenely – was growing and he felt sure that his dream of remaining in power for another four years was more and more likely to come true. The two old political warhorses called a joint press conference two days later. Side by side on the podium at Prime Minister's Office, both men were in obvious good spirits in responding to the pertinent – as well as the impertinent – questions posed by the gathered journalists.

> "Mr. Sharon, aren't you concerned that your new ally, Mr. Peres, will drag you to the left and force you to make new territorial concessions?"

Sharon replied with a laugh that was soon shared by Peres and others in the room: "Look at me, look at my size. Do you really think I can be moved that easily, even by a man named Shimon Peres?" He went on, saying:

> "Listen, I don't underestimate Shimon's physical strength. But he is an old friend, a few years my senior, that is true, and I have always respected him and admired his perseverance in the search for peace. If I am re-elected, Shimon Peres can have whatever position he wants in my government. As far as I am concerned he will be an equal partner, playing a central role in the peace process."

Peres, looking stiff and somewhat embarrassed, refused to answer any questions about the future of the Labor Party or the chances of its new leader, Amir Peretz, and merely added laconically, "The recent retreat from Gaza has encouraged me to join with Sharon in pursuing the peace process."

Meanwhile, there was another danger to confront: Tehran and its new leader Mahmoud Ahmadinejad, whose repeated public threats against Israel were extremely worrisome. The Iranian had already called for the annihilation of the Jewish state on October 26, 2005, in a speech entitled "A World Without Zionism;" Several days later he suggested the Jews of Israel should be moved to Europe, or even Alaska. A week after that, he denied the Holocaust ever took place. Ahmadinejad's many stupid and evil declarations in a short space of time were difficult to endure, especially since they came in the middle of the global crisis concerning Iran's quest for nuclear weapons. His words elicited sharp, immediate condemnations across the world... except in Arab and Muslim countries, where a pregnant silence could only be interpreted as mute approval.

Inside Israel, these revolting, provocative outbursts were page one news and a white-hot election issue; after all, the Iranians were already in up to their necks in the terrorism business, materially supporting Hamas and Islamic Jihad in the territories and consolidating their logistical and financial links with Hezbollah in Lebanon. Hamas leader Khaled Mashal had visited Tehran many times from his base in Syria, and there could be no doubt that he and the ayatollahs were not discussing measures to increase ecotourism between Damascus and Tehran!

Israel had until now remained in the background of the international push to contain Iran, playing the role of a consultant, but the new rant was too much. Openly threatened by the ayatollahs and the Iranian military, Israel had to react. It demanded the Iranian nuclear question be taken up with firmness and prudence by the United Nations Security Council with a view to sanctioning Iran and opening the possibility of quarantining of the obscurantist regime. What was regrettable was that the international community had taken so long to awaken to the clear danger the Iranian path represented. Since the time when the Shah was still on the Peacock throne and Ayatollah Khomeini freely preached anti-Semitic bile in sermons from his French sanctuary at Neauphle-le-Château near Paris, tolerated by President Valery Giscard d'Estaing, Israel had often warned of the risk to the world these people represented. Now, the count-down to atomic weapons was out in the open, in spite of Iranian obfuscation.

The Israeli Chiefs of Staff believed that the high level enrichment of uranium required to make atomic weapons began in March, 2006. Had the point of no return already been reached, or was it close? Would Arik Sharon order the Israeli Air Force to destroy Iran's nuclear facilities, just as Menachem Begin had sent in his jets to bomb the Iraqi Osirak nuclear plant near Baghdad in 1981? Shimon Peres had been Begin's opponent in those times; now, he and Sharon were a team, but the question was openly posed in the run-up to the March, 2006 Israeli elections.

A military strike on Iran would be without a doubt much more complex and delicate in every sense. An operation of this magnitude could only be accomplished with the logistical and intelligence support of the United States. It would involve many successive waves of attack; the Saudis and the Jordanians would need to be on board, as would the Gulf States who were Iran's immediate neighbours. And there was a vast American army in Iraq to be concerned about. How would the Iranians react to such a punishing blow?

Contrary to the Iraqi Osirak nuclear installation setup, Iranian atomic sites were largely underground and hidden in twenty different regions of the country; international inspections and spy satellites were handicapped, limited in the information they could obtain. So while it was true that Israel possessed the means to eliminate Iran's nuclear capacity, it preferred to try diplomacy first and let the Western Powers – first and foremost the United States of America – take the lead.

If that path was unsuccessful, all options remained open. No solution could be excluded if there was imminent danger to the Jewish state and to world peace. The "Cold War" was ongoing, in any case, with Israel flexing its powers of dissuasion: *Hetz* (Arrow) anti-missile missile systems capable of downing Iranian Shahib 3 rockets, had been successfully tested. The Shahib 3 was a cruise missile with a range of 3,000 kilometers. Manufactured with the help of Russia and North Korea, it could target both civilian and military targets.

During his historic visit to Israel in April 2005, Russian President Vladimir Putin had been warned of the Iranian threat by Ariel Sharon, but he seemed unconvinced by Israeli arguments and considered the case made at the time by the Prime Minister to be overexaggerated. Of course, in the months that followed, Tehran's regime took a harder line, both inside the country and in its diplomatic relations with the rest of the world. The radicalization of Iran was less and less difficult to ignore; with a constant stream of bellicose declarations emanating from its leadership, and its well-established support of international terror, even going as far as to suggest that terrorists could themselves acquire nuclear weapons, that country was a blatant menace to peace in the region and in the world.

On December 7, 2005, a suffocating hot day despite the winter season, Ariel Sharon arrived at Sde Boker, the kibbutz where the founder of Israel, David Ben-Gurion, had lived. Ben-Gurion had always hoped his village would one day become a spiritual, cultural and scientific center, and on this day, Ariel Sharon, Shimon Peres and Amir Peretz had come to commemorate the anniversary of "the Old Lion's" passing. Ben-Gurion's tomb looked out onto one of the most beautiful canyons of the Negev Desert. Ariel Sharon was dressed for the occasion in a dark suit and wore a large black kippa on his head. For him, Ben-Gurion was a spiritual leader, a man Sharon had admired, a man he would like to be seen as having emulated. He often quoted Ben-Gurion, reminding Israelis that he had also been ready to make painful concessions in order to reach a true peace with the Arabs. Most of the Territories including the Sinai, Gaza and the West Bank were open to negotiation as long as Israel retained Jerusalem and the Golan Heights. Sharon shared the same dream as Ben-Gurion: the development of the Negev. The desert region was vast, and could accommodate two million Jews working in agriculture and another two million in industry. From the security and demographic points of view, the Negev potential was enormous. Now Ariel Sharon, with the help of Shimon Peres, would leave no stone unturned to ensure that this gigantic project would become a reality in the coming years.

The thinking behind this plan was based on the Arab population explosion. Rather than support the status quo and maintain a geographic Greater Israel in which the Jewish population would be constantly sinking in proportion to the Arabs, the two venerable politicians saw that the Jewish character of the State of Israel and its military and economic power could only be maintained by abandoning some territory to the Palestinians and excluding them from Israel and Israeli rule. The historical mission of the Israeli state was not, in any case, compatible with the pursuit of ruling a hostile and dangerous Palestinian population several million strong. "Greater Israel" would be achieved by Israelis being on the cutting edge of agriculture, science and technology; fathoming the secrets of nature and raising the human spirit to new heights was a better use of the resource that was an unshakeable belief in the cause of the Jewish people and its universal values of justice.

The vision was a grand one; would the seventy-eight year-old Ariel Sharon have the capacity, energy and means to bring David Ben-Gurion's dream to reality? The old shepherd from Kfar Malal emphatically believed so. But meanwhile, the political circus dragged on. The election campaign saw ever more surprising – some said grotesque – somersaults of ideology and self-interest: Tzachi Hanegbi, the interim Likud President and son of the conservative Israeli "Pasionaria" Geula Cohen, resigned and publicly declared his support for Sharon, "the only leader capable of negotiating the right concessions." Hanegbi's mother, a well-known figure in diehard conservative circles, had been born in Jerusalem in 1925 to a Yemeni father and a Moroccan mother. During the British Mandate in Palestine she had been the spokesperson of the clandestine Lehi movement led by Yitzhak Shamir. In later years as a Knesset Member from 1974 to 1992, she had founded the ultra-conservative Tehia (Renaissance) splinter party along with a physician – Yuval Neeman – and General Raphael Eitan. Tehia had been dissolved in 1992.

Forty-eight hours later it fell to Defense Minister Shaul Mofaz to renounce his earlier decision to run for the Likud presidency. Only a few days earlier, Mofaz had turned down Sharon's offer of staying on as Defense Minister and Vice President of the Council of Ministers if he would follow the P.M. into Kadima. Mofaz called a press conference at the Beit Sokolov Press Center in Tel-Aviv (also, by the way, the headquarters of the spokesperson for Tsahal, the military censorship department and the government press and photo archives) at which he made a dramatic, through-the-window entrance citing security problems. As the room broke out in laughter at this unusual way of communicating the news, Mofaz sternly declared, "I'm supporting Sharon. The Likud militants have become extremists." This was the same man who had, the previous evening, sent letters of encouragement to all the Likud membership in which he declared:

> "Likud is my home, and here I will remain. It is simply unthinkable to abandon one's home. I will remain with you until we defeat the Kadima leftists and Ariel Sharon, who is cynically using the army for political and electoral purposes."

How Mofaz must have cursed his handlers. During the press conference, this forthright and honest neophyte in the unclean world of politics had to answer for his electoral flip-flop. How much, people wondered, was the word of an army chief worth? Mofaz had been one of the best Chiefs of Staff Tsahal had ever seen, but now, Sharon could conclude the man could not be trusted – and certainly not trusted with the Defense Portfolio again. In fact, Sharon was musing about naming a woman to the position, perhaps Tzipi Livni, who had proved her abilities as Justice Minister. If France could have a female Defense Minister, well, why not Israel? It would be an innovating decision for Tsahal, and probably not hurt either at the ballot box. Israeli women were loyal voters.

In addition to Justice, Tzipi Livni took on Foreign Affairs after the departure of Silvan Shalom; would she continue as head of Israeli Diplomatic Corps in the years to come, pursuing the work of Golda Meir? She was certainly qualified for the job, and had every chance of pulling it off. Mofaz, by contrast, was not an electoral plum. The circumstances of his departure from Likud left a bad taste in the mouth of public opinion. The polls showed he brought little to Kadima in terms of adding seats to its Knesset tally. In fact, what he added was more grist to the mill of public cynicism. Politicians in Israel were looked upon by the citizenry with the same sneer found in France, Canada, the United States and, in fact, most democracies.

The Likud war of succession was now a two man contest between Silvan Shalom and Benjamin Netanyahu. Bibi was - somewhat unjustly - caricaturized as an extremist, and suffered the outrage of being accused of having stolen money from the poor and the retirees during his term as Finance Minister for Sharon. Shalom, no stranger to back-room brawls, was willing to go to any depths to further his chances. He tried long and hard to divide the Sephardic members, knowing that Netanyahu probably needed them all to win the election. Bibi, by contrast, had the support of the Etsel old guard, the men and women who had fought the British in Palestine and remained loyal followers of the ideology of Jabotinsky and Begin. Outgoing Ministers Landau, Livnat and Levy also came out for Netanyahu, who, to his credit, avoided personal polemics and campaigned on the political weakness of Shalom. Netanyahu's considerable efforts were an uphill battle to close the Likud ranks, for he knew perfectly well that many more Likud partisans would move to Sharon's side if the old man won the general elections. That was just the way of politics.

Another polemic erupted concerning Sharon's true intentions for Jerusalem. Despite his constant affirmations to the contrary, one of his advisers, Kalman Gayer, seemed to indicate that he might not be opposed, under certain circumstances, to seeing the eternal capital of the Jewish people divided. In a *Newsweek* interview, Gayer went as far as affirming that Ariel Sharon would even be willing to give the Palestinians up to ninety percent of the territories in a final peace deal. The interview unleashed a political firestorm and called forth quick and forceful denials from both Gayer and his boss.

"These are grotesque fabrications. It's ridiculous. Never, ever will I ever sign an agreement that divides the eternal capital of the Jewish people. And my adversaries know this perfectly well," roared Sharon.

Was it just a tempest in a teacup? Who really knew the truth of the matter? Sharon's political adversaries hammered on the theme that the Prime Minister was lying. After all, they repeated, he had also sworn never to leave Gaza, and look what happened there. He was a man, they said, not to be trusted.

The problem with at least Kalman Gayer's denials was that, with typical American efficiency, *Newsweek* had him on tape.

The Jerusalem question was neatly turned into an ethnic-tinged poll the same day in the pages of *Yediot Aharonot*. The poll found that forty-nine per cent of Israelis, including Israeli Arab citizens, were ready for an agreement to share Jerusalem. It was a de facto declaration of separation and became the "battle theme" of the election campaign of leftist former Minister Yossi Beilin who sincerely believed it was the answer to finally reaching peace with the Palestinians.

For the Amir Peretz/Labor camp, the issue they brought before the public concerned what they called Sharon's cynical misuse of the military. In a radio interview on Kol Israel, Motti Morel - Peretz's strategic adviser - said:

> "Sharon continues the targeted assassinations of Palestinian militants to encourage escalation and in order that security and defense remain foremost in the minds of voters. He's just trying to make people forget about OUR issues, i.e. the social rift in the country and the economic crisis we face."

Kadima supporters were disgusted at the cheap remarks...but Amir Peretz never even came close to issuing an apology.

Ethics were conveniently put aside for the campaign: denial followed affirmation, insidious behavior and low blows were common currency, everything seemed to be allowed, nothing too base could be ignored in the quest for enough votes to win a seat in the Knesset. A real Middle Eastern bazaar. In fact, that's where the candidates often spent their time, shaking hands in the outdoor markets, chatting up the buyers and sellers, munching on a ripe tomato or a pepper, gesticulating using a leg of chicken or a fish for emphasis. The rule was: Please the public, and be sure to set out your party's ideological wares as prettily as possible next to the butcher, the fishmonger or the spice merchant. Oh, and get it in on camera and in time for the evening news. Who cared if politicians horsed around, looking ridiculous? Smiles had to be glued on – happy clown time – until events suddenly turned the laughter to tears.

Chapter 18

The Final Battle

Life is an endless struggle.
Voltaire

It was December 18, 2005, at exactly 7 pm Ariel Sharon was in his office with Shimon Peres, just returned from Strasbourg, France, where he had been the honored guest of the European Jewish Congress. The two old friends were nearing the end of an amicable conversation, when Sharon, who seemed all of a sudden distracted and not really listening to what Peres had to say, rose abruptly and ended their talk. He summoned his secretary, signed an urgent letter destined for the diplomatic pouch and with a taut smile on his lips, confided, "You know, I'm not sure what is the matter, but for the last few minutes I haven't been feeling very well."

His secretary, Marit Danone, blanched when she saw how ashen he looked, and quickly gave the Prime Minister a glass of water then hurried to the telephone and dialed Sharon's son:

"Your father is ill, Gilad," she said. "What should I do?"

"Don't panic, for one. Bring him discretely to the Tel Hashomer Hospital. I'll call his personal physician, Doctor Bolislav Goldman. Put Papa in his official car; we have to avoid an ambulance if at all possible."

Gilad spoke in a deeply worried, trembling voice. His father, who had by now turned from pale to florid, somehow made it down to his car and with obvious difficulty, succeeded in getting in on his own. He could hardly speak, not even a few mumbled words to the paramedic who sat next to him in the vehicle which now roared off at high speed, accompanied by the security detail. Sirens wailing, the convoy literally tore down the highway that led to the hospital. In the rear seat, Ariel Sharon maintained a stony calm. Then the car phone broke into the silence as the vehicle neared the village of Abu Gosh: it was Dr. Goldman, ordering the convoy to make a U-turn and instead head directly for the closest hospital, Hadassah Ein Karem.

Fifteen minutes later the Prime Minister's car arrived at the hospital's emergency entrance. Spurning the gurney that had been held ready for him, dizzy, his legs suddenly giving out, Ariel Sharon somehow remained ambulatory and was able to walk, not without considerable effort, to the trauma center. The best available doctors were there and immediately ordered a blood test, brain scan and heart ultrasound. The Prime Minister, like many people of his generation, was uncomfortable at showing his body to strangers, but the medical hardware was ready and there was really no choice but to quickly disrobe.

News in Israel travels fast. Outside the hospital, there was soon a considerable number of journalists and cameramen gathered in the confusion and the winter cold. Numerous police and watchful Shin Beth agents, weapons unholstered, surrounded the crowd. Inside, the Neurology Department had by now become a veritable crisis center, with security at a very high level. Sharon's sons Omry and Gilad had managed to avoid the paparazzi and find a discrete way into the hospital. They were determined not to leave their father's side until the crisis was resolved one way or another. Inbal, Gilad's wife, was also present. Television and radio networks all broke into their regularly scheduled programming to carry live – and for the most part vague – telephone commentary from their correspondents. It was a moment of total confusion, with no images available for the television news, and no precise information as to the exact nature of Sharon's condition. All anyone could state and restate was that there was no imminent threat to the Prime Minister's life. But there was no official statement. No one could say much of anything, but everyone was showing grave concern for Sharon's situation. In the absence of a clear statement from the medical or political authorities, speculation of the wildest kind was rampant. As the minutes went by, the country practically stopped dead in its tracks. No one could offer the slightest clue as to why Sharon had been rushed to hospital. No diagnosis filtered out from behind the closed doors. But everyone looked very, very worried. Had he been shot? Had there been an attempted assassination? Those who had seen the P.M. during the morning had reported nothing unusual. He had performed his usual tasks normally; no one had noticed anything out of the ordinary, or seen weakness of any kind. He had been the guest of friends on the weekend for a hearty meal, but that was in his habitual pattern of behavior. Sunday – the beginning of the work week in Israel -- had been an exceptionally busy day with a scheduled Cabinet meeting, but that too was a normal event. And in any case, as the commentators repeated, Sharon was a well-known workaholic. So what had happened here? Memories of the Rabin assassination quickly morphed into rumors of all kinds. The people of Israel, shocked into paralysis by the news, held their breath and waited.

If Israel was a democracy, Ariel Sharon had come to represent its pinnacle, an absolute force on the political and diplomatic scenes. Power was firmly concentrated in his hands. He who had emerged as the symbol of Israel's might, now in a fleeting instant had become no more than another distressed object for the scanners and ultrasound machines to study, an amalgam of brain cells, muscles and bones to be analyzed. But in a strange way it was as if the State of Israel itself was being examined in all its intimate details. Where was Israel going, and what was Ariel Sharon thinking in this moment of crisis?

After forty-five minutes of silence that seemed to last forever, a very emotional hospital spokesperson finally confirmed in Hebrew and English that, according to preliminary test results, the Prime Minister had suffered a mild stroke, but that he remained conscious. Adding, "Thank you very much," the spokesperson turned and walked away, leaving the reporters and commentators to voice their questions to each other: "Was the blood clot a danger to Sharon's brain, or to his heart? Was this mild thrombosis liable to reoccur? Were drugs being prescribed to treat him that could influence his decision-making capabilities? "

To those questions and many others there were to be, for the time being, no answers. One thing was certain, however: the political agenda of the state was in limbo. Official visits were put off. The Czech President was asked to postpone his arrival until a more propitious moment. Sharon's hospitalization had stupefied the country as a whole but it was also an event of deep concern to leaders of countries around the world. Thousands of get-well messages arrived at the hospital, from friend and foe alike. Many Arab states sent their best wishes for a prompt recovery.

As if things had not been in enough of a state of flux, Sharon's stroke added a whole new dimension of anxiety to Israel's political life. Would his illness be one more event in Ariel Sharon's long history of dramatic interventions in the affairs of state? How would his condition affect the Likud primary? Who would emerge as the new Likud leader? What political clout would Kadima have if its leader needed to campaign from a hospital bed? How could the Kadima train leave the station if its chief engineer was in a state of paralysis?

While the projectors were all focused on the fourth floor "Aleph" surgical wing of the Hadassah Hospital, Sharon's spokesperson let out that he had spent a comfortable night and that his state of health was good, under the circumstances. The doctors were also reassuring and opined that there was little likelihood of a recurrence: Ariel Sharon would be able to resume his functions after a few days' rest and the battery of cardiology tests he was presently undergoing.

Although for the moment no official photo was released, the Prime Minister was apparently joking with his doctors and sent a recorded message through his spokesperson that he was ready to "go forward," a play on words of *Kadima*. The laconic message had been scripted in detail, taking into account the fact that an election campaign was under way. As for the absence of photos, there was no desire on the part of Sharon's handlers to show him on a hospital bed in pajamas and slippers, surrounded by his doctors.

There were plenty of Israelis, of course, who were not waiting for the official photos to make his state of health an election issue. Many Knesset Members and jurists called for more transparency and suggested that political leaders be required to produce a "health report card" on a regular basis. In the past, they reminded voters, Israelis had not been informed of Golda Meir's fatal leukemia nor Moshe Dayan's colon cancer; Menachem Begin had been hospitalized more than once for cardiac problems and for a stroke. Not that there was anything unusual about this in world political circles: Roosevelt, Kennedy, Brezhnev, Tito, De Gaulle, Mitterrand and countless other leaders had all kept medical secrets from the people they governed. In Sharon's case, various candidates suggested during campaign debates that he would need to be more prudent and go on a crash diet to ensure he remained capable of governing in the coming months and years. Israel's survival depended on its leaders being in good health.

By Ariel Sharon's second night in hospital he was able to stay up until midnight discussing matters with his advisers and even watching televised accounts of his own condition. It was, as fate would have it, also the night of the Likud Primary, and the contest between Benjamin Netanyahu and Silvan Shalom went right down to the wire, with appeals to voters continuing even as the count went on. Who would run the party and cure it of "Sharonism?" In the end, the results were unsurprising: despite a very low turnout, "Bibi" was elected party president. He gave his victory speech in the early morning hours, surrounded by his wife Sarah and his lieutenants Uzi Landau and David Levy. The loser, Silvan Shalom, called to offer his congratulations and support. He would not, he said, follow Sharon into Kadima.

But Likud's public image had been sharply tarnished with Sharon's departure. It had become a party riven by extremism, with the ascension of messianic activists and other suspect groups driving away the party's traditional constituency and causing a real decline in credibility. In order to recover what it had lost, Likud would need to return to its roots and become a center-right movement based on conservative pluralism. Would Netanyahu be able to carry it off before the date of the elections? He certainly was not lacking in ambition, nor in personal conviction, but could he impose party discipline and gain the confidence of enough voters to avoid a crushing defeat at the polls?

All parties were happy to see the Prime Minister return home after a total of forty hours in hospital: the doctors found him an empathetic but high-maintenance patient, while the patient himself could hardly wait to be back in his usual element.

As he left the clinic with a broad grin on his face, Sharon thanked the doctors - who counted an Israeli Arab among them - and the nursing staff for their professionalism and kindness. To the numerous reporters who crowded the hospital's exit he added a sarcastic "thank you" for their devoted interest in his state of health:

> "I now have to go 'Forward' and my agenda is filled to the brim. But thanks for caring."

His agenda was indeed filled to the brim. In addition to his regular duties he now had to deal with the portfolios abandoned by ten ministers who had resigned when he founded Kadima. But his doctors had been rigorous in their orders, and he went, as they had advised, not to the Sycamores Ranch but to his Jerusalem residence to rest while keeping as close to the hospital as he could in case of a relapse. He would have to wait until his physicians gave the OK before seeing his sheep again.

When he arrived home, he was surprised to discover that a totally changed dietary regime awaited him. Gone were the hamburgers and fatty meats, the falafels, pita and french fries. Sweets and other similar treats were out, too. He was now going to subsist on whole grains, fruits and vegetables, a terrifying – for him – development. But his weight was 118 kilos – about 260 pounds – a great deal for his 5'7" frame. If he had lost 6 pounds during his hospitalization, he still had a high cholesterol level – 203 mg/dl – and he received twice daily injections of anti-coagulants. Clexan and Thyroxin were being employed to treat a hyperthyroid condition, and his cardiologists were seeing a coronary bypass operation as needed in the near future.

President George Bush suggested he take up sports and stop eating fast food. Italian Prime Minister Sylvio Berlusconi offered his summer residence for convalescing, and even French President Jacques Chirac weighed in, writing:

> "Mr. Prime Minister,
>
> I have learned that as a result of a health accident you are being closely followed by your physicians. I would like to offer my wishes for a prompt recovery and assure you of my complete friendship. I trust we will soon have the opportunity to continue the fruitful dialogue we began during your recent visit to Paris."

Sharon must have been salivating as he read these words: he still remembered the sumptuous feasts the Frenchman had put on for him in the City of Lights. In the meantime, he quickly returned to something resembling his normal workload. Even while he was hospitalized he was kept up to date on security and defense matters and on ongoing operations targeting Palestinian militants. Whatever the outcome of his health problems, Ariel Sharon, as a grand master of political poker, knew that the die was cast and the election campaign had begun well for Kadima.

The election was highly unusual for Israel in that three, and not just two, major political formations were seriously competing to form the next government. Now, to the traditional left-right equation was added a party overtly courting the pragmatic center. And yet, none of the three real contenders could pretend they had hopes of winning an absolute majority. Whatever the final outcome, some kind of coalition arrangement would have to be found. That certainty left open all sorts of end-game horse-trading possibilities with splinter parties, but no amount of pre-election manipulations could dictate the final outcome.

The political arena had been, to put it metaphorically, re-surfaced. Even if Sharon won, could he maintain discipline among his gladiators, dictate the political agenda with his media savvy and keep his opponents off balance? Would his historical capriciousness return to the forefront? Was it certain that the music-loving general whose favorite piece was the 1812 Overture by Tchaikovsky would remain in charge of the next order of battle? If politics is a game of inches with no guarantees, Sharon's adversaries still knew that, health problems aside, he could play a strong hand and as Prime Minister could initiate spectacular moves unavailable to the opposition. So they focused on his health, his age, and his physical frailty. The campaign would be hard fought in the coming days and weeks.

On the home front, Sharon's sons Gilad and Omry, his daughter-in-law Inbal and his doctors maintained a skeptical optimism. He would probably beat his political adversaries, they conceded, but the risk of another attack due to the stress of the campaign was tangible. Sharon's advisers, counselors and handlers believed he would carry both the election and overcome his health risks. *As he always had.* He was, they believed, solid as a rock, with proven tenacity and imbued with a strong winner's streak. Large numbers of militants were coming over to Kadima now, attracted by Sharon's strong personality. Well-known Israelis such as the former head of Shin Beth, Avi Dichter, also rallied to his side, and many politicians, now convinced he was going to win, emerged as fervent supporters, leading the more cynical wags to comment that the rats, far from leaving the ship, were now boarding *en masse*.

What seemed to be happening was that Israelis were going to give Kadima more than forty seats in the Knesset. At least that is what the polls indicated, and in the annals of Israeli politics it would be a spectacular first. Kadima members were ecstatic as trend lines showed Likud falling apart and Labor in a free fall among decided voters. Perhaps encouraged by this news, Ariel Sharon quickly – too quickly – returned to a full schedule. It was too much and too soon for a convalescing man of his age.

Unusually, Hannukah fell on Christmas Day in 2005, and Ariel Sharon, at the conclusion of the weekly Cabinet meeting, before leaving for home at sunset, lit the first candle on the Menorah symbolizing the victory of the Maccabees and the miracle of light in the Temple of Jerusalem. At the end of the ceremony, traditional doughnuts filled with jam were served; with a gleeful look, the Prime Minister approached the treat-filled serving plates and said to his Ministers – most of whom had already begun to stuff their faces – "Go ahead, my friends, eat, enjoy, but be careful not to exaggerate. As for me, my doctors have forbidden this little pleasure of life and it is only with the greatest reticence and out of respect for your pleasure that I can even offer myself a tiny bite."

Far from the meeting rooms and council tables, the military situation in the field was deteriorating by the day, with new terrorist attacks being undertaken by the masked men in the West Bank and Gaza. Some were nipped in the bud. Others, unfortunately were at least partially successful. On December 29 a young Israeli officer near Netanya took a suicide bomber into custody before he could blow himself up in a school just as students were taking part in a Hannukah celebration. Major carnage was averted, but the officer was killed along with the bomber when the Palestinian pressed the device's trigger.

From Gaza, Palestinians were still firing Qassam missiles on Sderot and the outskirts of Ashkelon. Miraculously, there were no victims, but now the rockets were reaching further into Israel, to the Northern West Bank and the Affoula region near Megiddo and the Nir Yaffe moshav. It was the first time since 1956 that Nir Yaffe, peopled mostly by Israelis of Tunisian origin, had been attacked, and residents took it very seriously. Sharon's plan to accelerate construction of a security wall to make it more difficult for terrorists to infiltrate Israel became a much-supported priority for the worried residents of the area's agricultural settlements. On the Northern border, Hezbollah had acquired new Russian missiles bought from Damascus, certainly with the tacit approval of Moscow, and Aharon Ze'evi Parkash, Israel's chief of military intelligence, accused the Russians of not respecting the commitments made to Jerusalem concerning this type of weaponry.

Faced with the escalation, Sharon consulted with his chiefs of staff and the heads of Mossad, Shin Beth and civilian police, and settled on a response to the provocation. An air force attack on southern Lebanon would get the message across to Beirut without upping the ante beyond acceptable levels. The Government of Lebanon did not want any new confrontation, and in fact wanted the Syrians definitively gone from their country and no longer pulling strings from across the border. Lebanese Druze and Christian groups, fearing a resurgent Hezbollah, demonstrated in the streets of the capital in front of the Lebanese Parliament, and the daily newspapers took a strong stand, especially when new revelations concerning the assassination of Rafik Hariri surfaced.

Former Syrian Vice President Abdel Halim Khaddam, a venerable politician and former right-hand man of the late Hafez al-Assad, now seventy-three years of age, formally accused the thirty-nine year old current Syrian president, al-Assad junior, of having orchestrated the killing. Khaddam, from his Paris exile, declared in a New Year's Eve interview on the Saudi-financed Al-Arabia television news network that the successful attempt on Hariri's life could not have been undertaken without al-Assad's direct authorization. Furious, Bashar al-Assad denied the charges and accused Khaddam of being a pathological liar and true traitor to the Syrian fatherland. Khaddam's response had a definite Freudian flavor to it:

"Assad is suffering from mental troubles. He should urgently seek help from a psychoanalyst."

Khaddam had evolved into a self-described specialist in investigations of the psychic process and had voluntary supplied French and U.S. intelligence with important, even precious, information on the way the new al-Assad regime functioned. His information on the "little lion of Damascus" – the name Assad means "lion" in Arabic – and his knowledge of the inside world of Syrian politics made Khaddam not only a valuable asset for the West, but a prime target for Syrian intelligence agents in the French capital. He was protected around-the-clock by bodyguards and agents of the French equivalent of the F.B.I., the D.S.T.

The German weekly *Der Speigel* revealed at about the same time that the United States had drawn up a plan to take out Iranian nuclear sites and that the CIA had already informed Turkey, Jordan, Saudi Arabia and Pakistan that successive waves of American bombers could take off from U.S. bases at any time. This information, published on the last day of the year, was taken extremely seriously by all parties. Was it a warning, leaked by the Bush White House as a way of diverting attention from the mess in Iraq? Was there truly an operational plan in place? Or was it one more episode in the ongoing psywar campaign between Uncle Sam and the Iranian Mullahs? No one could be sure, but in Jerusalem and the European capitals within range of Iranian rocketry, the threat was taken seriously. In the midst of it all, Shin Beth arrested an Israeli Arab who had been recruited by Iranian intel to run for the Knesset. Other arrests in the case were expected to follow.

Sharon felt that circumstances were right for a major operation against the people who were launching missiles on Israeli villages and their surroundings – including on his own Sycamores Ranch – and authorized Operation Blue Skies which was to target the northern part of the Gaza strip that had become the launch pad for Palestinian rocket attacks. Several months before, in September 2005, Tsahal had demolished all buildings in this area and declared it a "no-go" military zone, similar to the security belt established in Southern Lebanon in the 1980s. The zone was meant to put distance between the missile launchers and their targets; thousands of Arabic-language flyers were dropped on the surrounding inhabited areas, warning the population to stay away from the forbidden zone: "Any Palestinian," the tracts read, "who enters this zone will be considered a suspect and risks being killed."

Other draconian measures were undertaken, such as the use of spy drones, commando raids and dragnets. The Gaza border with Egypt was also closed. Tsahal patrols were increased with a view to stopping terrorists and Sinai arms smugglers from entering the area; a secondary target was the network of Bedouin drug and human traffickers who brought Eastern European prostitutes across the desert on camelback. It was a Thousand and One Nights fantasy gone mad: caravans of Al-Qaeda weapons, messianic fundamentalist Islamic warriors, drugs and merchants of the sex trade plying their way across the naked desert wasteland in the dark of night.

At midnight, December 31, 2005, a new year began. It was greeted with fireworks and optimism by Israelis. Ariel Sharon, convalescing at home, could look back on the year gone by with some satisfaction. The economy of the nation had improved, and if social disparity had not been eliminated, at least unemployment had declined, purchasing power had risen, taxes had gone down and economic growth was up five per cent. The stock market had risen too, and bank profits were considerably better than they had been the previous year. Despite the threat of the terrorists, the all-important tourism sector was flourishing; Jews and Christians, North Americans and Europeans, even Asians were filling the country's hotels and returning with a better understanding of what Israel was all about. As importantly, they were leaving behind foreign currency that bolstered the nation's reserves and strengthened the Israeli shekel.

There was good reason to look to the future with confidence. Ariel Sharon had stayed the course and it had paid off. His personal image had improved worldwide. His people were solidly behind him and his strategy for peace and prosperity, and were about to re-elect him for another four years. Security in the country had dramatically improved since Sharon had become Prime Minister. A confidential Shin Beth report confirmed that 2005 had seen a sixty per cent drop in fatalities and injuries from suicide bombings as compared to 2004. On the downside, Shin Beth estimated that approximately fifty human bombs were in circulation at any one time, ready to sow death and destruction whenever their handlers ordered them to explode. It was a terrifying statistic, but according to Shin Beth analysts it had proven practically impossible to reduce this number, for new recruits were always coming into play as the Israeli police and intelligence forces picked up the spoor of one or another of the current bombers.

Still, efficient intelligence and merciless, 7/24 hunting down of the homicide bombers and, just as importantly, their "cat's paw" handlers had resulted in tens of bloody, spectacular terror attempts being forestalled. Inter-agency communications had dramatically improved and were now on a real-time information network. As soon as information – from whatever source – came in to any department, all operational screens were immediately advised, right up to the ones in the Prime Minister's office.

Cooperation between the various branches of Israel's security forces had reached such efficient levels that foreign security services including those of France, but especially the United States – which was confronted by a similar situation in the mess that was Iraq – came to learn from what the Israelis had accomplished.

The threat that was perhaps the most troubling, and the least contained, concerned the Qassam missiles, and Israel knew for a fact that at least three hundred rockets had come into Gaza from the Sinai since Israel's evacuation in September 2005; there was also more than five tons of high explosives to be worried about, five thousand Kalashnikov machine guns and hundreds of side arms and munitions. Sharon only knew one way of dealing with Muslim extremists willing to kill innocent men, women and children, and that was with the language of implacable, overwhelming force. There was no way he was going to allow these hateful men to break Israeli society apart and plunge the country into the hellfire they sought to unleash.

The Sharon doctrine could not have been clearer: the security of

Israel would come before the need to make peace with the Arabs. No backtracking on this could even be considered, much less implemented, and his instructions were strict on the matter. "Defendable borders for Israel" was a concept that was mulled over and discussed in great detail, and a confidential report was produced for the Prime Minister on this truly existential matter. The document directly addressed the fact that Israel remains one of the rare countries in the world to have never possessed safe, recognized, defendable and definitive borders. It was a situation that Sharon wanted remedied.

The document gave a global analysis of the strategic, diplomatic and judicial aspects of the new configuration of the State of Israel and the threats to its population, which for the most part resides along the Mediterranean coast. The nerve centers of the Jewish state, including Ben-Gurion International Airport near Tel-Aviv, were clearly at risk from missile strikes. Israel's Jordanian neighbor also figured prominently in the report that considered the fragile political balance of power within that country – and within Egypt and Iraq as well – in the face of the rapid growth of Islamic fundamentalism. The report's authors, General Yacov Amidror and Ambassador Dory Gold, looked additionally at the question of maintaining military control of the Jordan Valley.

Upon his return from the White house with a letter of assurances to Israel of April 14, 2004, signed by President Bush, Sharon explained the significance of the US document to the Knesset:

> "There is American acknowledgment that in any final status agreement there will not be Israeli withdrawal to the 1967 lines. This acknowledgement appears in two ways: understanding the facts determined by the large Israeli settlement blocs such as making it impossible to return to the 1967 lines, and implementation of the concept of defendable borders."

Sharon even repeated the term "defendable borders" in English, for emphasis.

On January 3, 2006, in spite of having a very full agenda, Ariel Sharon decided to meet with two Japanese editors from the influential Tokyo newspaper *Nikkei Shimbun*, along with Eli Garshowitz, their correspondent in Israel. The interview covered a lot of territory, and Sharon, glasses perched on his nose and comfortably seated behind his desk, responded with humor to the journalists' many questions concerning recent events. Talking about issues of peace and security he optimistically declared that with the help of God he would continue on with the Roadmap negotiations with Abu Mazen, and added that he hoped to make an official visit to Japan right after the Israeli elections. It was to be Sharon's last interview, for several hours later, his doctors called a press conference to announce that the Prime Minister would undergo cardiac bypass surgery during which a heart catheter would be inserted and that for a period of about three hours he would be under total anesthesia. The operation itself was described as routine by current standards, but the physicians added that all surgery presented some risk, especially for a man of the Prime Minister's age and weight. Still, the doctors - among Israel's best - remained confident and affirmed their belief that all should go well.

The evening television news on the private channel 10 did not even lead with this story, preferring instead to headline the gathering storm concerning accusations of three million dollars in bribes putatively handed to the Sharon family by an Austrian billionaire. It was a complicated story relating to illegal 1999 campaign financing, and at this point in time, old hat. Many saw it as a transparent, politically motivated attempt to eat away at Sharon's lead in the polls, but the hook the story hung on was the resignation letter Omry Sharon - the one directly accused in the case - had delivered to the president of the Knesset earlier in the day.

The story was page one news in the next day's papers, which went into great detail about the supposed financial misdeeds of the Sharon family. Israeli radio and television stations sensationalized the story all day long, eliciting comments from unscrupulous, "outraged" politicians who, seeing a chink in the Prime Minister's armor, called the Sharon clan an "Israeli Mafia" and went as far as to term Ariel

Sharon a "mob boss." It was an embarrassing example of how the thirst for power can lead people to abominable verbal abasement. Sharon, for his part, decided to remain above the fray.

Even though he felt disgust and profound sadness at the calumny, the Prime Minister went on with his normal routine and did not react in public although he obviously was in turmoil at the news. Perhaps he was most saddened at how his adversaries had conveniently forgotten the biblical nostrum of not attacking a man in distress, whether it was due to sickness or accident. Surely the Jews, of all people, needed to show the world they conducted themselves with dignity and mutual respect. But Sharon could see, and regret, what he bitterly confided to the author of this book as the fratricidal, needless – and useless – hatred Jews had shown other Jews throughout history. The writings of the ancient historian Yossef Ben Matityahu (known to the Romans as Flavius Joseph) were filled with examples of this misfortune. The current crop of critical books by a new generation of Israeli historians concerning Israel's more recent combat troubled the Prime Minister as much, if not more. "There were mistakes made, of course," he said, "but Tsahal never pursued a doctrine of killing innocents. There is nothing 'sacred' about armed conflict. Why these people have opened a campaign of hatred against their fellow Jews is beyond me. We are all, in the end, brothers-in-arms."

By the end of the day, in response to the media firestorm, ordinary Israelis had decided to speak up: thousands of faxes and phone calls came in to the Office of the Prime Minister, wishing him a successful operation and a quick return to running the affairs of state. In an ironic aside to his Deputy Prime Minister Ehud Olmert, Sharon said, "I'm putting you in charge of the country for only three hours. Be wise, and patient, and don't take any decisions or change the furniture around. And keep my staff on, is that clear?" Olmert took the message as a sardonic way of spitting in the devil's face, and the men, who enjoyed a profound mutual respect, shared a hearty laugh.

Ariel Sharon then returned to his beloved Sycamores Ranch to shake off the stress of the day, and prepare himself for his imminent hospitalization. Shin Beth agents were already on patrol at the hospital, awaiting their boss and riding herd on the journalists and television cameramen from around the world who were waiting for a story. At the ranch, the patient took a light meal and conversed with his sons and grandchildren. A paramedic gave him a Clexan injection to reduce the risk of coagulation and took his blood pressure, which was a little high. But everything was within acceptable parameters and Sharon, calm if a little anxious about the operation, prepared to retire for the evening. Suddenly, at eight twenty-five, he felt severe chest pain and an emergency call was placed to his physicians. The director of the Beer Sheva Hospital – the closest medical facility to the ranch – was told to prepare to receive the Prime Minister immediately. Doctor Shlomo Segev arrived within twenty minutes and took the decision to transfer Sharon by ambulance to Jerusalem's Hadassah Hospital. He had good and valid reasons for his decision: the Prime Minister's medical records were at Hadassah, and so was the Shin Beth security force. The seventh floor of the facility had been transformed into a veritable fortress in anticipation of Sharon's upcoming surgery, too.

Inside the ambulance, Ariel Sharon was prone, extremely weak, and while still conscious, suffering greatly. A cardiogram showed that his heart was distressed. With his son Gilad and his physician at his side, the vehicle's sirens wailing, the stricken leader was taken at high speed to the Hadassah Ein Karem hospital. When the ambulance rolled up at the emergency entrance at ten fifty-six pm, the Prime Minister was in critical condition and was immediately taken to the operating room, surrounded by his security detail. One agent, armed, scrubbed, and wearing a hospital green gown and a surgeon's cap, maintained radio contact with the security command center as events transpired. The operating room was fully equipped with the most up-to-date surgical lamps, imaging equipment and computer screens displaying the Prime Minister's vital signs.

As the minutes went by, everyone in the room could not have been more conscious of the importance of their tasks to the nation. Each second could be a critical one, each decision fateful. But the surgeons were consummate professionals and left their emotions at the surgery door. Doctor Felix Umansky, an Argentinian Jew, supervised the operation. Born in Buenos Aires, he had over the course of a brilliant thirty-year career saved hundreds of human lives. Outside the hospital, a concerned silence was displayed by the crowd of reporters, shivering in the cold night air. At eleven thirty, hospital director Shlomo Mor Yoseff gave the official diagnosis:

"Prime Minister Ariel Sharon has suffered a new cerebral hemorrhage. He is in critical condition, fully anesthetized and on a respirator."

Israel Maimon, the Secretary of the Government, then announced that Ehud Olmert was, as of that moment, the Interim Prime Minister of Israel.

That night, few Israelis slept. The country was praying for a miracle. Listening to the radio and watching live television coverage of the tragic events, the citizens of Israel were in shock, worried sick, hoping that the next bit of news would be more optimistic. The country was suddenly plunged into total disarray, and whatever their political stripe or religious beliefs, Israelis were united in their concern for their leader. The real news dripped out while rumors abounded, and in the country's synagogues and before the Wailing Wall, rabbis donned their prayer shawls and dovened, reciting the psalms in which they sought comfort and encouragement.

Eight hours had gone by since the surgery began. In the early hours of the morning, Ehud Olmert convened the Cabinet in an atmosphere heavy with anxiety. Only fifteen hours before, Ariel Sharon had laughingly handed Olmert the keys to the country, putting him in charge of the State, its secrets and ultra-confidential documents, and the red line to its most powerful weaponry. Around the Cabinet table, grown men were freely crying. The Army Chief of Staff Dan Halutz and Yuval Diskin, head of Shin Beth, had their head in their hands, in profound shock, wordless. Ehud Olmert chaired the meeting from a seat next to the now empty chair usually occupied by Ariel Sharon.

"We all pray for the Prime Minister," he began, almost choking on the words. "This is a painful, difficult and complex situation for us, but the government is functioning and the State of Israel will pursue its activities with no interruption and all current affairs will be dealt with normally." If the transfer of power was accomplished smoothly, and in a spirit of great solidarity, there was yet an emptiness that filled the room, a void named Ariel Sharon. It was as if a respected father had suddenly departed, leaving his children to fend for themselves.

In moments of crisis, Ariel Sharon could always be counted on to offer creative responses to the most difficult problems. When Israel was in danger, he had always been there. *But no more*. It was the first time since 1948 that he was unable to respond to the call of his country: his powerful spirit was silent, and his brain locked down. No one could say what would happen now.

Outside Israel, the clearly worried international community closely followed the Israeli leader's departure from the scene. After all was said and done, he was the man who had put the peace process back on the rails by disengaging from Gaza. Even in the Islamic world – apart from the joyful reaction of extremists who danced in the streets and handed out sweets at the tragic news – Ariel Sharon was respected as a man of his word, a man who could be counted upon to keep his agreements. In Cairo, Amman, and throughout the Arab world, leaders affirmed that despite the crimes Sharon had committed against them, it was better for everyone that he survived.

George W. Bush issued a statement calling Sharon a good man, a strong man with a vision for making peace. European leaders like France's Jacques Chirac called for the continuation of his courageous initiatives and assured Israel of French support and solidarity.

In times of crisis, the Israeli nation has always come together as one. With the Jews of the diaspora, Israel forms a great family that has seen its share of quarrels, unions, happiness and grief. But in the end, solidarity and unity are the bricks and mortar that define what it is to be a Jew. The Sharon crisis was a family crisis: the head of the tribe and *hassaba shel ahuma* – grandfather of the nation – was in dire straits; the people of Israel now lined up to support him and pray for his recovery.

The Hadassah hospital had become the nerve center of the country. Israelis hung on every word, every gesture of the medical spokespersons. Sharing a common sense of existential concern, Israelis of differing political affiliations joined the crowds milling about in front of the hospital, craving the slightest bit of news that might filter out. Thousands of supportive telephone messages came in from around the world, including one from Sharon's estranged sister Dita Scheinermann in New York. Letters, e-mail, childrens' drawings and gifts arrived in great number. Rose-colored balloons were set loose to float up to the seventh floor of the hospital in the hope they would encourage Sharon to awaken and admire the spectacle.

The Hadassah Hospital patients, at first anguished by the news, gradually felt a resurgence of hope. The hospital itself had been turned into a magnet for pilgrims hoping to cure the Prime Minister through their faith. Everyone in the land, it seemed, had health on their minds, from the youngest schoolchildren to aging hypochondriacs. All three television networks abandoned their usual programming and carried "all Ariel, all the time." Sharon was shown in older shots, smiling, in good shape, empathetic. The best images of his long life were shown in a televised carousel: pictures of his younger years, film clips of Sharon the military man, the family man, the sheep rancher, the loving husband dancing with his wife to a romantic waltz, the caring grandfather playing with his grandchildren were all shown for Israelis in an outpouring of emotions that left no one indifferent. Grandmothers shared their tears with their daughters and granddaughters; grandfathers and their sons and grandsons embraced in a spontaneous show of feeling that, from the cynical viewpoint of the political organizer, could hardly have been better orchestrated.

The show of support reminded some of the kind of reaction one might expect if a Grand Rabbi or a Pope was in mortal danger. Yet

Sharon was an avowed agnostic, and Israel was not a dictatorship given over to the cult of personality. Still, the crowd reaction, almost pathological in scope, could hardly have been more tangible. Sharon's long, active career was now in the shadow world, with painful and unpredictable events still to come. Ironically, his hospital stay while in a comatose state, was in the department named after Shlomo Argov, the Israeli Ambassador to London who had been the victim of an Palestinian assassination attempt at the beginning of the nineteen eighties that resulted in the Sharon-led invasion of Lebanon. Argov passed away in 2003, after twenty years in a coma.

In an attempt to not forego any chance to help their father, Sharon's sons Omry and Gilad played his favorite classical music in his hospital room, but the Mozart sonatas, sacred compositions and even the delightful *Eine Kleine Nachmusik,* all pieces he had adored, were not sufficient to pull Arik from his coma. But the boys did not give up: they also played recordings of his own voice giving the speeches that had made him famous, or the orders of battle and radio exchanges made during the Suez attack that made him a hero of the October War. Nothing that might help was ignored.

During the crisis, Ehud Olmert took the reins of power astutely and smoothly. At age 61, this former mayor of Jerusalem and serious fan of the Betar Yerushalaim soccer team was a man who smoked cigars and loved to travel. Born in Benjamina to the north of Tel-Aviv, to refugees from the Chinese city of Shanghai who had come to Palestine in 1933, Olmert himself had four children who did not always see eye-to-eye with their father who was well known to identify with the Israeli nationalist right. Still, Olmert had supported Sharon's courageous decision to disengage from Gaza and offer the Palestinians a real opportunity to found their own independent state.

In a strange but symbolic coincidence, Olmert lived on Kaf Tet (November 1947), a street named for the date of the historic United Nations resolution concerning the partition of Palestine. The house, situated in the upscale Katamon district, had been purchased from Olmert in April, 2004 by the American philanthropist Daniel Abraham for 2.6 million dollars. Since that time he had remained in the home as a lessee, paying a monthly rent of $2250.00 The transaction's ethics was called into question inasmuch as Abraham, a friend of numerous Israeli leaders, was also close to William Jefferson Clinton and had often proposed his services in the cause of peace. On numerous occasions, Abraham had been seen in Arab capitals, on semi-official business. After the 2006 March elections and with the state of health of Ariel Sharon still not improving, the government of Israel officially declared that the former Prime Minister was no longer able to assume his responsibilities and Olmert, now no longer just Israel's interim leader, finally decided it was time to move into the official residence of the Prime Minister on Balfour Street.

Olmert had studied psychology, philosophy and law. As a lawyer, he had been instrumental in the fight against corruption and the influence of the Mafia in Israel. Elected at the tender age of twenty-nine, Ehud Olmert held the record of the being the youngest member of the Knesset, and as Mayor of Jerusalem from 1993 to 2002, he often said his role model was New York Mayor Rudolf Giuliani. While he was mayor he had shown a proclivity for supporting the Judaisation of Jerusalem and had always been close to the ultra-orthodox political parties. But he was also a savvy politician and used to the manipulation common to Israeli politics. Now, a firm supporter of Sharon and disengagement, Olmert was in the pragmatic conservative center, with moderate views clearly opposed to those held by his principal rival, Bibi Netanyahu.

The men had in fact long been adversaries. When Bibi resigned as Finance Minister in Ariel Sharon's government he was replaced by Olmert. The two were, moreover, not on speaking terms, but they had reconciled somewhat in the light of recent events. In general, though, Ehud Olmert was known as a caustic, cold and cynical man who gave no quarter and was accustomed to giving free rein to his predilection for vengeance. As Minister in charge of Public Television he had achieved considerable notoriety through the brutal firing of the President of the Israeli State Radio and TV networks. Now, Olmert had to come to grips with the challenge of his life. Was he capable of rising to the occasion and overcoming the bitter aftermath of the election campaign? How would he deal with the criticism that was sure to confront him, and finally, how would he react to U.S. pressure to advance the peace process?

As the logical heir to Ariel Sharon's policies, Olmert had every chance of serving a full term as Prime Minister of Israel and implementing the next steps in the disengagement plan which called for Israel, absent a serious Palestinian negotiating partner, to set its final borders unilaterally. Still, the Middle East was a powder keg, and running the very complex apparatus of the State of Israel a task that demanded not only technical expertise but considerable political adroitness as well. The polls showed that "Sharonism" was alive and well, and Kadima was expected to win forty-five Knesset seats, while the Likud would be reduced to rump status. Of course, all election polls are subject to electors changing their minds, and decision day was still in the future. Ariel Sharon was indeed Kadima's best card, and Reuven Adler, the party's chief strategist and longtime friend of the Prime Minister, was determined to maintain Sharon at the top of the party's list of candidates despite his pitiful current condition. Sharon's face may have been on all of Kadima's posters, but in truth, there was no chance he could, at least for the foreseeable future, exit his coma and return to an active life. Even if a miracle occurred and he regained consciousness, there was a high probability of brain damage, and certainly, a long period of convalescence to be dealt with.

So, it was logical to ask if "Sharonism" and Kadima could survive Ariel Sharon. Nostalgics could imagine a convalescing, wise old man living out his years on the Sycamores Ranch, surrounded by his sheep and the fields through which he loved to stroll, being consulted on occasion for this or that policy decision. But was it just a pipe dream? What would happen with Shimon Peres if the man he followed to Kadima was no longer there, and for that matter, how many of the party militants would be tempted to return to Bibi Netanyahu and the Likud? What about the new leader of Labor, Amir Peretz: would he take a stab at setting up his own ruling coalition now that the Old Man was no longer active? Nothing was certain except that everything was possible. The elections were weeks away, and more than one observer expected more low blows to occur in what was also an election involving a change in generations. The charismatic generals like Dayan, Rabin, Weizman and Sharon would no longer be in charge of the destiny of Israel. Nor for that matter would the Holocaust survivors be at the helm. A page in history was turning, and as it turned, many new faces would have to prove themselves worthy.

Questions were also being asked about the medical decisions that had been taken in Ariel Sharon's case. Why had he been allowed to leave hospital so quickly and return to his habitual, punishing schedule? Should the physicians not have used their medical authority to enforce rest on this man of action? After all, Arik was highly medicated and at risk. Perhaps he should have been given a lower dose of anti-coagulants, and kept under more strict observation. Then too, the period of time between the onset of symptoms and his arrival at the hospital was questioned, as was the last-minute change of destination and physicians. Why was a medical specialist not kept with him 24/7, given the risks of his condition and his importance to the nation? Why was a helicopter not kept at the ready to speed him to the hospital in minutes? When a stroke occurs, each second is vital to the patient's survival.

Just as it had been when Yitzhak Rabin was assassinated, questions were many, and immediate answers few. A commission of inquiry might look into the matter, but by then it would be an issue for historians. It was true that the transparency of the Hadassah hospital authorities in sharing news of the Prime Minister's state of health was, compared to the situation in European countries, exemplary. But legitimate questions would long remain and require serious answers.

As for the peace process, fundamental issues still separated the parties and there was a palpable fear of the chance of a resolution between Israel and the Palestinians falling into a coma as deep as the one clutching Ariel Sharon. Many thought the matter was now in the hands of all-powerful Jehovah and Allah the Merciful.

Chapter 19

The Last Act

The end is also the point of origin.
Thomas Stearns Eliot

Since the birth of Israel in 1948, Ariel Sharon has had an undeniable influence on the history of his region of the world. Born a Sabra and raised in a kfar – an independent agricultural village, not a kibbutz – he learned the value of discipline, physical labor and the importance of being a unique individual. He, like his parents, was uninterested in the values of collectivism and from his years as a child was a loner. In fact he cultivated the attributes of discretion and mystery, enjoying the thrill of keeping secrets. In his life, he seldom shared his true opinions, kept his thoughts and his property to himself, and took military command and political decisions on his own. His health was his own and not the public's business. Sharon was a man of action, who played his cards close to his chest, unwilling to reveal his intentions or his plans for implementing them until the moment was ripe for action, when he would act with force and determination in what he alone judged to be the best interests of the country (and, as some critics cynically added, in the best interests of his own career).

Ariel Sharon participated in all of Israel's great wars with its Arab neighbors; often praised as a national hero, sometimes fiercely criticized for his involvement in less lofty actions, he was a man often admired, sometimes detested, but always looked to with consideration and respect. Hardly a page in Israel's history had been written without his name on it.

At the birth of Israel, when Benjamin Netanyahu was in his mother's womb and Ehud Olmert a kindergarten student, Ariel Sharon was already a man of twenty who knew how to fight and carried a rifle on his shoulder. During the war of independence he was gravely wounded at the battle of Latroun; he recovered and continued to fight for the Jewish state, always in the front lines, displaying exemplary courage. During the 1950s as leader of a paratroop commando unit he led spectacular raids on Arab targets that sometimes had horrible collateral damage. By the age of twenty-five, Ariel Sharon was already famous and his picture often appeared in the newspapers alongside his hero, David Ben-Gurion, and the generals of the army command.

In 1956 he parachuted into the Sinai; in 1967 he was the first to arrive on the shores of the Suez Canal during the Six Day War. In 1973, with Israel staring into the face of disaster, he crossed the same canal and encircled the Egyptian Third Army, forcing the enemy to surrender. Yet in 1982 he summoned the strength to remove all Israeli presence from the Sinai Peninsula that was being returned to Egypt. Three months later he attacked Lebanon to rid Beirut of Yasser Arafat's Palestine Liberation Organization in an alliance with Lebanese Christians. He paid a huge political price for this alliance when the Christians massacred unarmed Palestinians in refugee camps near the Lebanese capital. It would be years before he could re-establish himself as a force in Israeli politics.

But he did not despair, it was not in his nature. He stoically faced family tragedy and health problems, always making his plan of attack as a trained military man. Like the Caucasus warriors of legend, he feared nothing. A master strategist and tactician, he knew he needed to leave politics for a time in order to return stronger than ever. When he came back it was as Agriculture and Housing Minister, then added the portfolio of National Infrastructures to his responsibilities. He became a champion of the settlers' movement, building new settlements in Gaza and the West Bank over the course of fifteen years.

As a politician in the ranks of the Opposition, he had his own caucus, organizing his supporters and mobilizing his activists within the Likud Party, holding back when he judged it necessary, willing to suffer small losses in order to be victorious in the more important battles. One step backward, two forward, always in movement, dynamic and audacious, Ariel Sharon was known for his capricious decisions which made him difficult to pin down. He knew how to surprise his adversaries and was prepared to be brutal and emotionless in dividing to conquer. Sly as an old fox, Sharon employed ruse, vagueness and half-truths to reach his goals and was often on the edge of ethics, morality and fair play. Judicial enquiries followed him like a shadow.

Although his engagement in the great causes of the Jewish people and the Jewish state was unerring, he did not defend any precise ideology and was not a disciple of either Russian Socialism or the conservative doctrines of Jabotinsky, the spiritual founder of the Herut Party – today's Likud. Sharon was not an ideologue, nor an intellectual, nor a political romantic. He was a man of the soil, moved by its bounty, and loving his family and close friends.

Boundlessly energetic and a man of great personal charisma, he acted out of conviction and a personal sense of justice. Tenderness in politics was definitely not his strong suit. He was thick-skinned, suspicious by nature but charming, and a man who listened courteously to his interlocutors. He was good at quickly determining the qualities, strengths and weaknesses of negotiating partners and immediately perceiving the intentions of his adversaries – which was of great value in the political arena. But he could also be vengeful, even vicious, when contradicted or faced with obstructionism.

With his qualities and his faults, his pride, his arrogance and his frank talk, Ariel Sharon was a typical Sabra. He charged ahead, beating the bushes before him, pushing into the fog of politics and the military without preoccupation, willing to confront obstacles as they emerged. He was not himself a sportsman but adored challenge and competition. As a driver, he seemed unable to find the brake pedal or respect stop signs, and with a heavy foot on the accelerator would consistently run red lights to arrive at his destination before all others.

He was a proud and pretentious man, seldom choosing to directly confront his mediocre adversaries. He preferred to let them criticize him and bark as much as they wanted; possessed of a quiet sense of power he knew the chicanery always stops in the end, and he knew how to win. If someone showed a lack of personal respect or criticized him in public, that person could expect the silent treatment for a long time. Forgiveness was rare, and always obtained at a price. Ariel Sharon, as everyone he ever met found out, had a very long memory.

He was, in sum, a pragmatist, tenacious but flexible according to circumstances. His down-to-earth realism became the foundation of a global vision, and he always looked to Israel not as it was, but as he felt it should become. Those who called him an egocentric were right, but his intentions lay in the direction of the interests of society at large, even though he always took care of his friends. He was always willing to change directions and opinions. After all, as Moshe Dayan once proclaimed, "Only the donkey never changes his opinion. And he'll always remain an ass."

Sharon's mentor, David Ben-Gurion, was a philosopher, a moralist and a visionary. Arik had not such pretence, but he did resemble Ben-Gurion in other ways: he possessed courage and determination, charisma and creative pride, always seeking to act in accordance with his words. Ben-Gurion was a self-taught man, slim and physically strong, with a powerful spirit, a practitioner of Yoga who admired the Bible and read Plato. He led an austere life, never had much money in his pocket, and claimed that his best friends were the classics he constantly read. David Ben-Gurion was comfortable in the collective life style of the kibbutz. His life intersected with Ariel Sharon's in their common love for the Negev Desert and for the sheep they both raised.

Sharon had been an average student, not part of the intellectual or social elite nor a prince-in-waiting. His father was an obstinate man, a loner who lived on the margins of society, and like his father, Sharon built his ranch and his career through perseverance and force of will. He never surrounded himself with a brain trust or with thinkers in the literary genre. For him, the present was the field from which the crops of the future would grow and be harvested.

He certainly was a materialist and enjoyed the good life, caustic humor and abundant meals. He took great pride in his ranch, which was valued at over ten million dollars, and felt a great brotherhood with the Texas cowboys of Hollywood westerns he had admired in his youth. The Sycamores Ranch prospered in a region where villages were often poor and settled with newly-arrived immigrants. In a sense, Ariel Sharon was the local lord of the manor, a dominant and materialistic gentleman who believed that profits were not to be shared. The wealth he created was to remain in the family. Although he was no expert in economics, he knew how to save and accumulate wealth.

His taste in books ran to biographies of great men and accounts of the grand battles of military history. He was complementary to David Ben-Gurion, and more than one Israeli held out the hope that he could finish his mentor's work: Ben-Gurion had founded the Jewish state, Ariel Sharon would finally define its permanent borders.

Sharon was not a religious man, in fact he was an avowed agnostic who did not always eat kosher. He traveled on the Sabbath. He did not fast on Yom Kippur. Raised in the Jewish tradition, he had received a liberal education and had a broad general culture. For him, the Talmud was quite compatible with the classics of literature, the study of the Torah and the works of great composers like Mozart, Brahms and Vivaldi. If the sacred texts were a part of his life, they enjoyed no exclusive privileges in his life where they shared pride of place with his fascination for the practical realization of Zionism and the bounty of the good earth.

The Bible, according to Sharon, was not sacred in the religious sense but represented the fascinating history of the Jewish people with its great victories and terrifying defeats, its joys and sadness, its universal values, fundamental laws, crimes and punishments.

The months preceding his illness were difficult for him. Leaving Likud in 2005 and founding Kadima had fatigued him, The new Ariel Sharon had obviously aged, and his traditional energy and ambitions were waning. But he poured whatever energy he had left into his work, pushing on like the old bulldozer he was often called. He remained Israel's bulwark, a providential statesman. He laughed about remaining in power until 2008, when he could celebrate the 60th anniversary of the State of Israel as the oldest Head of State of the democratic countries of the world, convinced he would resolve the political difficulties he faced and draw the permanent borders of his country. Despite the hostility, extremism and violence Israel faced, Sharon remained confident he would sign his own peace treaty with the Palestinians and achieve the national goals he had set for his nation.

But Arik Sharon was an unpredictable man, and his life was unpredictable also, carrying him away from active politics before he was ready to go, and making it impossible for him to achieve his dream. And yet he was, out of all the leaders of Israel, undeniably the best placed to shoulder the responsibilities of the moment and carry out some of the most important decisions in current history. He had never ceased to surprise both his friends and adversaries with his ability to bounce back from adversity. After all, he had overcome serious war injuries, and even a stroke had not slowed him down. But the second cerebral hemorrhage proved more than even he could deal with, and like all men, Sharon could not escape his destiny.

His sudden departure left Israel in the lurch, with confusion and concern over the future of the country rampant. A page in history was being turned, with new leaders coming to the fore to confront difficult issues. All Israelis yearned to be shown that like Arik Sharon, they would be capable of taking audacious, perhaps painful decisions and bring the nation to a lasting peace.

Epilogue

On March 28, 2006, Israelis showed little enthusiasm as they went to cast their votes in a record low turnout. The entire Sharon family spent the morning at the hospital, by the bed where Ariel was still in a deep coma, spectral, unmoving, at the mercy of his doctors and The Creator. His children, one Agnostic, the other a Believer, both prayed for his recovery. But the battle seemed lost this time around; a miracle would be needed to reverse the tragic situation. The old shepherd, general, and politician had finally reached the point of no return.

Sharon's doctors were pessimistic as to the outcome but were considering another operation – his third since being hospitalized. Remorse and regret overshadowed the usually upbeat Hadassah Hospital, considered one of the best in the world. The original decisions in the case were now being scrutinized and questions asked as to whether everything had been done to save him. In the halls of government, different, more macabre questions were asked: "When will they pull the plug and let him die? Is it humane to keep him alive in a vegetative state? Has he not already suffered enough in his family life and on the field of battle?" It was a delicate question to contemplate, but an ineluctable one in more than one respect.

Religion is a dominant force in Israeli life, and euthanasia forbidden in the Jewish religion. The moral and spiritual structure of the country generally looked upon the medical procedure not as a deliverance, but to put it simply, assassination. God's will, it was said, had to be endured in silence and with bowed head.

If the old man was unconscious, his spirit seemed alive, omnipresent in the election polling stations. The country waited, holding its breath, to see if Ehud Olmert and Kadima would show the pollsters to be right. Less than a thirty-seat showing would make life very difficult for Kadima and would virtually guarantee that a stable ruling coalition would be unattainable. But election day was also a holiday in Israel and many families took advantage of the time off not only to vote but also go shopping or for a drive in the country. Shopping centers were jammed; many stores were projecting a doubling of their usual sales despite – or perhaps because of – the political uncertainty in the air: in addition to its many other complex attributes, Israel remains a pulsing consumer society.

Smoke wafted through the squares and public gardens of the country, carrying the aroma of kebabs and grilled sausages to the noses of countless citizens taking the day off. Political posters covered walls, fences, even store windows and a veritable fleet of cars painted in party colors ferried voters to and from the polling stations. Each citizen was seen as a precious commodity in play by the party volunteers eager not to miss a single possible vote; people were called and recalled as they day wore on and the names of those who had voted already were struck from the watch lists. Text messaging to cell phones reached an all-time high as users were solicited by each party in turn. The elderly, the sick, and the wounded war veterans became remarkably popular all of a sudden; even if they were on their deathbeds there was sure to be a way to get them out to vote. As Andy Warhol might have said, it was their fifteen minutes of fame, because the rest of the time they were the forgotten, the part of society whose distress usually left the state indifferent. Kings for a day! Then back to being beggars.

Security measures were draconian, with more than 25,000 police officers, soldiers, night watchmen and volunteers of all sorts on a state of alert. These forces were present to ensure peace and public order during the election, but of course, they were especially vigilant for any possible terror attacks. Military intelligence and Shin Beth had picked up precise information on more than sixty suicide bombers on the loose in the West Bank, aiming to infiltrate Israel proper and blow themselves up in the densely populated urban areas of the country, a terrifying threat with which to contend.

Happily, no major incident took place, and the election vigilance paid off. At 8 pm, the polling stations across the country closed their doors and the counting began. Streets were deserted, with most Israelis glued to their television screens waiting for the results in a kind of existential anxiety. In the absence of hard news, the rumor mills were running at full tilt, one story being quickly contradicted by another. As the trend became obvious, the anchors of all three networks came on the air and calmly communicated the peoples' choice.

The makeup of the new Knesset, as it appeared using projections of early vote tabulations, was significantly different from what had been anticipated. The first surprise was the relatively disappointing results for Kadima, which only elected twenty-nine to parliament, not the forty-two-plus voter surveys taken after Sharon's second hospitalization had predicted. The success of Avigdor Liberman's Russian language party Israel Beiteinu was another eye-opener. Liberman, former director of the Prime Minister's Office under Benjamin Netanyahu, won the same number of seats as the Likud party that had been in power for most of the years since 1977. Never in Israeli history had two fledgling parties enjoyed such success. Amir Peretz' Labor Party retained its core support and would be second to Kadima in the Knesset. With only twelve members in the new Knesset, post-Sharon Likud had suffered a crushing defeat; so, probably had the political ambitions of Bibi Netanyahu. In a sense this was unfair, since Netanyahu's policy of austerity when he was Finance Minister under Sharon had saved the Israeli economy from ruin less than three years earlier, but it had galvanized opposition to him among less fortunate Israelis who went on to vote "anybody but Bibi."

The collapse of Likud was an obvious consequence of the public wrangling within the party since Sharon left; in particular, the open quarrel between Netanyahu and his opponent Silvan Shalom had proven distasteful to many voters in the Likud constituency. Shalom had an irritating, Napoleonic style and was given to pettiness and base behavior; Israelis also recalled that his policies as Finance Minister had left the country in less than mint condition. As Foreign Minister, he suffered the ignominy of seeing his Prime Minister bypass him and conduct all business with the White House and the U.S. State Department through Washington Ambassador Dany Ayalon and Sharon's personal adviser Dov Weissglass. Since that time, Shalom was not even on speaking terms with the two men.

Shalom's wife was also hard to take, and it was no state secret that the useless and petty quarrels the couple initiated were without precedent in the history of Israel. Out of the loop as far as sensitive and vital decisions concerning the United States went, Shalom was also, and frequently, criticized within his own department, in newspaper editorials and by foreign embassies. With no little irony, it was caustically remarked that at the Foreign Ministry, Shalom's wife Judy wore the pants. Daughter of newspaper magnate Noah Moses, Judy Shalom accompanied her husband everywhere on his trips abroad and had the last word on certain diplomatic and ambassadorial appointments. Still, a fair appreciation of her husband must recognize that his influence within Likud was far from negligible, and that his support in the Sephardic community remained strong.

Whatever the case, on the morning after the 2006 elections it had become clear that the dream of Israeli conservative nationalism symbolized by Jabotinsky and Begin was in decline.

The protest vote also favored the Retirees Party, whose policies of improving the conditions of the elderly won support from many young electors. This party, quite unique in Israeli politics, was headed by the 72 year-old former Mossad officer Rafi Eitan, who had participated in the 1961 capture of Adolf Eichmann in Buenos Aires. In November 1985, Eitan had also hired Jonathan Pollard, an American Jew born on August 7, 1954, and a United States Naval analyst with a high security clearance, as an espionage agent. When Pollard was arrested, the affair resulted in serious stress on the U.S.-Israeli relationship, and resulted in a shakeup in the Israeli secret service as well. Tried and sentenced to life in prison for treason, Pollard - now prisoner 09185 - has been incarcerated for more than twenty years. Despite the close relationship between the two allies and numerous Israeli requests for clemency, no sitting United States president has chosen to grant Pollard amnesty.

As to the non-religious centrist Shinnui Party led by former journalist and close friend of Ehud Olmert Tomy Lapid, it now proved to be a spent force, dropping from fifteen Knesset seats to none! Of course, under Israel's system of proportional voting, which has withstood protest and attempts at reform and is notorious for its maddening lack of cohesiveness, this phenomenon was not entirely unprecedented.

The new Knesset would have more religious members (36) and more former military men (12, including one woman) with a higher average education than the previous parliament. Unfortunately, only seventeen women candidates in all (compared to twenty-one outgoing) were returned as members to the 17th Knesset. Still, the women of Israel could take pride in the fact that for the first time, the Knesset President would be female. Kadima member Dalia Ithzik was elected to that august position unanimously and with no abstentions, on the first ballot.

Of real concern to observers and politicians alike was the low electoral turnout. The choice of abstention was rightly seen as proof of a widening gap between the governing and the governed, especially disaffected youth, and would need serious reflection on the part of the political class. Voting for the Eitan-led Retirees Party, for example, was an obvious way to show that no political formation had any legitimacy. The morose campaign had demonstrated that people were fed up with the polarized ideological combat that had characterized previous elections. Something new was required: new leaders, new ideas, a new framework for Israeli democracy was being called for by citizens yearning for their confidence in the system to be restored.

In any case, the collapse of Likud meant the end of the national debate on Eretz Israel established on both banks of the Jordan River. The left-wing Meretz Party led by Yossi Beilin saw its dream of immediate peace with the Palestinians at any price also go down the drain as it only elected five member to the Knesset. In a real sense, Ariel Sharon's Kadima had carved out an ideological center, a territorial compromise "third way," imbued with pragmatism and *realpolitik*. The election could rightly be seen as a national referendum on ending ideological cleavage within Israel, and in this context, it was only natural that Kadima and Labor would join forces in a coalition to govern the country. Of course, Peretz had his own agenda, and even if he would not take the Social Affairs portfolio, he still had a platform on which he had been elected, and took very seriously his promise to offer Israelis security of a social nature, as well as the existential security that had been front and center for many years.

Olmert was far from being a charismatic leader, nor did he possess the authoritative ways of Ariel Sharon, but since Arik's strokes, he had shown himself quite capable of applying Sharon's doctrines. The unauthorized settlement of Amona had been dismantled on Olmert's orders, and two weeks before election day he had authorized the audacious raid on Jericho Prison to capture the terrorist leader Ahmed Saadat and others who were about to be released in defiance of an agreement made several years earlier between Israel, The US, the European Union and the Palestinian Authority.

In his victory speech, Olmert was clear:

> "A new chapter in the history of Israel has begun. It will allow our country to set its final borders while remaining a Jewish state with a Jewish majority."

This obviously meant continuing on the road set out by Ariel

Sharon, with compromise and painful territorial concessions on the table and the evacuation of populations living outside the final borders understood. The goal was to allow Israelis within the final borders of the country proper to realize their dream of living in peace and security. But this was the Israeli side of things. There was also the new Hamas government which had a majority in the Palestinian parliament to take into account, and Hamas seemed intent on pursuing their disastrous policy of denying Israel's right to exist, refusing to recognize the accords with Israel signed by previous Palestinian governments, and in general, being determined to miss another historical chance at Palestinian statehood.

Hamas, founded in Egypt by the Imam Hassan al Banna, is a Muslim brotherhood whose allegiance to Allah is total. The Palestinian branch of Hamas was created by the late Sheikh Ahmed Yassin and in its founding charter of August 18, 1988 declared itself committed as a resistance movement to seeing "Islam erase Israel from the land." Today, Hamas has found an uncontestable ally and brother-in-arms in this aim: the Iran of the Ayatollahs. In its 1990 White Paper setting out its ideology to be accomplished in stages, Hamas stated clear goals:

– Pursuit of armed struggle and violence until the last Zionist has left Palestine;

– Stress that Islam is the solution to the Palestinian problem;

– Refuse all negotiation with Israel and reject all American plans;

– Islamic religious government is to be the only acceptable leadership for the Palestinians.

Now, thanks to the democratic process, fundamentalist Islam, long gnawing at the gates of Israel, had become legitimized, and in part, the Bush administration in Washington was responsible, having dictated Western democratic norms on a region and people to whom they were completely foreign. George Bush's dream of a Greater, Democratic Middle East would prove to be a utopian vision of the Arab world. Even in the West, how could one forget that Adolf Hitler came to power in 1933 in democratic elections? The sad fact here was that at the very moment when Ariel Sharon was doing all he could to avoid legitimizing and empowering Hamas in this chaotic region, the international community including Europe and the USA pressured Israel into allowing elections that led to exactly this outcome. Democracy is a fruit to be tasted slowly, to appreciate its fine flavor, but forced down the throat it can also lead to choking; in no case can the democratic ideal be used to justify terror and absolve terrorists.

Shin Beth and the CIA had been wrong in their projections of the Palestinian elections: they had both predicted a PLO victory under Abu Mazen, proving once again that even the most efficient intelligence services can misjudge the intentions of the voters in a highly politicized election. Politicians and chiefs of state, take note. Recent history abounds in cases where intelligence agencies have made wrong predictions, notably in Iraq, Iran, and Lebanon. The rise of Shiite fundamentalism in particular has proven to be a particular puzzle for the West. Among the Palestinians, rage had been growing for years at the open corruption and disastrous management of the billions received from the European Community and other Western states. Violent settling of accounts took place after the death of Yasser Arafat as it became obvious to all that Israeli occupation was in many respects no more than a pretext and far from the only cause of the misery of Palestinians.

Now that Hamas was in power, and with Israel no longer in Gaza, the Palestinian private sector was quickly following suit and evacuating to Jordan, where investments could be made in a predictable environment. Amman was now full of Palestinian and Israeli businessmen. Hamas also had a choice: remain a movement dedicated to the destruction of Israel and become isolated from the world community most responsible for funding the Palestinian state, or change gears, shoulder its state responsibilities, renounce violence and hatred, break with foreign terror groups like Al-Qaeda and begin sincere negotiations with Israel in order to form, with Egypt and Jordan, a more modern and moderate Middle East. Palestinian Authority President Abu Mazen was weak, and seemingly incapable of pulling his people out of anarchy and chaos.

In point of logical fact, governing Palestine will prove to be impossible for Hamas if they obstinately pursue their blind, intransigent politics. Simple good sense and political wisdom dictate a move to moderation, demilitarization of power and the territory, and sincere peace negotiations in the absence of which Palestinians will remain in the abyss of distress while Israel, with no partner, will on its own set final borders. If such were to happen, no one could fault Israel for being responsible for the mess in Palestine, and no Foreign Ministry or Embassy could denounce the unilateral measures taken by the Olmert administration.

The opening ceremony of the new Knesset took place on Monday, April 17, 2006. An honor guard in sky blue uniforms was lined up on the esplanade to welcome the new representatives of the people of Israel. The ceremony was set to begin at precisely 4 pm in the presence of the Israeli President and the oldest Knesset member, Shimon Peres, who would have the privilege of presiding over the solemn event. (Eleven days later, the *Yediot Aharonot* daily would reveal that Peres had received $320,000 in impermissible, quota-busting election contributions from three American Jews. An investigation had been initiated by the State Controller's Office and the Government Prosecutor indicated that a judicial procedure might be undertaken. Those close to Peres vigorously denied allegations of impropriety but in the political milieu, some suggested it might be time for the old war-horse to resign and leave politics.) Shimon Peres had a unique career in contemporary history, remaining the last statesman on the planet to have exercised official functions for more than fifty years. During his long career, he realized enormous projects for Israel including the construction of the Dimona nuclear reactor, financed to a great extent through donations from the Diaspora. Estimates of the funds he collected for Israel over the years go as high as 15 billion dollars.

At the same time as the choices of Israel's democracy were celebrating in the spring air fragrant with almond flowers, and families were taking advantage of the fine day and Passover holiday to enjoy life, another homicide bomber suddenly blew himself up in Neve Shaanan street at the entrance to a popular restaurant. The bomb was powerful and full of nails and ball bearings, the carnage horrifying. Bodies were torn into shreds and thrown through the air, body parts dotted the sidewalk, and the wounded were counted by the dozen. The panic was punctuated by the screaming of victims and the sirens of ambulances hurrying to the site of the explosion. Those still able to talk were crying out for their loved ones. The TV networks had cameras on the scene within minutes, but alas, as horrible as it was, it was just one more replay of a tragic scene known too well by too many Israelis.

In the Knesset, the joy of the newly elected quickly turned to sadness. How could anyone abide this terror any more? The issue seemed all the more insoluble as it hit right at the heart of Israeli democracy where the political, legal, cultural, economic, and military leaders of the country were all together. This was the first attack since the Hamas election and an obvious targeted test for the new Olmert government. To his credit, Olmert remained calm and the decided that the ceremony would continue. After all, there could be no question of the dignity and the faith of an entire people being destroyed by the violent acts of a madman. The representatives of the people of Israel were gathered to raise the flag of freedom and to underscore their will to give no quarter to the saboteurs of peace, these "Mad Bombers of Allah."

The stands were full of honored guests, the trumpets sounded and president Moshe Katsav declared the new session open. Together, the elected sat in the shape of an enormous Menorah, symbol of the Jewish state. One by one, they rose and swore allegiance to the State of Israel, a political act of faith made in person, in public, and shown live across the country on television. The 17th Knesset was officially open, with the historic decisions to be debated and taken in the chamber of Israeli democracy weighing heavily on the participants.

The Tel-Aviv suicide bombing was claimed by Islamic Jihad, but it was ordered and cynically planned by Hamas in Damascus as a clear strategic decision taken to attempt to plunge the region back into chaos and create international sympathy for the Palestinians – and direct attention away from Syria and Iran when the West was focusing on both countries, the former for its involvement in terror and assassination in Lebanon, the latter for its quest for the Bomb.

Since September 11, 2001, Ariel Sharon had pretty well enjoyed a free hand in responding to terror. Israel was an active part of the international attempts to stamp out Al Qaeda and other such groups, and George Bush had shown faith in leaving the country alone to take such decisions. But Ehud Olmert was a new Prime Minister and needed to feel his way through the complex world in which he was now a major player. If he was hesitant to act without consulting the Americans on this new incident, he was also prudent and turned down suggestions from his advisers to quickly set up a state visit to Washington. After all, the popularity of Mr. Bush was at a low, and if he did go to meet the president he would need to go with something in hand; he needed a little time to prepare.

Olmert was conscious of the risks responding in kind to the Hamas provocation entailed but he was even more attentive to not letting Israeli public opinion believe he had bent to foreign – especially American – pressure. He had yet to announce his Cabinet: this was no time to start things off with a faux pas. On the other hand, George Bush was a true friend of Israel and it would be best that the "painful decisions" to be made come before the end of the president's second term. Olmert decided the best policy would be to dispatch his Foreign Minister Tsipi Livni to Washington. This would demonstrate his intentions of pursuing Sharon's policies and maintaining the American priority in the ongoing peace process. The current tension in the region made this profession of faith even more important at this crucial time.

The results were quite satisfactory. The United States froze the fifty million dollars it paid each month to pay the 140,000 Palestinian government employees, and Secretary of State Condoleeza Rice embarked on a tour of European capitals to ensure they also took a strong stand against Hamas. The French, whose relations with Washington had been chilly since the American invasion of Iraq, changed tactics, with President Jacques Chirac – whose underlying policies remained as they had been – having figured out that it was smarter to get along with George W. Bush than to confront him. If the Iraq business had cooled down the French-American relationship, well, there were other issues that could patch it up, like the common struggle against terror, the Syrian file, and especially the Iranian nuclear question. If the Yanks remained to be convinced that France was no longer an ally not to be trusted and punished for its anti-American betrayal over Saddam Hussein, France was at least eager to demonstrate that it was back in the fold. Chirac's improved relations with Israel, in this respect, were anything but a hindrance.

Could a new and strong Washington-Paris-Jerusalem triangle emerge form the current situation? It would, in an important way depend on Chirac himself, a long-time practitioner of the political zig-zag. France was in the throes of an economic swamp and an extremely serious social crisis. Its large Muslim population with enormous unemployment among young men of North African and African descent was seen as a fertile soil for home-grown terrorists, and the riots of the fall of 2005 made Chirac even more prudent than usual. He had to appear to be doing all things at the same time and offending no one, while defending the principles of the French Republic.

French Jews, long a seamless part of French society, were more than concerned by the rise of anti-Semitic incidents. Synagogue fire-bombing, graveyard desecration and mugging of religious Jews wearing traditional clothing quickly evolved into attacks on Jewish soccer teams and most horrifying of all, the kidnap killing of Ilan Halimi, a Jewish cell phone salesman who worked near the Père Lachaise cemetery in Paris. Mass demonstrations in the French capital and throughout the country called for more social vigilance and government intervention to stop things from getting out of hand.

French citizens of Arab descent were now pressuring Chirac about the situation in Palestine, and he decided to officially receive Abu Mazen, the Palestinian President, at the Elysee Palace, where the Frenchman would propose that a special Palestinian relief fund be created at the World Bank.

In Israel, negotiations were progressing concerning the makeup of the new Cabinet. Kadima signed an official alliance with Rafi Eitan's Retirees Party and thus had a 36-seat bloc in the Knesset. With this agreement hand, Prime Minister Olmert struck a coalition accord with Amir Peretz and the Labor Party. According to the terms of the coalition, the government was to determine the permanent borders of Israel as a democratic state with a Jewish majority. The frontiers were to be negotiated with the Palestinian Authority if possible, but discussion could only be entertained with Hamas if this group renounced violence and recognized the State of Israel. Absent a viable Palestinian partner, the future Government of Israel would take unilateral measures. The Labor Party gave its support to the dismantling of dozens of small and isolated colonies of settlers; these men, women and children would be brought back into the larger colonies on land destined to be within the permanent borders of Israel. Olmert also succeeding in bringing the Sephardic religious Shas party into his coalition by promising a new chapter in Israeli social policy.

The government would set up a vast program intended to reduce social injustice, improve the health system, and contribute to the unity of the citizens of Israel. A significant reform of the educational system was also promised, as was a plan to develop the Negev and Galilee. Jerusalem would be maintained as the political, cultural, and economic center of the State of Israel. Some points would remain in contention such as the final amount of the minimum guaranteed income, but on the whole, there was much nodding of heads.

Olmert's agreement with the Labor Party and negotiating style did go down smoothly with many members of Kadima. His decision to cede several key Ministries to Labor, including Defense, was seen as a slap in the face to Shaul Mofaz. Despite promises made by Ariel Sharon to Professor Uriel Reichmann concerning the Education portfolio, this was also given to Labor. Forty-eight hours later, Reichmann made his mark on the Knesset by resigning. It was the shortest term in Knesset history!

The agreement added several new twists to Israeli tradition. In offering Amir Peretz the Defense portfolio, Olmert broke with the habit of giving this vital nomination to a military man. Would Peretz be up to running military and security matters with a dangerous and hostile Palestinian government in place thirty kilometers from Tel-Aviv? How would he deal with the Iranian nuclear menace?

Questions about this nomination came from many quarters. Was Peretz the right man in the right place at the right time? Was it appropriate for Israel, at this dangerous and delicate hour, to have both the Prime Minister and the Defense Minister lacking in personal military history? It wasn't as if there was any shortage of ex-generals in the Labor Party: Ben Eliezer, Ayalon, Sneh, Vilnahi and Yatom, to name but a few, all experienced in the Defense of the country. Israeli political horse-trading was behind this, no one could doubt that, but still, the price of preserving a solid coalition seemed to be inordinately high.

Olmert maintained that the defense of the country was no longer a war of borders with Egypt, Syria, and Jordan, but took place instead in the cities, towns and villages of Israel and the enemy was terror. Viewed from this angle, the role of the civilian police became of capital importance and along with it, the role of municipal administrations. The police too, were going to be in the front lines of the disengagement implementation. It all made sense to the Prime Minister who put all his political weight behind the concept of unity; his Cabinet would comprise thirty ministers and he had maneuvering room to cede several key portfolios to his coalition partners. If a civilian was named to Defense, well Tsahal was, after all an army of the people in which reservists were in the majority. Amir Peretz would no doubt rely on the advice of the highly capable chiefs of staff including army head Dan Halutz.

In celebrating the 58th anniversary of the birth of their country on May 3, 2006, Israelis could not but reflect on the fact that theirs was the only country in the world without recognized and secure borders, the only land not to have known a single day of veritable peace, the only one where no citizen could go peacefully about his life without worrying about a bomb exploding in his face, and the only nation where the majority of its people lived abroad. The Star of David flag was unfurled throughout the land, from South to North, in solemn memory of the 20,506 soldiers who gave their lives so that Jews could live in their own land. For the first time, Ariel Sharon was absent from the cemetery ceremonies honoring his fallen comrades. Israel felt in a sense orphaned and the moment was sad and difficult to face. This was a day of reflection on an unfinished history full of hope and bitterness, life and death. After the solemnity and the gathering in prayer, sadness gave way to hope, then to joy, dancing, and singing, hearts light with the chance of a happy future as the fireworks broke showers of light into the night skies of the Holy Land.

That is the way of Israel, and the way of the world. Things change. We think of the future, of the generations to come. The Sharon era was passing, and the Olmert Era beginning, with hope. *Hatikva.*

Chronology

Dear reader, this is in no way intended to be an exhaustive chronology. It is merely, and modestly, a selection of events in his life and of the major events in the history of Israel and the Middle East that influenced the military and political career of Ariel Sharon.

1928

Ariel (Arik) Sharon, son of Shmuel and Vera Scheinermann is born in Kfar Malal, Palestine.

1929

August – Anti-Jewish Arab pogroms in Jerusalem (133 killed, 230 injured) and Hebron (60 killed).

1933

Adolf Hitler seizes power in Germany.

1934

September – Little Ariel goes to school for the first time.

1936

Beginning of the Arab uprising in Palestine.

1939

Publication of British Mandate White Paper forbidding Jews to immigrate to Palestine; World War II begins.

1940

France capitulates to Nazi Germany and is divided at the Loire River into a northern, occupied zone, and a southern, unoccupied zone. Lebanon and Syria under the rule of the French Vichy government. Gestapo and SS comb Paris for Jews, Communists and Resistance fighters.

1941

Ariel Scheinermann celebrates his Bar-Mitzvah and enters secondary school at the Geula Lyceum in Tel-Aviv.

1942

Arik joins the Haganah paramilitary forces at the age of 14.

1944

Ariel promoted Corporal, in charge of a unit of 11 soldiers.

1945

Ariel, now a lieutenant, in charge of a unit of fifty soldiers.

1947

Ariel Scheinermann takes part in his first military operations targeting Arabs.

United Nations November 29 resolution on the partition of Palestine.

1948

May 14, Proclamation of the end of the British Mandate and the birth of the State of Israel

Dissolution of clandestine groups and creation of Tsahal (Israel Defense Forces)

First war opposing Israel and seven Arab states (Egypt, Transjordan, Syria, Lebanon, Iraq, Saudi Arabia and Yemen)

Ariel Scheinermann named captain in the Alexandroni Division

May 26, Ariel Scheinermann gravely wounded in the Battle of Latroun

1950

Ariel Scheinermann promoted to rank of Brigade Commander. His first superior officer is Yitzhak Rabin. Several months later, Ariel is named Intelligence officer of the Tsahal Command Center.

1951

King Abdallah of Jordan assassinated on the Esplanade of Mosques in Jerusalem.

Ariel Scheinermann catches malaria; first trip to Paris, London, and New York.

1952

Death of Chaim Weizman, first President of Israel. Yitzak Ben Tsvi succeeds him.

Ariel Scheinermann enters the Faculty of History at the Hebrew University of Jerusalem.

1954

March 29, Ariel Scheinermann marries Margalith in a ceremony presided over by a military rabbi.

Creation of Commando Unit 101, led by Ariel Scheinermann.

October 16 – Spectacular raid on the village of Kibya. Twelve Jordanian soldiers and sixty-nine Palestinian women and children are killed.

First encounter with David Ben-Gurion. From now on, Ariel Scheinermann would be known as Arik Sharon.

Commando unit 101 is attached to the 890th Parachute Brigade.

Ben-Gurion retires to his kibbutz. Moshe Sharett becomes Prime Minister of Israel.

Moshe Dayan named Tsahal Chief of Staff.

Military operation on Nebi Shemuel near Jerusalem, led by Arik Sharon.

1955

David Ben-Gurion comes out of retirement to lead Israel once more, naming himself as Defense Minister.

Spectacular raid led by Sharon on the Egyptian Military Headquarters in Gaza. Thirty-six Egyptian soldiers perish and twenty-eight are injured; Israel loses eight dead and thirteen wounded.
Raid led by Sharon in the Nitsana (No Man's Land) region near the Egyptian Border. Eight-one Egyptian soldiers are killed and fifty-five taken prisoner. Israeli paratrooper losses are five dead and thirty-five wounded.

Operation Kineret against Syria in Tiberiad. Fifty-four Syrian soldiers perish and thirty are taken prisoner.

1956

Operation Kalkylia led by Arik Sharon in the West Bank, with heavy losses: 18 Israelis killed and 68 wounded. Jordan lost 90 killed and more than one hundred wounded.

Golda Meir replaces Moshe Sharett as Foreign Minister
Sharon receives a delegation of French paratroopers.

October-November: France, England and Israel attack Nasser's Egypt in the Suez War. Arik Sharon sees action in the Sinai fighting, parachuting into the Mitla Pass with his troops.

December 27, Margalith Sharon gives birth to Arik's son Gury.

December 31, Shmuel Scheinermann passes away.

1957

Israel leaves the Sinai Peninsula and the Gaza Strip

A madman throws a grenade in the Knesset, lightly wounding David Ben-Gurion and Golda Meir.

Sharon leaves for London and military studies.

1958

United States military intervention in Lebanon

1959

Ben-Gurion forms the 9th Government of Israel.

1960

Historic meeting between David Ben-Gurion and German Chancellor Konrad Adenauer

Ben-Gurion visits Paris and meets Charles De Gaulle.

Ben-Gurion reveals in the Knesset that Israel has built a Nuclear Reactor in the Negev with the help of France, leading to a polemic with the U.S.A.

Mossad agents seize Nazi fugitive Adolf Eichmann in Argentina.

1961

New elections in Israel see the Mapai (Labor) Party lose 5 seats, but Ben-Gurion remains in power as Prime Minister.

1962

Margalith Sharon dies in an auomobile accident near Jerusalem.

Civil war in Yemen, Egyptian military intervenes

Adolf Eichmann is tried, sentenced to death and – in the first and only such incident – executed by Israeli authorities.

1963

Ben-Gurion resigns, Levy Eshkol become Prime Minister of Israel

Yitzhak Rabin named to lead Tsahal.

Arik Sharon named to chief of staff of the Northern Command.

Sharon weds deceased wife Margalith's younger sister, Lily.

1964

Birth of Omry Sharon, first son of Lily and Arik

Prime Minister Levy Eshkol visits Paris, received by De Gaulle

Creation of the Palestine Liberation Organisation and publication of its charter.

1965

Tunisian president Habib Bourguiba calls for Arab states to recognize Israel

Israel and West Germany establish full diplomatic relations.

David Ben-Gurion founds a new political party, Rafi, but winds only ten seats in the next elections.

Arik Sharon becomes Tsahal chief of military instruction.

1966

New government led by Levy Eshkol. Abba Eban becomes Foreign Minister.

An Iraqi pilot defects to Israel in a Mig-21.

Syria and Israel exchange fire on the northern border.

Moshe Dayan becomes military correspondent in Vietnam.

Birth of Gilad Sharon, younger son of Lily and Arik.

1967

Seven Syrian Migs shot down by Israel fighter planes.

Egypt's Nasser begins blocade of the Red Sea Straits of Tiran

First National Unity Government in Israel

France embargoes all arms deliveries to the Middle East.

Six Day War. General Arik Sharon leads combat in the Sinai.

Resolution 242 voted by the United Nations General Assembly.

The three "no's" at the Khartoum summit: "No" to the recognition of the State of Israel, "No" to negotiations and "No" to peace.

Tragic death of Gury Sharon, Arik's child with Margalith, in a firearms accident. The child was only eleven.

1968.

Car bomb explodes in Jerusalem. Twelve are killed, fifty-two injured.

An El-Al civil jet is taken to Algiers by Palestinian pirates.

Tsahal raid on Beirut. Thirteen planes are destroyed.

1969

Levy Eshkol dies, Golda Meir becomes Prime Minister.

Coup d'État in Libya brings Moammar Khaddafi to power.

The Cherbourg naval affair: Israeli crews successfully exfiltrate five already paid for missile boats from a French shipyard of Cherbourg in one of military history's greatest stories of daring, resourcefulness, drama, and ingenuity. France had embargoed delivery of the boats after a policy change.

Sharon named Chief of Southern Command.

War of Attrition begins along the Suez Canal.

1970

Black September massacre of Palestinians by Jordanian Military.

Israeli National Unity Government collapses.

Gamal Nasser dies; Anwar Sadat becomes President of Egypt.

1971

Jordanian Prime Minister Wasfi Tal is assassinated by a Palestinian in Cairo.

1972

Japanese Red Army attack on Ben-Gurion Airport: 26 dead, 81 wounded.

Massacre of Israeli wrestling team by Palestinian terrorists at Munich Olympics.
Assault on Sabena airliner held by Palestinian terrorists at Ben-Gurion Airport.

Ariel Sharon resigns his military position and joins the Liberal Party beforing founding Likud.

1973

Commando operation in Beirut against Palestinian leaders.

The October, or Yom Kippur, War. Reserve General Arik Sharon crosses the Suez Canal with a tank brigade and captures the Egyptian Third Army.

David Ben-Gurion dies at age eighty-four.

International Middle East Peace Conference convened in Geneva.

Sharon elected to the Knesset. Named to the Foreign Affairs and Defense Committee.

1974

Secret Rabin-Peres-Allon meeting wih King Hussein of Jordan

Disengagement accords with Egypt and Syria

Hostage taking at Maalot near the Lebanese border: sixteen children killed and sixty-eight wounded.

Golda Meir andMoshe Dayan resign. Rabin becomes Prime Minister, with Shimon Peres at Defense.

Arik Sharon resigns seat in Knesset.

1975

Civil war breaks out in Lebanon.

Suez Canal re-opens

United Nations General Assembly equates Zionism with racism.

Yitzhak Rabin chooses Sharon as adviser.

1976

Israel launches raid to free pirated airliner passengers at Entebbe, Uganda. Benjamin Netanyahu's brother, one of the commandos, is killed during the operation.

Israel and the European Community sign first accord.

"Day of the Land" demonstrations by Israeli Arabs turn violent.

Attack on El Al passengers at Istanbul airport. Four dead, twenty-four wounded.

Government crisis in Israel. Rabin resigns.

Sharon forms new Shlom Tsion party.

1977

Elections in Israel see Menachem Begin take victory and become Prime Minister. Shlom Tsion wins only two Knesset seats.

Egyptian President Anwar El-Sadat's historic visit to Jerusalem.

1978

Sharon folds the Shlom Tsion Party and rejoins Likud as Minister of Agriculture and President of the Ministerial Committee for settlements in the Territories.

Camp David Peace Accords signed with Egypt.

Golda Meir passes away.

Anwar Sadat and Menachem Begin awarded Nobel Peace Prize.

1979

Fall of the Shah of Iran. Arch-conservative Ayatollah Ruhollah Khomeini seizes power in Iran. Egyptian-Israeli Peace Treaty signed.

First official visit of Sharon to Egypt.

1980

Venice Declaration on the middle East

Iran-Iraq War

Terrorist attack on the Union Libérale Israëlite Synagogue on rue Copernic in Paris: 3 killed, 12 wounded.

France calls for Palestinian self-determination and for PLO participation in the peace negotiations.

1981

François Mitterrand elected President of the French Republic.

Israeli jets destroy the Iraqi Osirak nuclear reactor near Baghdad.

October 6 assassination of Anwar el-Sadat during a military parade

Moshe Dayan passes away.

New elections in Israel won by Likud: Arik Sharon named Defense Minister.

1982

French President Mitterrand on historic visit to Jerusalem.

Arik Sharon supervises Israel's retreat from the Sinai and the evacuation of Yamit.

Lebanese War. Sharon leads Israeli tanks into Beirut, chasing Arafat and the PLO out.

Lebanese Christian leader Bashir Gemayel assassinated in a car bomb attack. Lebanese Christian forces perpetrate massacre of Palestinian in Sabra and Shatilla refugee camps.

Kahn Commission lays blame for the massacre at Sharon's feet. Sharon reigns from second Begin Cabiuet.

1983

Menachem Begin, now ill, definitively leaves power and is replaced by Yitzhak Shamir.

1984

At Sharon's initiative, a National Unity government is formed. Shimon Peres named Prime Minister for a rotating two years, to be followed by Shamir.

Arik Sharon is now Minister of Housing.

Sharon wins defamation suit against *Time Magazine.*

1985

Mossad organizes Operation Moses to rescue seven thousand five hundred Falasha Jews from Ethiopia.

Initial Tsahal retreat from Beirut and the Chuf Mountains.

Cruise ship Achille Lauro taken over by Palestinian terrorists who kill U.S. wheelchair-bound Leon Klinghofer by throwing him overboard.

1986

Shimon Peres on state visit to Morocco.

Sharon accuses Peres of secretly negotiating an international peace conference with Arab leaders including Saddam Hussein.

Yitzhak Shamir, now Prime Minister, rejects the idea and fires Peres.

1987

Shimon Peres, now Foreign Minister of Israel. Signs a secret agreement in London with Jordan's King Hussein. Apprised of the signature, an outraged Shamir annuls it. Sharon forms his own caucus within Likud.

Beginning of First Intifada in Gaza and the West Bank. Defense Minister Rabin is initially indifferent to the possible consequences of the uprising and uses force to put down "the war of stones."

1988

King Hussein of Jordan renounces his country's sovereignty over the West Bank.

Arafat renounces terrorism and recognizes Israel's right to live in peace and security with its neighbours.

Israeli President Chaim Herzog visits France.

Israeli elections result in Shamir forming a new National Unity government with Sharon Minister of Commerce and Industry

Sharon's mother, Vera Scheinermann, dies at age 88.

1989

Arafat-Mitterrand meeting at the Elysée Palace in Paris.

Sharon resigns, unity government collapses.

1990

Iraq invades Kuweit.

East Germany collapses and is absorbed in to West Germany.

Massive exodus of Russian Jews to Israel. Sharon is placed in charge of welcoming and settling them.

Violent fighting breaks out on the Temple Mount, Esplanade of thr Mosques. Twenty-one Arabs are killed.

1991

First Gulf War. Iraq fires Scud missiles at Israel. Sharon demands an overwhelming response; Shamir government takes a moderate stand.

Fourteen thousand four hundred more Falasha Jews are spirited from Ethiopia. Sharon is in charge of housing them.

United Nations General Assembly annuls its earlier resolution equating Zionism with racism.

1992

China establishes diplomatic relations with Israel.

Menachem Begin dies at age 79.

Israeli Embassy and Jewish cultural center in Buenos Aries attacked by Iranian-sponsored terrorists: five killed, 81 wounded.

Labor Party wins elections and Yitzhak Rabin becomes Prime Minister. Shimon Peres gets Foreign Ministry, Arik Sharon in Opposition.

Benjamin Netanyahu elected to head Likud.

Ezer Weizman, once Likud but now Laborite, become the seventh President of Israel.
Israel expels four hundred Hamas activists.

1993

Operation “Settling of Accounts” in Lebanon.

Oslo Accords signed at the White House.

Palestinians massacred by crazed Israeli settler at the Cave of the Patriarchs in Hebron.

1994

The Declaration of Washington ends state of belligerency between Jordan and Israel.

Opening of an Israeli Liason Office in Rabat, Morocco.

1995

Suicide attack at Beth Lid, near Netyana, kills 20 Israeli soldiers.

Yitzhak Rabin assassinated by a Jewish extremist.

Shimon Peres named interim Prime Minister.

1996

First ever Palestinian elections held in the West Bank and Gaza.
Peace negotiations begin with Syria.

Israeli Liason Office opens in Tunis.

Suicide bombing in Jerusalem leaves 25 dead and 51 wounded.

Suicide attack in Ashkelon: two dead and thirty-one wounded.

International conference on anti-terrorism opens in Sharm el-Sheik.

Grapes of Wrath offensive targets Hezbollah.

Early elections in Israel. Benjamin Netanyahu becomes Prime Minister. Ariel Sharon takes Infrastructure portfolio.

French President Jacques Chirac on state visit to Israel. Violence breaks out in Jerusalem.

1997

Two suicide bombings in Jerusalem: 20 dead, more than one hundred wounded.

Mossad aborts killing of Hamas leader Khaled Mashal in Amman. As a consequence, relations between Israel and Jordan become very tense. Sharon personally intervenes with King Hussein.

Arik Sharon on state visit to China and Mongolia.

1998

David Levy resigns as Foreign Minister and is replaced by Sharon.

Israel celebrates the 50th anniversary of Independence.

Israel signs an agreement at the White House for returning thirteen per cent of the West Bank to the Palestinians including the City of the Patriarchs, Hebron. Sharon participates in face to face negotiations with Yasser Arafat at the Wye River Plantation.

Official visit to Israel by Mauritanian Foreign Minister who is received by Sharon at the Sycamores ranch.

1999

King Hussein of Jordan dies of cancer. Sharon attends state funeral in Amman.

State visit by Sharon to China.

State visit by Sharon to Russia.

State visit by Sharon to the Vatican. Audience with Pope John Paul II.

Sharon's residence at the Sycamores Ranch destroyed by fire resulting from an electrical short circuit. Material damages heavy but no loss of life.

Labor Party wins Israeli elections, Ehud Barak becomes Prime Minister. Sharon, in Opposition, becomes new head of Likud,

Israel opens Embassy in Nouakchott, Mauritania.

2000

Final evacuation of Israeli forces from southern Lebanon.

Sharon's wife Lily dies from lung cancer after 37 years of marriage. Her death will leave Sharon in deep solitude.

Ehud Barak opens negotiations with Syria with President Bill Clinton as intermediary.
Camp David peace negotiations between Barak and Arafat.

French Prime Minister Lionel Jospin on state visit to Israel. Violent incidents at Bir Zeit in the West Bank.

President Clinton meets with Syrian strongman Hafez al-Assad in Geneva.

Al-Assad dies shortly thereafter and is replaced by his son Bashar, a London-trained opthalmologist.

Paris peace negotiations collapse, French President Jacques Chirac irate.

Ariel Sharon, head of Knesset Opposition, takes well-publicized walk on Temple Mount.

Second Intifada starts in the territories.

George W. Bush wins U.S. presidential elections.

Morocco and Tunisia break diplomatic relations with Israel in solidarity with Second Intifada.

2001

February 6 – Ariel Sharon elected Prime Minister of Israel.

September 11 – Al Qaeda terrorists strike World Trade Center in New York and Pentagon. Thousands die in collapse of skyscrapers as Osama Bin Laden's suicide operatives succeed in hitting the American homeland.

President George W. Bush orders U.S. military into Afghanistan to depose Taliban fundamentalist government. Coins phrase, "Axis of Evil" (Afghanistan, Iraq, Iran).
October 17– Israeli Minister of Tourism, General Rehavam Ze'evi is assassinated.

October 20 – West Bank Fatah chief Marwan Bargouti is arrested.

October 21 – President George W. Bush states for first time that he favors the creation of a Palestinian state.

2002

January 10 – Israeli naval unit 13 intercepts cargo ship on Red Sea, loaded with weapons secretly ordered by Arafat.

March 27 – Attack on Park Hotel in Netanya on the eve of Passover. Thirty killed.

March 30 – Operation Ramparts(*Homat Magen*) in West Bank. Arafat's headquarters – the Mukhata – is encircled, and Arafat isolated until the end of his life.

April 9 – Heavy combat in West Bank Jenin refugee camp. Fourteen Israeli soldiers and 56 Palestinians killed, twenty-seven wounded.

April 14 – Atack on ancient synagogue in Djerba, Tunisia, kills German tourists and locals.

June 23 – Palestinian terrorist leader Salah Shahde is killed by Israeli aviation.

June 24 – President Bush unveils his "vision" for the Middle East.

2003

January 7 – Israeli daily *Haaretz* publishes page one article on supposed corruption involving Sharon and his sons. In the ensuing scandal and investigation, Sharon defends himself well and no charges are laid, but his son Omry is accused.

February 28 – Arik Sharon reelected as Prime Minister. His Likud Party seats 38 in Knesset to 19 for Labor.

March 18 – United States and coalition forces invade Iraq and depose Saddam Hussein and Baath Party. Hussein eventually found hiding in a spider hole and taken into custody, beginning an excruciatingly long legal process.

June 4 – Summit in Aqaba between George Bush, Ariel Sharon, Abu Mazen and King Abdallah of Jordan.

August 19 – Suicide bombing in Jerusalem kills 23.

September 17 – Publication of the "Quartet Roadmap" plan for peace by the United States, the United Nations, the European Union and Russia.
December 18 – First declaration by Sharon on disengagement with Palestinians.

2004

March 11 – Train bombing in Madrid. Two hundred two killed, more than one thousand injured.

March 14 – Twin attacks in port of Ashdod. Ten killed, twenty wounded.

March 22 – Hamas spiritual chief Ismail Yassin killed by Israeli aviation.

April 14 – Bush-Sharon meeting in Washington followed by exchange of letters.

April 17 – New Hamas chief Abdel Aziz Rantisi killed by Israeli aviation.

May 3 – Disengagement plan rejected by Likud Party.

May 11 – Thirteen Israeli soldiers killed in Gaza.

May 13 – Operation Rainbow in Rafah.

May 22 – Sharon meets secretly with King Abdallah of Jordan.

July 9 – International Court of Justice in the Hague declares Israeli security fence illegal and calls for it to be removed.

July 10 – Benjamin Netanyahu demands a referendum prior to disengagement. Demonstrations throughout Israel. Rebellion against Sharon within Likud.

August 31 – Twin attack on Beersheva. Sixteen dead and one hundred injured.

October 25 – Knesset gives approval to Sharon plan for disengagement. Grave crisis in Likud.

November 1 – Suicide attack on central market in Tel-Aviv. Three dead, forty wounded.

November 11 – Yasser Arafat dies in Paris hospital at age 75.

December 16 – Vast demonstration against Sharon's disengagement plam.

Wave of anti-Semitic incidents in Europe, especially France. Sharon openly calls for French Jews to emigrate to Israel. Strong polemic with French government. Unease among French Jews.

2005

January 8 – Abu Mazen is democratically elected President of the Palestinian Authority, succeeding Yasser Arafat. A new page is turned in Middle Eastern politics.

January 10 – The Knesset approves Arial Sharon's coalition with the Labor Party.

January 20 – George W. Bush begins his second term as President of the United States.

February 6 – New Secretary of State Condoleeza Rice visits Jerusalem and Ramallah.

February 8 – Sharm el-Sheik summit meeting between Sharon and George Bush, Hosni Mubarak, Abu Mazen and King Abdallah of Jordan. Abu Mazen proclaims Intifada over.

February 14 – Former Lebanese Prime Minister Rafik Harari assassinated in Beirut car bomb attack. Syria widely suspected to have orchestrated the attack.

February 16 – Knesset approves compensation plan for settlers evacuating Gaza.

March 16 – Israel transfers security control of Jericho and Tulkarem in the West Bank to Palestinian Authority.

July 22 – Sharon hosts Condoleeza Rice for talks at his Sycamores Ranch.

July 27 – Sharon on official visit to Paris; received with full state honors at Elysée Palace by Jacques Chirac.

August 7 – Israeli Finance Minister Netanyahu resigns and is replaced by Ehud Olmert.

August 15 – The disengagement plan is fully implemented in Gaza and the northern West Bank. Fifty thousand soldiers and police officers take three weeks to evacuate settlers and move their belongings.

September 1 – Signature of agreement to open Rafah border crossing. An Egyptian battalion and European Union inspectors to supervise movement of persons and goods between Gaza and Egypt.

September 12 – Final evacuation of all Israeli forces from Gaza, after an occupation that lasted 38 years, All Israeli settlements destroyed and wiped off the map.

September 24 – Qassam rockets fired at Sderot, causing 6 wounded. Israel retaliates against Hamas terrorist targets.

October 16 – Palestinian attack on Gush Etsion causes three young Israeli deaths.

October 21 – United Nations report accuses Syria of involvement in the death of Rafik Harari.

October 26 – Newly elected Iranian President Mahmoud Ahmadinejad calls for Israel to be wiped off the map. Suicide attack in a Hadera market north of Tel-Aviv causes five deaths and leaves 28 injured.

November 9 – Amir Peretz beats Shimon Peres in Labor Party elections.

November 14 – The State of Israel commemorates the tenth anniversary of the assassination of Prime Minister Yitzhak Rabin. Many foreign dignitaries attend ceremony, including former U.S. President Bill Clinton.

November 21 – Ariel Sharon provokes the Knesset to be dissolved and calls for early elections.

November 23 – Sharon resigns as president of Likud Party and forms a new center-right party, Kadima (Forward). Struggle to succeed him as Likud head begins.

December 2 – Shimon Peres leaves Labor Party to join Sharon in Kadima. Election campaign begins in total confusion. Polls suggest Sharon and Kadima easy winners and collapse of Likud.

Israel announces ninth successful launch of its Metz anti-missile missile capable of intercepting and destroying Scuds and Iranian Shahib missiles with a range of 1,300 kilometers.

December 5 – Suicide bombing in Netanya leaves 4 dead and 24 injured. Israel locks down the territories and launches reprisal attacks in the West Bank and Gaza.

December 10 – Israeli professor Israel Auman of Jerusalem awarded Nobel Prize in Economics, the eighth time an Israeli has received this distinction. The seventy-five year-old Orthodox Jew attends the Stockholm ceremony with his twenty-six children and his new wife!

December 11 – Defense Minister Shaul Mofaz leaves Likud and joins Kadima.

December 18 – Sharon hospitalized after a stroke. Forty hours later he leaves the Hadassah Hospital in Jerusalem smiling and in apparent good shape.

December 19 – Benjamin Netanyahu wins Likud elections and replaces Arik Sharon as president of that party.

2006

January 4 – Ariel Sharon rushed to hospital in critical condition

January 5 – Ehud Olmert named interim Prime Minister and leader of Kadima to ensure continuity of authority.

January 11 – Anti-Semitic attack in Moscow synagogue during prayers leaves 11 wounded.

January 13 – Tsipi Livni named Foreign Minister, replacing Sylvan Shalon after his resignation. Livni is the first woman to fill this position since Golda Meir, "Israel's grandmother." Livni had been Justice Minister in the Sharon government and four years in the Mossad.

January 14 – Ariel Sharon still in critical condition and in a deep coma. His time on the political scene over, a page of Israel's history ends in sadness and disarray.

January 15 – Israeli government under Ehud Olmert authorizes Palestinian elections in East Jerusalem despite protest by Likud and extremist right.

Violent demonstrations by settlers in Hebron confronting Israeli police.

Serious concern worldwide as Iranian President refuses to renounce the nuclear option despite European and U.S. pressure. United Nations Security Council takes up the Iranian dossier.

Sheik Jaber, Kuwaiti Emir, dies at age 79. After ruling his country since 1978, he suffered a stroke in 2001, and functioned at a diminished level since that date.

January 16 – Shimon Peres resigns his Knesset seat in a legal and tactical move allowing him to run in the next elections on the Kadima ticket. The legendary Labor Party leader had been a member of parliament since 1959.

Ariel Sharon moves his eyelids and opens his eyes for a few seconds.

January 19 – Suicide bombing in Tel-Aviv: twenty wounded. The kamikaze attacker had been sent by the Islamic Jihad group prepared in Damascus and financed by Iran as an attempt to sabotage the elections in Israel and Palestine.

Violent demonstrations by Arab Israelis in Wadi Ara on the Tel-Aviv-Affula highway following the death of a young Arab delinquent. Islamic movements trt to exploit this police error on the eve of elections.

President Jacques Chirac proclaims in a speech to his military, "France reserves the right to respond in a non-conventional (ie, nuclear) fashion to any terrorist attacks on its interests. " Jerusalem appreciates this firm, dissuasive declaration at a time when the Iranian president was visiting Damascus and Osama Ben Laden reappeared on videotape threatening Europe, the United States and Israel anew.

January 20 – Ehud Olmert warns Iran. Tsahal Chief of Staff Dan Halutz reiterates that the nuclear threat from Iran represents a question of life or death for Israel. A delegation of Israeli officers led by the head of the Atomic Energy Commission leaves for Moscow to try and convince the Russians to intervene with the Iranians.

January 21 – Benjamin Netanyahu, head of Likud, affirms Israel's right to defendable borders and its need to control the Jordan Valley in particular.

January 22 – Labor Party head Amir Peretz declares that Israel will never return to its pre-1967 borders.

January 23 – Israeli Foreign Minister Tsipi Livni affirms that the Palestinian refugee issue will be settled within the framework of the creation of a Palestinian state.

January 24 – Ehud Olmert declares it preferable to arrive at an agreement with the Palestinians before evacuating further territory, adding "We need to abandon land to preserve a Jewish majority in Israel."

January 25 – Legislative elections in Palestine results in surprising majority victory for Hamas. Abu Mazen announces the resignation of his Fatah government. Widespread concern in Israel as the government affirms unwillingness to deal with a Palestinian Hamas-led government.

March 14 – Siege of the Jericho prison in the West Bank. Units backed by tanks enter the prison abandoned by foreign observers and capture many terrorists including Ahmed Saadat, responsible for the assassination of Israeli Tourism Minister Rehavan Ze'evi in October 2001.

March 28 – Legislative elections in Israel. Kadima wins low turnout victory and Ehud Olmert named to head new government.

April 14 – Sharon officially declared unfit to assume his responsibilities. His personal effects are moved from the official residence of the Prime Minister on Balfour Street in Jerusalem to his Sycamores Ranch in the Negev Desert.

April 17 – Passover suicide bombing in Tel-Aviv: nine killed, sixty-six wounded.

April 24, 2006 – Triple bomb attack in the Red Sea resort town of Dahab in the Egyptian Sinai results in 23 dead and sixty wounded.

April 25 – Israel launches a new spy satellite on a Russian rocket; on-board camera can resolve images down to 70 centimeters or about 27 inches.

May 3 – Israel Independence Day. On this 58th anniversary of the founding of the Jewish state, the population has reached more than seven million of which 1,387,000 are Israeli Arabs. Twenty-two thousand one hundred twenty three Jews lost their lives in wars and hostile actions since the first Jewish pioneers arrived in Palestine in 1860.

May 4 – Prime Minister Ehud Olmert presents his government to the Knesset.

Appendix

Documents of historical interest

1

Government meeting at the P.M.'s office in Jerusalem about the Prime Minister's statement on the Roadmap.

(25/05/2003)

A.The Government of Israel, today (Sunday), 25.5.03, considered the Prime Minister's statement on the Roadmap, as well as Israels comments on its implementation. Following its deliberations, the Government, by a majority vote, resolved:

Based on the 23 May 2003 statement of the United States Government, in which the United States committed to fully and seriously address Israels comments to the Roadmap during the implementation phase, the Prime Minister announced on 23 May 2003 that Israel has agreed to accept the steps set out in the Roadmap.

The Government of Israel affirms the Prime Ministers announcement, and resolves that all of Israels comments, as addressed in the Administrations statement, will be implemented in full during the implementation phase of the Roadmap.

A list of the comments forwarded by Israel for the review of the Administration in the United States has been attached to this decision.

B. The Government also resolved, concerning the issue of the refugees, as follows:

The Government of Israel today accepted the steps set out in the Roadmap. The Government of Israel expresses its hope that the political process that will commence, in accordance with the 24 June 2002 speech of President Bush, will bring security, peace and reconciliation between Israel and the Palestinians.

The Government of Israel further clarifies that, both during and subsequent to the political process, the resolution of the issue of the refugees will not include their entry into or settlement within the State of Israel.

Israel's Roadmap reservations

Prime Minister Ariel Sharon's Cabinet on Sunday approved the "road map" - a three-phase plan that calls for a settlement freeze and an end to terror attacks in the first stage, a Palestinian state with temporary borders in the second, and a final-status agreement by 2005. The vote was 12-7 with four abstentions at the end of a stormy six-hour debate.

Israel attached 14 reservations to the road map, which the U.S. has promised to "fully and seriously address," but this promise was not an assurance that all of Israel's demands would be met. The following is the text of the reservations:

Primary themes of Israel's remarks

1. Both at the commencement of, and during the process, and as a condition to its continuance, calm will be maintained. The Palestinians will dismantle the existing security organizations and implement security reforms during the course of which new organizations will be formed and act to combat terror, violence and incitement (incitement must cease immediately and the Palestinian Authority must educate for peace).

These organizations will engage in genuine prevention of terror and violence through arrests, interrogations, prevention and the enforcement of the legal groundwork for investigations, prosecution and punishment. In the first phase of the plan and as a condition for progress to the second phase, the Palestinians will complete the dismantling of terrorist organizations (Hamas, Islamic Jihad, the Popular Front, the Democratic Front, Al-Aqsa Brigades and other apparatuses) and their infrastructure; collection of all illegal weapons and their transfer to a third party for the sake of being removed from the area and destroyed; cessation of weapons smuggling and weapons production inside the Palestinian Authority; activation of the full prevention apparatus and cessation of incitement.

There will be no progress to the second phase without the fulfillment of all above-mentioned conditions relating to the war against terror. The security plans to be implemented are the Tenet and Zinni plans. [As in the other mutual frameworks, the road map will not state that Israel must cease violence and incitement against the Palestinians].

2. Full performance will be a condition for progress between phases and for progress within phases. The first condition for progress will be the complete cessation of terror, violence and incitement. Progress between phases will come only following the full implementation of the preceding phase. Attention will be paid not to time lines, but to performance benchmarks (time lines will serve only as reference points).

3. The emergence of a new and different leadership in the Palestinian Authority within the framework of governmental reform. The formation of a new leadership constitutes a condition for progress to the second phase of the plan. In this framework, elections will be conducted for the Palestinian Legislative Council following coordination with Israel.

4. The Monitoring mechanism will be under American management. The chief verification activity will concentrate upon the creation of another Palestinian entity and progress in the civil reform process within the Palestinian Authority. Verification will be performed exclusively on a professional basis and per issue (economic, legal, financial) without the existence of a combined or unified mechanism. Substantive decisions will remain in the hands of both parties.

5. The character of the provisional Palestinian state will be determined through negotiations between the Palestinian Authority and Israel. The provisional state will have provisional borders and certain aspects of sovereignty, be fully demilitarized with no military forces, but only with police and internal security forces of limited scope and armaments, be without the authority to undertake defense alliances or military cooperation, and Israeli control over the entry and exit of all persons and cargo, as well as of its air space and electromagnetic spectrum.

6. In connection to both the introductory statements and the final settlement, declared references must be made to Israel's right to exist as a Jewish state and to the waiver of any right of return for Palestinian refugees to the State of Israel.

7. End of the process will lead to the end of all claims and not only the end of the conflict.

8. The future settlement will be reached through agreement and direct nego-

tiations between the two parties, in accordance with the vision outlined by President Bush in his 24 June address.

9. There will be no involvement with issues pertaining to the final settlement. Among issues not to be discussed: settlement in Judea, Samaria and Gaza (excluding a settlement freeze and illegal outposts); the status of the Palestinian Authority and its institutions in Jerusalem; and all other matters whose substance relates to the final settlement.

10. The removal of references other than 242 and 338 (1397, the Saudi Initiative and the Arab Initiative adopted in Beirut). A settlement based upon the road map will be an autonomous settlement that derives its validity therefrom. The only possible reference should be to Resolutions 242 and 338, and then only as an outline for the conduct of future negotiations on a permanent settlement.

11. Promotion of the reform process in the Palestinian Authority: a transitional Palestinian constitution will be composed, a Palestinian legal infrastructure will be constructed and cooperation with Israel in this field will be renewed. In the economic sphere: international efforts to rehabilitate the Palestinian economy will continue. In the financial sphere: the American-Israeli-Palestinian agreement will be implemented in full as a condition for the continued transfer of tax revenues.

12. The deployment of IDF forces along the September 2000 lines will be subject to the stipulation of Article 4 (absolute quiet) and will be carried out in keeping with changes to be required by the nature of the new circumstances and needs created thereby. Emphasis will be placed on the division of responsibilities and civilian authority as in September 2000, and not on the position of forces on the ground at that time.

13. Subject to security conditions, Israel will work to restore Palestinian life to normal: promote the economic situation, cultivation of commercial connections, encouragement and assistance for the activities of recognized humanitarian agencies. No reference will be made to the Bertini Report as a binding source document within the framework of the humanitarian issue.

14. Arab states will assist the process through the condemnation of terrorist activity. No link will be established between the Palestinian track and other tracks (Syrian-Lebanese).

Prime Minister's Office
Communications Department

משרד ראש הממשלה
אגף התקשורת

2

A Performance-Based Roadmap to a Permanent Two-State Solution to the Israeli-Palestinian Conflict

The U.S. State Department April 30 released the text of the "roadmap" to a permanent solution to the Israeli-Palestinian conflict. The roadmap specifies the steps for the two parties to take to reach a settlement, and a timeline for doing so, under the auspices of the Quartet - the United States, the European Union, the United Nations, and Russia.

Following is the text of the Roadmap:

Office of the Spokesman
Washington, DC
April 30, 2003

The following is a performance-based and goal-driven roadmap, with clear phases, timelines, target dates, and benchmarks aiming at progress through reciprocal steps by the two parties in the political, security, economic, humanitarian, and institution-building fields, under the auspices of the Quartet [the United States, European Union, United Nations, and Russia]. The destination is a final and comprehensive settlement of the Israel-Palestinian conflict by 2005, as presented in President Bush's speech of 24 June, and welcomed by the EU, Russia and the UN in the 16 July and 17 September Quartet Ministerial statements.

A two-state solution to the Israeli-Palestinian conflict will only be achieved through an end to violence and terrorism, when the Palestinian people have a leadership acting decisively against terror and willing and able to build a practicing democracy based on tolerance and liberty, and through Israel's readiness to do what is necessary for a democratic Palestinian state to be established, and a clear, unambiguous acceptance by both parties of the goal of a negotiated settlement as described below. The Quartet will assist and facilitate implementation of the plan, starting in Phase I, including direct discussions between the parties as required. The plan establishes a realistic timeline for implementation. However, as a performance-based plan, progress will require and depend upon the good faith efforts of the parties, and their compliance with each of the obligations outlined below. Should the parties perform their obligations rapidly, progress within and through the phases may come sooner than indicated in the plan. Non-compliance with obligations will impede progress.

A settlement, negotiated between the parties, will result in the emergence of an independent, democratic, and viable Palestinian state living side by side in peace and security with Israel and its other neighbors. The settlement will resolve the Israel-Palestinian conflict, and end the occupation that began in 1967, based on the foundations of the Madrid Conference, the principle of land for peace, UNSCRs 242, 338 and 1397, agreements previously reached by the parties, and the initiative of Saudi Crown Prince Abdullah - endorsed by the Beirut Arab League Summit - calling for acceptance of Israel as a neighbor living in peace and security, in the context of a comprehensive settlement. This initiative is a vital element of international efforts to promote a comprehensive peace on all tracks, including the Syrian-Israeli and Lebanese-Israeli tracks.

The Quartet will meet regularly at senior levels to evaluate the parties' performance on implementation of the plan. In each phase, the parties are expected to perform their obligations in parallel, unless otherwise indicated.

Phase I: Ending Terror And Violence, Normalizing Palestinian Life, and Building Palestinian Institutions – Present to May 2003

In Phase I, the Palestinians immediately undertake an unconditional cessation of violence according to the steps outlined below; such action should be accompanied by supportive measures undertaken by Israel. Palestinians and Israelis resume security cooperation based on the Tenet work plan to end violence, terrorism, and incitement through restructured and effective Palestinian security services. Palestinians undertake comprehensive political reform in preparation for statehood, including drafting a Palestinian constitution, and free, fair and open elections upon the basis of those measures. Israel takes all necessary steps to help normalize Palestinian life. Israel withdraws from Palestinian areas occupied from September 28, 2000 and the two sides restore the status quo that existed at that time, as security performance and cooperation progress. Israel also freezes all settlement activity, consistent with the Mitchell report.

At the outset of Phase I:

Palestinian leadership issues unequivocal statement reiterating Israel's right to exist in peace and security and calling for an immediate and unconditional cease-fire to end armed activity and all acts of violence against Israelis anywhere. All official Palestinian institutions end incitement against Israel.
Israeli leadership issues unequivocal statement affirming its commitment to the two-state vision of an independent, viable, sovereign Palestinian state living in peace and security alongside Israel, as expressed by President Bush, and calling for an immediate end to violence against Palestinians everywhere. All official Israeli institutions end incitement against Palestinians.

Security

Palestinians declare an unequivocal end to violence and terrorism and undertake visible efforts on the ground to arrest, disrupt, and restrain individuals and groups conducting and planning violent attacks on Israelis anywhere.

Rebuilt and refocused Palestinian Authority security apparatus begins sustained, targeted, and effective operations aimed at confronting all those engaged in terror and dismantlement of terrorist capabilities and infrastructure. This includes commencing confiscation of illegal weapons and consolidation of security authority, free of association with terror and corruption.

GOI takes no actions undermining trust, including deportations, attacks on civilians; confiscation and/or demolition of Palestinian homes and property, as a punitive measure or to facilitate Israeli construction; destruction of Palestinian institutions and infrastructure; and other measures specified in the Tenet work plan.

Relying on existing mechanisms and on-the-ground resources, Quartet representatives begin informal monitoring and consult with the parties on establishment of a formal monitoring mechanism and its implementation.
Implementation, as previously agreed, of U.S. rebuilding, training and resumed security cooperation plan in collaboration with outside oversight board (U.S.-Egypt-Jordan). Quartet support for efforts to achieve a lasting, comprehensive cease-fire.

All Palestinian security organizations are consolidated into three services reporting to an empowered Interior Minister.
Restructured/retrained Palestinian security forces and IDF counterparts pro-

gressively resume security cooperation and other undertakings in implementation of the Tenet work plan, including regular senior-level meetings, with the participation of U.S. security officials.

Arab states cut off public and private funding and all other forms of support for groups supporting and engaging in violence and terror.
All donors providing budgetary support for the Palestinians channel these funds through the Palestinian Ministry of Finance's Single Treasury Account.

As comprehensive security performance moves forward, IDF withdraws progressively from areas occupied since September 28, 2000 and the two sides restore the status quo that existed prior to September 28, 2000. Palestinian security forces redeploy to areas vacated by IDF.

Palestinian Institution-Building

Immediate action on credible process to produce draft constitution for Palestinian statehood. As rapidly as possible, constitutional committee circulates draft Palestinian constitution, based on strong parliamentary democracy and Cabinet with empowered Prime Minister, for public comment/debate. Constitutional committee proposes draft document for submission after elections for approval by appropriate Palestinian institutions.

Appointment of interim Prime Minister or Cabinet with empowered executive authority/decision-making body.

GOI fully facilitates travel of Palestinian officials for PLC and Cabinet sessions, internationally supervised security retraining, electoral and other reform activity, and other supportive measures related to the reform efforts.
Continued appointment of Palestinian ministers empowered to undertake fundamental reform. Completion of further steps to achieve genuine separation of powers, including any necessary Palestinian legal reforms for this purpose.

Establishment of independent Palestinian election commission. PLC reviews and revises election law.

Palestinian performance on judicial, administrative, and economic benchmarks, as established by the International Task Force on Palestinian Reform.
As early as possible, and based upon the above measures and in the context

of open debate and transparent candidate selection/electoral campaign based on a free, multi-party process, Palestinians hold free, open, and fair elections.

GOI facilitates Task Force election assistance, registration of voters, movement of candidates and voting officials. Support for NGOs involved in the election process.

GOI reopens Palestinian Chamber of Commerce and other closed Palestinian institutions in East Jerusalem based on a commitment that these institutions operate strictly in accordance with prior agreements between the parties.

Humanitarian Response

Israel takes measures to improve the humanitarian situation. Israel and Palestinians implement in full all recommendations of the Bertini report to improve humanitarian conditions, lifting curfews and easing restrictions on movement of persons and goods, and allowing full, safe, and unfettered access of international and humanitarian personnel.

AHLC reviews the humanitarian situation and prospects for economic development in the West Bank and Gaza and launches a major donor assistance effort, including to the reform effort.

GOI and PA continue revenue clearance process and transfer of funds, including arrears, in accordance with agreed, transparent monitoring mechanism.

Civil Society

Continued donor support, including increased funding through PVOs/NGOs, for people to people programs, private sector development and civil society initiatives.

Settlements

GOI immediately dismantles settlement outposts erected since March 2001. Consistent with the Mitchell Report, GOI freezes all settlement activity (including natural growth of settlements).

Phase II: Transition – June 2003-December 2003

In the second phase, efforts are focused on the option of creating an independent Palestinian state with provisional borders and attributes of sovereignty, based on the new constitution, as a way station to a permanent status settlement. As has been noted, this goal can be achieved when the Palestinian people have a leadership acting decisively against terror, willing and able to build a practicing democracy based on tolerance and liberty. With such a leadership, reformed civil institutions and security structures, the Palestinians will have the active support of the Quartet and the broader international community in establishing an independent, viable, state.

Progress into Phase II will be based upon the consensus judgment of the Quartet of whether conditions are appropriate to proceed, taking into account performance of both parties. Furthering and sustaining efforts to normalize Palestinian lives and build Palestinian institutions, Phase II starts after Palestinian elections and ends with possible creation of an independent Palestinian state with provisional borders in 2003. Its primary goals are continued comprehensive security performance and effective security cooperation, continued normalization of Palestinian life and institution-building, further building on and sustaining of the goals outlined in Phase I, ratification of a democratic Palestinian constitution, formal establishment of office of Prime Minister, consolidation of political reform, and the creation of a Palestinian state with provisional borders.

International Conference: Convened by the Quartet, in consultation with the parties, immediately after the successful conclusion of Palestinian elections, to support Palestinian economic recovery and launch a process, leading to establishment of an independent Palestinian state with provisional borders. Such a meeting would be inclusive, based on the goal of a comprehensive Middle East peace (including between Israel and Syria, and Israel and Lebanon), and based on the principles described in the preamble to this document.

Arab states restore pre-intifada links to Israel (trade offices, etc.).

Revival of multilateral engagement on issues including regional water resources, environment, economic development, refugees, and arms control issues.

New constitution for democratic, independent Palestinian state is finalized and approved by appropriate Palestinian institutions. Further elections, if required, should follow approval of the new constitution.

Empowered reform Cabinet with office of Prime Minister formally established, consistent with draft constitution.

Continued comprehensive security performance, including effective security cooperation on the bases laid out in Phase I.

Creation of an independent Palestinian state with provisional borders through a process of Israeli-Palestinian engagement, launched by the international conference. As part of this process, implementation of prior agreements, to enhance maximum territorial contiguity, including further action on settlements in conjunction with establishment of a Palestinian state with provisional borders.

Enhanced international role in monitoring transition, with the active, sustained, and operational support of the Quartet.

Quartet members promote international recognition of Palestinian state, including possible UN membership.

Phase III: Permanent Status Agreement and End of the Israeli-Palestinian Conflict – 2004 - 2005

Progress into Phase III, based on consensus judgment of Quartet, and taking into account actions of both parties and Quartet monitoring. Phase III objectives are consolidation of reform and stabilization of Palestinian institutions, sustained, effective Palestinian security performance, and Israeli-Palestinian negotiations aimed at a permanent status agreement in 2005.

Second International Conference: Convened by Quartet, in consultation with the parties, at beginning of 2004 to endorse agreement reached on an independent Palestinian state with provisional borders and formally to launch a process with the active, sustained, and operational support of the Quartet, leading to a final, permanent status resolution in 2005, including on borders, Jerusalem, refugees, settlements; and, to support progress toward a comprehensive Middle East settlement between Israel and Lebanon and Israel and Syria, to be achieved as soon as possible.

Continued comprehensive, effective progress on the reform agenda laid out by the Task Force in preparation for final status agreement.

Continued sustained and effective security performance, and sustained, effective security cooperation on the bases laid out in Phase I.
International efforts to facilitate reform and stabilize Palestinian institutions

and the Palestinian economy, in preparation for final status agreement.

Parties reach final and comprehensive permanent status agreement that ends the Israel-Palestinian conflict in 2005, through a settlement negotiated between the parties based on UNSCR 242, 338, and 1397, that ends the occupation that began in 1967, and includes an agreed, just, fair, and realistic solution to the refugee issue, and a negotiated resolution on the status of Jerusalem that takes into account the political and religious concerns of both sides, and protects the religious interests of Jews, Christians, and Muslims worldwide, and fulfills the vision of two states, Israel and sovereign, independent, democratic and viable Palestine, living side-by-side in peace and security.

Arab state acceptance of full normal relations with Israel and security for all the states of the region in the context of a comprehensive Arab-Israeli peace.

Prime Minister's Office
Communications Department

משרד ראש הממשלה
אגף התקשורת

3

Address by Prime Minister Ariel Sharon at the Fourth Herzliya Conference

(December 18, 2003) (Translated from Hebrew)

Good Evening,

I congratulate the organizers of this conference for the important and interesting gathering which you have held here. During the past three days, you have been discussing Israel's situation. I, as Prime Minister, am responsible for the planning and implementation of the measures which will shape Israel's character during the next few years.

We are all entrusted with the duty of shaping the face of the Jewish and democratic State of Israel a state where there is an equal distribution of the burden, as well as the acceptance of rights and shouldering of duties by all sectors, through different forms of national service. A state where there is a good and efficient education system which educates a young generation imbued with values and national pride, which is capable of confronting the challenges of the modern world. A country whose economy is adapted to the advanced global market of the 21st century, where the product per capita crosses the $20,000 line and is equal to that of most developed European countries. An immigrant-absorbing state which constitutes a national and spiritual center for all Jews of the world and is a source of attraction for thousands of immigrants each year. Aliyah is the central goal of the State of Israel.

This is the country we wish to shape. This is the country where our children will want to live.

I know that there is sometimes a tendency to narrow all of Israel's problems down to the political sphere, believing that once a solution is found to Israel's problems with its neighbors, particularly the Palestinians, the other issues on the agenda will miraculously resolve themselves. I do not believe so. We are facing additional challenges, which must be addressed the economy, educating the young generation, immigrant absorption, enhancement of social cohesion and the improvement of relations between Arabs and Jews in Israel.

Like all Israeli citizens, I yearn for peace. I attach supreme importance to taking all steps, which will enable progress toward resolution of the conflict with the Palestinians. However, in light of the other challenges we are faced with, if the Palestinians do not make a similar effort toward a solution of the conflict I do not intend to wait for them indefinitely.

Seven months ago, my Government approved the Roadmap to peace, based on President George Bush's June 2002 speech. This is a balanced program for phased progress toward peace, to which both Israel and the Palestinians committed themselves. A full and genuine implementation of the program is the best way to achieve true peace. The Roadmap is the only political plan accepted by Israel, the Palestinians, the Americans and a majority of the international community. We are willing to proceed toward its implementation: two states, Israel and a Palestinian State living side by side in tranquility, security and peace.

The Roadmap is a clear and reasonable plan, and it is therefore possible and imperative to implement it. The concept behind this plan is that only security will lead to peace. And in that sequence. Without the achievement of full security within the framework of which terror organizations will be dismantled it will not be possible to achieve genuine peace, a peace for generations. This is the essence of the Roadmap. The opposite perception, according to which the very signing of a peace agreement will produce security out of thin air, has already been tried in the past and failed miserably. And such will be the fate of any other plan which promotes this concept. These plans deceive the public and create false hope. There will be no peace before the eradication of terror.

The government under my leadership will not compromise on the realization of all phases of the Roadmap. It is incumbent upon the Palestinians to uproot the terrorist groups and to create a law-abiding society, which fights against violence and incitement. Peace and terror cannot coexist. The world is currently united in its unequivocal demand from the Palestinians to act toward the cessation of terrorism and the implementation of reforms. Only a transformation of the Palestinian Authority into a different authority will enable progress in the political process. The Palestinians must fulfill their obligations. A full and complete implementation will at the end of the process lead to peace and tranquility.

We began the implementation of the Roadmap at Aqaba, but the terrorist organizations joined with Yasser Arafat and sabotaged the process with a series of the most brutal terror attacks we have ever known.

Concurrent with the demand from the Palestinians to eliminate the terror organizations, Israel is taking and will continue to take steps to significantly improve the living conditions of the Palestinian population: Israel will remove closures and curfews and reduce the number of roadblocks; we will improve freedom of movement for the Palestinian population, including the passage of people and goods; we will increase the hours of operation at international border crossings; we will enable a large number of Palestinian merchants to conduct regular and normal economic and trade relations with their Israeli counterparts, etc. All these measures are aimed at enabling better and freer movement for the Palestinian population not involved in terror.

In addition, subject to security coordination, we will transfer Palestinian towns to Palestinian security responsibility.

Israel will make every effort to assist the Palestinians and to advance the process.

Israel will fulfil the commitments taken upon itself. I have committed to the President of the United States that Israel will dismantle unauthorized outposts. It is my intention to implement this commitment. The State of Israel is governed by law, and the issue of the outposts is no exception. I understand the sensitivity; we will try to do this in the least painful way possible, but the unauthorized outposts will be dismantled. Period.

Israel will meet all its obligations with regard to construction in the settlements. There will be no construction beyond the existing construction line, no expropriation of land for construction, no special economic incentives and no construction of new settlements.

I take this opportunity to appeal to the Palestinians and repeat, as I said at Aqaba: it is not in our interest to govern you. We would like you to govern yourselves in your own country. A democratic Palestinian state with territorial contiguity in Judea and Samaria and economic viability, which would conduct normal relations of tranquility, security and peace with Israel. Abandon the path of terror and let us together stop the bloodshed. Let us move forward together towards peace.

We wish to speedily advance implementation of the Roadmap towards quiet and a genuine peace. We hope that the Palestinian Authority will carry out its part. However, if in a few months the Palestinians still continue to disregard their part in implementing the Roadmap then Israel will initiate the unilateral security step of disengagement from the Palestinians.

The purpose of the Disengagement Plan is to reduce terror as much as possible, and grant Israeli citizens the maximum level of security. The process of disengagement will lead to an improvement in the quality of life, and will help strengthen the Israeli economy. The unilateral steps which Israel will take in the framework of the Disengagement Plan will be fully coordinated with the United States. We must not harm our strategic coordination with the United States. These steps will increase security for the residents of Israel and relieve the pressure on the IDF and security forces in fulfilling the difficult tasks they are faced with. The Disengagement Plan is meant to grant maximum security and minimize friction between Israelis and Palestinians.

We are interested in conducting direct negotiations, but do not intend to hold Israeli society hostage in the hands of the Palestinians. I have already said we will not wait for them indefinitely.

The Disengagement Plan will include the redeployment of IDF forces along new security lines and a change in the deployment of settlements, which will reduce as much as possible the number of Israelis located in the heart of the Palestinian population. We will draw provisional security lines and the IDF will be deployed along them. Security will be provided by IDF deployment, the security fence and other physical obstacles. The Disengagement Plan will reduce friction between us and the Palestinians.

This reduction of friction will require the extremely difficult step of changing the deployment of some of the settlements. I would like to repeat what I have said in the past: In the framework of a future agreement, Israel will not remain in all the places where it is today. The relocation of settlements will be made, first and foremost, in order to draw the most efficient security line possible, thereby creating this disengagement between Israel and the Palestinians. This security line will not constitute the permanent border of the State of Israel, however, as long as implementation of the Roadmap is not resumed, the IDF will be deployed along that line. Settlements which will be relocated are those, which will not be included in the territory of the State of Israel in the framework of any possible future permanent agreement. At the same time, in the framework of the Disengagement Plan, Israel will strengthen its control over those same areas in the Land of Israel which will constitute an inseparable part of the State of Israel in any future agreement. I know you would like to hear names, but we should leave something for later.

Israel will greatly accelerate the construction of the security fence. Today we can already see it taking shape. The rapid completion of the security fence will enable the IDF to remove roadblocks and ease the daily lives of the Palestinian population not involved in terror.

In order to enable the Palestinians to develop their economic and trade sectors, and to ensure that they will not be exclusively dependent on Israel, we will consider, in the framework of the Disengagement Plan, enabling in coordination with Jordan and Egypt the freer passage of people and goods through international border crossings, while taking the necessary security precautions.

I would like to emphasize: the Disengagement Plan is a security measure and not a political one. The steps which will be taken will not change the political reality between Israel and the Palestinians, and will not prevent the possibility of returning to the implementation of the Roadmap and reaching an agreed settlement.

The Disengagement Plan does not prevent the implementation of the Roadmap. Rather, it is a step Israel will take in the absence of any other option, in order to improve its security. The Disengagement Plan will be realized only in the event that the Palestinians continue to drag their feet and postpone implementation of the Roadmap.

Obviously, through the Disengagement Plan the Palestinians will receive much less than they would have received through direct negotiations as set out in the Roadmap.

According to circumstances, it is possible that parts of the Disengagement Plan that are supposed to provide maximum security to the citizens of Israel will be undertaken while also attempting to implement the Roadmap.

Ladies and Gentlemen,

My life experience has taught me that for peace, as well as for war, we must have broad consensus. We must preserve our unity, even in the midst of a difficult, internal debate.

In the past three years, the Palestinian terrorist organizations have put us to a difficult test. Their plan to break the spirit of Israeli society has not succeeded. The citizens of Israel have managed to step into the breach, support each other, lend a helping hand, volunteer and contribute.

I believe that this path of unity must be continued today. Whether we will be able to advance the Roadmap, or will have to implement the Disengagement Plan, experience has taught us that, together, through broad national consensus, we can do great things.

Let us not be led astray. Any path will be complicated, strewn with obstacles, and obligate us to act with discretion and responsibility. I am confident that, just as we have managed to overcome the challenges of the past, we will stand together and succeed today.

We will always be guided by the words of Prime Minister David Ben-Gurion, who said, on the day after the Declaration of Independence:

> "These days, our purpose is only to build the State of Israel with love and faith, in Jewish brotherhood, and to defend it with all our spirit, and as long as necessary. We are still in the midst of a difficult battle, one that has two fronts: political and military. Let us not embellish our deeds and, of course, our words, with gran-

> diose names. We must remain humble. We achieved what we have achieved by standing on the shoulders of previous generations, and we accomplished what we have accomplished by preserving our precious legacy, the legacy of a small nation which has endured suffering and tribulations, but which is, nevertheless, great and eternal in spirit, vision, faith and virtue."

I am also a great believer in the resilience of this small, brave nation, which has endured suffering and tribulations. I am confident that, united in the power of our faith, we will be able to succeed in any path we choose.

Thank you very much, and happy Hannukah.

Prime Minister's Office
Communications Department

משרד ראש הממשלה
אגף התקשורת

4

Prime Minister Ariel Sharon's Statement At the White House

Wednesday, April 14, 2004

I want to thank you, Mr. President, for your warm welcome and your strong support and friendship for the State of Israel.

I came to you from a peace-seeking country. Despite the repeated terror attacks against us, the people of Israel continues to wish for the achievement of a viable peace, in accordance with our Jewish tradition, as outlined by Israel's prophets.

Our people desires to be known for its achievements in the fields of culture, science and technology, rather than in the battlefield.

We are committed to make any efforts to develop our country and society for our own benefit and for the benefit of the peoples of the region.

In our meeting today, I presented to you the outlines of my disengagement plan.

It will improve Israel's security and economy and reduce friction and tension between Israelis and Palestinians.

My plan will create a new and better reality for the State of Israel, and it also has the potential to create the right conditions to resume negotiations between Israel and the Palestinians.

I was encouraged by your positive response and your support for my plan.

In that context, you handed me a letter that includes very important statements regarding Israel's security and its wellbeing as a Jewish state.

You have proven, Mr. President, your ongoing, deep and sincere friendship to the State of Israel and to the Jewish people.

I believe that my plan can be an important contribution to advancing your vision, which is the only viable way to achieve peace and security in the Middle East.

I wish to end with a personal note.

I myself have been fighting terror for many years and understand the threats and costs from terrorism.

In all these years, I have never met a leader as committed as your are, Mr. President, to the struggle for freedom and the need to confront terrorism wherever it exists.

I want to express my appreciation to you, for your courageous leadership in the war against global terror and your commitment and vision to bring peace to the Middle East.

Thank you.

the White House
President George W. Bush

For Immediate Release
Office of the Press Secretary
April 14, 2004

5

Statement by the President

I remain hopeful and determined to find a way forward toward a resolution of the Israeli-Palestinian dispute.

The Israeli Plan:

I welcome the disengagement plan prepared by the Government of Israel, under which Israel would withdraw certain military installations and all settlements from Gaza, and withdraw certain military installations and settlements in the West Bank. These steps will mark real progress toward realizing the vision I set forth in June 2002 of two states living side by side in peace and security, and make a real contribution toward peace.

I am hopeful that steps pursuant to this plan, consistent with this vision, will remind all states and parties of their own obligations under the roadmap.

The Path to Peace:

I believe certain principles, which are very widely accepted in the international community, show us the path forward: The right of self defense and the need to fight terrorism are equally matters of international agreement. The two-state vision and the roadmap for peace designed to implement it, command nearly universal support as the best means of achieving a permanent peace and an end to the Israeli occupation that began in 1967. United Nations Security Council resolutions have repeatedly spoken of the desirability of establishing two independent states, Israel and Palestine, living side by side within secure and recognized borders.

Having these principles in mind, the United States is able to make the following comments.

Peace Plans:

The United States remains committed to the vision of two states living side by side in peace and security, and its implementation as described in the roadmap. The United States will do its utmost to prevent any attempt by anyone to impose any other plan.

Security:

There will be no security for Israelis or Palestinians until they and all states, in the region and beyond, join together to fight terrorism and dismantle terrorist organizations. The United States reiterates its steadfast commitment to Israel's security, including secure, defensible borders, and to preserve and strengthen Israel's capability to deter and defend itself, by itself, against any threat or possible combination of threats. The United States will join with others in the international community to strengthen the capacity and will of Palestinian security forces to fight terrorism and dismantle terrorist capabilities and infrastructure.

Terrorism:

Israel will retain its right to defend itself against terrorism, including to take actions against terrorist organizations. The United States will lead efforts, working together with Jordan, Egypt, and others in the international community, to build the capacity and will of Palestinian institutions to fight terrorism, dismantle terrorist organizations, and prevent the areas from which Israel has withdrawn from posing a threat that would have to be addressed by any other means. The United States understands that after Israel withdraws from Gaza and/or parts of the West Bank, and pending agreements on other arrangements, existing arrangements regarding control of airspace, territorial waters, and land passages of the West Bank and Gaza will continue.

The Two-State Solution:

The United States remains committed to the two-state solution for peace in the Middle East as set forth in June 2002, and to the roadmap as the best path to realize that vision.

The goal of two independent states has repeatedly been recognized in international resolutions and agreements, and it remains a key to resolving this conflict. The United States is strongly committed to Israel's security and well-being as a Jewish state. It seems clear that an agreed, just, fair and realistic framework for a solution to the Palestinian refugee issue as part of any final status agreement will need to be found through the establishment of a Palestinian state, and the settling of Palestinian refugees there, rather than in Israel.

As part of a final peace settlement, Israel must have secure and recognized borders, which should emerge from negotiations between the parties in accordance with UNSC Resolutions 242 and 338. In light of new realities on the ground, including already existing major Israeli populations centers, it is unrealistic to expect that the outcome of final status negotiations will be a full and complete return to the armistice lines of 1949, and all previous efforts to negotiate a two-state solution have reached the same conclusion. It is realistic to expect that any final status agreement will only be achieved on the basis of mutually agreed changes that reflect these realities.

Palestinian Statehood:

The United States supports the establishment of a Palestinian state that is viable, contiguous, sovereign, and independent, so that the Palestinian people can build their own future in accordance with the vision I set forth in June 2002 and with the path set forth in the roadmap. The United States will join with others in the international community to foster the development of democratic political institutions and new leadership committed to those institutions, the reconstruction of civic institutions, the growth of a free and prosperous economy, and the building of capable security institutions dedicated to maintaining law and order and dismantling terrorist organizations.

Palestinian Obligations:

Under the roadmap, Palestinians must undertake an immediate cessation of armed activity and all acts of violence against Israelis anywhere, and all official Palestinian institutions must end incitement against Israel. The Palestinian leadership must act decisively against terror, including sustained, targeted, and effective operations to stop terrorism and dismantle terrorist capabilities and infrastructure. Palestinians must undertake a comprehensive and fundamental political reform that includes a strong parliamentary democracy and an empowered Prime Minister.

Israeli Obligations:

The Government of Israel is committed to take additional steps on the West Bank, including progress toward a freeze on settlement activity, removing unauthorized outposts, and improving the humanitarian situation by easing restrictions on the movement of Palestinians not engaged in terrorist activities.

As the Government of Israel has stated, the barrier being erected by Israel should be a security rather than political barrier, should be temporary rather than permanent, and therefore not prejudice any final status issues including final borders, and its route should take into account, consistent with security needs, its impact on Palestinians not engaged in terrorist activities.

Regional Cooperation:

A peace settlement negotiated between Israelis and Palestinians would be a great boon not only to those peoples but to the peoples of the entire region. Accordingly, all states in the region have special responsibilities: to support the building of the institutions of a Palestinian state; to fight terrorism, and cut off all forms of assistance to individuals and groups engaged in terrorism; and to begin now to move toward more normal relations with the State of Israel. These actions would be true contributions to building peace in the region.

Prime Minister's Office
Communications Department

משרד ראש הממשלה
אגף התקשורת

6

Letter from Prime Minister Ariel Sharon to US President George W. Bush

April 14, 2004

The Honorable George W. Bush
President of the United States of America
The White House
Washington, D.C.

Dear Mr. President,

The vision that you articulated in your 24 June 2002 address constitutes one of the most significant contributions toward ensuring a bright future for the Middle East. Accordingly, the State of Israel has accepted the Roadmap, as adopted by our government. For the first time, a practical and just formula was presented for the achievement of peace, opening a genuine window of opportunity for progress toward a settlement between Israel and the Palestinians, involving two states living side-by-side in peace and security.

This formula sets forth the correct sequence and principles for the attainment of peace. Its full implementation represents the sole means to make genuine progress. As you have stated, a Palestinian state will never be created by terror, and Palestinians must engage in a sustained fight against the terrorists and dismantle their infrastructure. Moreover, there must be serious efforts to institute true reform and real democracy and liberty, including new leaders not compromised by terror. We are committed to this formula as the only avenue through which an agreement can be reached. We believe that this formula is the only viable one.

The Palestinian Authority under its current leadership has taken no action to meet its responsibilities under the Roadmap. Terror has not ceased, reform of the Palestinian security services has not been undertaken, and real institutional reforms have not taken place. The State of Israel continues to pay the heavy cost of constant terror. Israel must preserve its capability to protect itself and deter its enemies, and we thus retain our right to defend ourselves against terrorism and to take actions against terrorist organizations.

Having reached the conclusion that, for the time being, there exists no Palestinian partner with whom to advance peacefully toward a settlement and since the current impasse is unhelpful to the achievement of our shared goals, I have decided to initiate a process of gradual disengagement with the hope of reducing friction between Israelis and Palestinians. The Disengagement Plan is designed to improve security for Israel and stabilize our political and economic situation. It will enable us to deploy our forces more effectively until such time that conditions in the Palestinian Authority allow for the full implementation of the Roadmap to resume.

I attach, for your review, the main principles of the Disengagement Plan. This initiative, which we are not undertaking under the roadmap, represents an independent Israeli plan, yet is not inconsistent with the roadmap. According to this plan, the State of Israel intends to relocate military installations and all Israeli villages and towns in the Gaza Strip, as well as other military installations and a small number of villages in Samaria.

In this context, we also plan to accelerate construction of the Security Fence, whose completion is essential in order to ensure the security of the citizens of Israel. The fence is a security rather than political barrier, temporary rather than permanent, and therefore will not prejudice any final status issues including final borders. The route of the Fence, as approved by our GovernmentÂ's decisions, will take into account, consistent with security needs, its impact on Palestinians not engaged in terrorist activities.

Upon my return from Washington, I expect to submit this Plan for the approval of the Cabinet and the Knesset, and I firmly believe that it will win such approval.

The Disengagement Plan will create a new and better reality for the State of Israel, enhance its security and economy, and strengthen the fortitude of its people. In this context, I believe it is important to bring new opportunities to the Negev and the Galilee. Additionally, the Plan will entail a series of measures with the inherent potential to improve the lot of the Palestinian Authority, providing that it demonstrates the wisdom to take advantage of this opportunity. The execution of the Disengagement Plan holds the prospect of stimulating positive changes within the Palestinian Authority that might create the necessary conditions for the resumption of direct negotiations.

We view the achievement of a settlement between Israel and the Palestinians as our central focus and are committed to realizing this objective. Progress toward this goal must be anchored exclusively in the Roadmap and we will oppose any other plan.

In this regard, we are fully aware of the responsibilities facing the State of Israel. These include limitations on the growth of settlements; removal of unauthorized outposts; and steps to increase, to the extent permitted by security needs, freedom of movement for Palestinians not engaged in terrorism. Under separate cover we are sending to you a full description of the steps the State of Israel is taking to meet all its responsibilities.

The government of Israel supports the United States efforts to reform the Palestinian security services to meet their roadmap obligations to fight terror. Israel also supports the American's efforts, working with the International Community, to promote the reform process, build institutions and improve the economy of the Palestinian Authority and to enhance the welfare of its people, in the hope that a new Palestinian leadership will prove able to fulfill its obligations under the roadmap.

I want to again express my appreciation for your courageous leadership in the war against global terror, your important initiative to revitalize the Middle East as a more fitting home for its people and, primarily, your personal friendship and profound support for the State of Israel.

Sincerely,

Ariel Sharon

the White House
President George W. Bush

7

Letter from US President George W. Bush to Prime Minister Ariel Sharon

April 14, 2004

His Excellency
Ariel Sharon
Prime Minister of Israel

Dear Mr. Prime Minister,

Thank you for your letter setting out your disengagement plan.

The United States remains hopeful and determined to find a way forward toward a resolution of the Israeli-Palestinian dispute. I remain committed to my June 24, 2002 vision of two states living side by side in peace and security as the key to peace, and to the roadmap as the route to get there.

We welcome the disengagement plan you have prepared, under which Israel would withdraw certain military installations and all settlements from Gaza, and withdraw certain military installations and settlements in the West Bank. These steps described in the plan will mark real progress toward realizing my June 24, 2002 vision, and make a real contribution towards peace. We also understand that, in this context, Israel believes it is important to bring new opportunities to the Negev and the Galilee. We are hopeful that steps pursuant to this plan, consistent with my vision, will remind all states and parties of their own obligations under the roadmap.

The United States appreciates the risks such an undertaking represents. I therefore want to reassure you on several points.

First, the United States remains committed to my vision and to its implementation as described in the roadmap. The United States will do its utmost to prevent any attempt by anyone to impose any other plan. Under the roadmap,

Palestinians must undertake an immediate cessation of armed activity and all acts of violence against Israelis anywhere, and all official Palestinian institutions must end incitement against Israel. The Palestinian leadership must act decisively against terror, including sustained, targeted, and effective operations to stop terrorism and dismantle terrorist capabilities and infrastructure. Palestinians must undertake a comprehensive and fundamental political reform that includes a strong parliamentary democracy and an empowered Prime Minister.

Second, there will be no security for Israelis or Palestinians until they and all states, in the region and beyond, join together to fight terrorism and dismantle terrorist organizations. The United States reiterates its steadfast commitment to Israel's security, including secure, defensible borders, and to preserve and strengthen Israel's capability to deter and defend itself, by itself, against any threat or possible combination of threats.

Third, Israel will retain its right to defend itself against terrorism, including to take actions against terrorist organizations. The United States will lead efforts, working together with Jordan, Egypt, and others in the international community, to build the capacity and will of Palestinian institutions to fight terrorism, dismantle terrorist organizations, and prevent the areas from which Israel has withdrawn from posing a threat that would have to be addressed by any other means. The United States understands that after Israel withdraws from Gaza and/or parts of the West Bank, and pending agreements on other arrangements, existing arrangements regarding control of airspace, territorial waters, and land passages of the West Bank and Gaza will continue.

The United States is strongly committed to Israel's security and well-being as a Jewish state. It seems clear that an agreed, just, fair and realistic framework for a solution to the Palestinian refugee issue as part of any final status agreement will need to be found through the establishment of a Palestinian state, and the settling of Palestinian refugees there, rather than in Israel.

As part of a final peace settlement, Israel must have secure and recognized borders, which should emerge from negotiations between the parties in accordance with UNSC Resolutions 242 and 338. In light of new realities on the ground, including already existing major Israeli populations centers, it is unrealistic to expect that the outcome of final status negotiations will be a full and complete return to the armistice lines of 1949, and all previous efforts to negotiate a two-state solution have reached the same conclusion. It is realistic to expect that any final status agreement will only be achieved on the basis of mutually agreed changes that reflect these realities.

I know that, as you state in your letter, you are aware that certain responsibilities face the State of Israel. Among these, your government has stated that the barrier being erected by Israel should be a security rather than political barrier, should be temporary rather than permanent, and therefore not prejudice any final status issues including final borders, and its route should take into account, consistent with security needs, its impact on Palestinians not engaged in terrorist activities.

As you know, the United States supports the establishment of a Palestinian state that is viable, contiguous, sovereign, and independent, so that the Palestinian people can build their own future in accordance with my vision set forth in June 2002 and with the path set forth in the roadmap. The United States will join with others in the international community to foster the development of democratic political institutions and new leadership committed to those institutions, the reconstruction of civic institutions, the growth of a free and prosperous economy, and the building of capable security institutions dedicated to maintaining law and order and dismantling terrorist organizations.

A peace settlement negotiated between Israelis and Palestinians would be a great boon not only to those peoples but to the peoples of the entire region. Accordingly, the United States believes that all states in the region have special responsibilities: to support the building of the institutions of a Palestinian state; to fight terrorism, and cut off all forms of assistance to individuals and groups engaged in terrorism; and to begin now to move toward more normal relations with the State of Israel. These actions would be true contributions to building peace in the region.

Mr. Prime Minister, you have described a bold and historic initiative that can make an important contribution to peace. I commend your efforts and your courageous decision which I support. As a close friend and ally, the United States intends to work closely with you to help make it a success.

Sincerely,

George W. Bush

Prime Minister's Office
Communications Department

משרד ראש הממשלה
אגף התקשורת

8

Address by Prime Minister Ariel Sharon to the Conference of Presidents of Major American Jewish Organizations

February 20, 2005

Mr. Jim Tisch, Chairman of the Conference of Presidents, Mr. Malcolm Hoenlein, Executive Vice Chairman of the Conference of Presidents,

Dear Friends,

Good evening. It is my great pleasure to welcome you here to Jerusalem, the eternal capital of the Jewish people and the united capital of the State of Israel forever.

I arrived here today directly from the meeting of the Government, a meeting in which an historic decision was made to implement the Disengagement Plan. Accordingly, with your permission, I would like to say a few words in Hebrew:

[TRANSLATED FROM HEBREW]

Today, the State of Israel took a decisive step for its future. The Government of Israel approved my proposal, and resolved to relocate the Israeli communities from the Gaza Strip and four communities in northern Samaria.

60 years have passed since I began to serve the people of Israel, beginning when I served as a company commander in B Company of the 32nd

Battalion of the Alexandroni Brigade until I gained the trust of the people when I was elected Prime Minister 4 years ago. During all those years, I made hundreds, if not thousands, of decisions. Many of them were fateful ones, some were life and death decisions. However, the decision regarding the Disengagement Plan was, for me, the most difficult one of all.

I accompanied the settlers of the Gaza Strip when I served as Head of the Southern Command, and then as a minister in the Governments of Israel. I was privileged to see the first greenhouse erected, the first field planted, homes built and children born. I was with them in their difficult moments, in their daily concerns of security needs, in their courageous stand when faced with mortar fire and terrorist attacks. As Prime Minister, as a citizen of the State of Israel, as a farmer - I am proud of them for their accomplishments, I am proud of them for their courage, I am proud of them for their great love of the land.

However, there are moments which demand leadership, determination and responsibility, even if it does not seem popular, even if the decision is difficult. My task as Prime Minister and our task as a Government is to see the big picture. In the wider view, the Disengagement Plan ensures the future of the State of Israel as a Jewish and democratic state, fortifies our security, strengthens our economy, improves our international standing and promotes the chance of peace in our region. The decision which the Government of Israel made today was a difficult one - a very difficult one. However, it is a decision of hope for the citizens of Israel - hope for a better future for all of us.

[CONTINUING IN ENGLISH]

I would like to thank you for being here in Israel and showing your solidarity. We are at a critical hour for Israeli society and its unity. In this sensitive and complicated period, there is great importance to the support and solidarity of the Jewish communities for the State of Israel. Your support of the State of Israel, your standing by our side, is important now, maybe more than ever.

Last Wednesday, the Knesset passed, by a large majority, the law which will allow for the implementation of the Disengagement Plan. And as I stated earlier, today my Government voted in favor of the implementation of the Plan. In light of these two decisions, we are now proceeding forward with preparations to leave the Gaza Strip; a process which will begin five months from today.

I said before in Hebrew that in all my years of service, I have made hundreds, if not thousands, of decisions, many in regards to life and death. But the decision about the Disengagement Plan is the most difficult of all. However, I am convinced that the step which was taken today is the right one in ensuring the future of Israel as a Jewish democratic state. It is the correct step to take as we aim to better our economy, strengthen our security and improve our international standing. The Disengagement Plan gives the Israeli people hope for a better future - hope for a better Israel.

We have many dreams and goals. We wish to absorb millions of new immigrants. We wish to be a place where all Jewish youth dream of realizing their future. We wish to stand as a symbol of pride to all Jews around the world. There is much work to be done in reaching these goals, but I am sure that today we took a big step forward in the fulfillment of this dream.

Two weeks ago, I stood in Sharm el-Sheikh alongside the President of Egypt, Mr. Hosni Mubarak, King Abdullah II of Jordan and the Chairman of the Palestinian Authority, Mr. Mahmoud Abbas. We agreed that there are many steps which we must take to advance the Middle East. In todayâ€™s Government decision, Israel proved that it is willing to make painful compromises and take great steps towards achieving peace. I said that many times, and I would like to repeat it today.

For a genuine and real peace, we are willing to make many painful compromises. But there is one thing we are not willing to make any compromise on, not now and not in the future. That is when it comes to the security of Israeli citizens and the security of the State of Israel. I say it there, and I will say it here again - when it comes to security, we are not going to make any compromises whatsoever. Not now, and not in the future. We hope that our neighbors will also have the courage to take bold steps. If each party takes the necessary steps, then a peaceful Middle East is a real possibility for the future. And I believe that we can realize this future.

Thank you

Prime Minister's Office
Communications Department

משרד ראש הממשלה
אגף התקשורת

9

Prime Minister Ariel Sharon's Speech at the United Nations Assembly

September 15, 2005

Translation

My friends and colleagues, heads and representatives of the UN member states,

I arrived here from Jerusalem, the capital of the Jewish people for over 3,000 years, and the undivided and eternal capital of the State of Israel.

At the outset, I would like to express the profound feelings of empathy of the people of Israel for the American nation, and our sincere condolences to the families who lost their loved ones. I wish to encourage my friend, President George Bush, and the American people, in their determined efforts to assist the victims of the hurricane and rebuild the ruins after the destruction. The State of Israel, which the United States stood beside at times of trial, is ready to extend any assistance at its disposal in this immense humanitarian mission.

Ladies and Gentlemen,

I stand before you at the gate of nations as a Jew and as a citizen of the democratic, free and sovereign State of Israel, a proud representative of an ancient people, whose numbers are few, but whose contribution to civilization and to the values of ethics, justice and faith, surrounds the world and encompasses history. The Jewish people have a long memory, the memory which united the exiles of Israel for thousands of years: a memory which has its origin in G-d's commandment to our forefather Abraham: "Go forth!" and continued with the receiving of the Torah at the foot of Mount Sinai and the wanderings of the children of Israel in the desert, led by Moses on their journey to the promised land, the land of Israel.

I was born in the Land of Israel, the son of pioneers – people who tilled the land and sought no fights – who did not come to Israel to dispossess its residents. If the circumstances had not demanded it, I would not have become a soldier, but rather a farmer and agriculturist. My first love was, and remains, manual labor; sowing and harvesting, the pastures, the flock and the cattle.

I, as someone whose path of life led him to be a fighter and commander in all Israel's wars, reaches out today to our Palestinian neighbors in a call for reconciliation and compromise to end the bloody conflict, and embark on the path which leads to peace and understanding between our peoples. I view this as my calling and my primary mission for the coming years.

The land of Israel is precious to me, precious to us, the Jewish people, more than anything. Relinquishing any part of our forefathers' legacy is heartbreaking, as difficult as the parting of the Red Sea. Every inch of land, every hill and valley, every stream and rock, is saturated with Jewish history, replete with memories. The continuity of Jewish presence in the Land of Israel never ceased. Even those of us who were exiled from our land, against their will, to the ends of the earth – their souls, for all generations, remained connected to their homeland, by thousands of hidden threads of yearning and love, expressed three times a day in prayer and songs of longing.

The Land of Israel is the open Bible, the written testimony, the identity and right of the Jewish people. Under its skies, the prophets of Israel expressed their claims for social justice, and their eternal vision for alliances between peoples, in a world which would know no more war. Its cities, villages, vistas, ridges, deserts and plains preserve as loyal witnesses its ancient Hebrew names. Page after page, our unique land is unfurled, and at its heart is united Jerusalem, the city of the Temple upon Mount Moriah, the axis of the life of the Jewish people throughout all generations, and the seat of its yearnings and prayers for 3,000 years. The city to which we pledged an eternal vow of faithfulness, which forever beats in every Jewish heart: "If I forget thee, O Jerusalem, may my right hand forget its cunning!"

I say these things to you because they are the essence of my Jewish consciousness, and of my belief in the eternal and unimpeachable right of the people of Israel to the Land of Israel. However, I say this here also to emphasize the immensity of the pain I feel deep in my heart at the recognition that we have to make concessions for the sake of peace between us and our Palestinian neighbors.

The right of the Jewish people to the Land of Israel does not mean disregarding the rights of others in the land. The Palestinians will always be our neighbors. We respect them, and have no aspirations to rule over them. They are also entitled to freedom and to a national, sovereign existence in a state of their own.

This week, the last Israeli soldier left the Gaza Strip, and military law there was ended. The State of Israel proved that it is ready to make painful concessions in order to resolve the conflict with the Palestinians. The decision to disengage was very difficult for me, and involves a heavy personal price. However, it is the absolute recognition that it is the right path for the future of Israel that guided me. Israeli society is undergoing a difficult crisis as a result of the Disengagement, and now needs to heal the rifts.

Now it is the Palestinians' turn to prove their desire for peace. The end of Israeli control over and responsibility for the Gaza Strip allows the Palestinians, if they so wish, to develop their economy and build a peace-seeking society, which is developed, free, law-abiding, transparent, and which adheres to democratic principles. The most important test the Palestinian leadership will face is in fulfilling their commitment to put an end to terror and its infrastructures, eliminate the anarchic regime of armed gangs, and cease the incitement and indoctrination of hatred towards Israel and the Jews.

Until they do so – Israel will know how to defend itself from the horrors of terrorism. This is why we built the Security Fence, and we will continue to build it until it is completed, as would any other country defending its citizens. The Security Fence prevents terrorists and murderers from arriving in city centers on a daily basis and targeting citizens on their way to work, children on their way to school and families sitting together in restaurants. This Fence is vitally indispensable. This Fence saves lives!

The successful implementation of the Disengagement Plan opens up a window of opportunity for advancing towards peace, in accordance with the sequence of the Roadmap. The State of Israel is committed to the Roadmap and to the implementation of the Sharm El-Sheikh understandings. And I hope that it will be possible, through them, to renew the political process.

I am among those who believe that it is possible to reach a fair compromise and coexistence in good neighborly relations between Jews and Arabs. However, I must emphasize one fact: there will be no compromise on the right of the State of Israel to exist as a Jewish state, with defensible borders, in full security and without threats and terror.

I call on the Palestinian leadership to show determination and leadership, and to eliminate terror, violence and the culture of hatred from our relations. I am certain that it is in our power to present our peoples with a new and promising horizon, a horizon of hope.

Distinguished representatives,

As I mentioned, the Jewish people have a long memory. We remember events which took place thousands of years ago, and certainly remember events which took place in this hall during the last 60 years. The Jewish people remember the dramatic vote in the UN Assembly on November 29, 1947, when representatives of the nations recognized our right to national revival in our historic homeland. However, we also remember dozens of harsh and unjust decisions made by United Nations over the years. And we know that, even today, there are those who sit here as representatives of a country whose leadership calls to wipe Israel off the face of the earth, and no one speaks out.

The attempts of that country to arm itself with nuclear weapons must disturb the sleep of anyone who desires peace and stability in the Middle East and the entire world. The combination of murky fundamentalism and support of terrorist organizations creates a serious threat that every member nation in the UN must stand against.

I hope that the comprehensive reforms which the United Nations is undergoing in its 60th anniversary year will include a fundamental change and improvement in the approach of the United Nations, its organizations and institutions, towards the State of Israel.

My fellow colleagues and representatives,
Peace is a supreme value in the Jewish legacy, and is the desired goal of our policy. After the long journey of wanderings and the hardships of the Jewish people; after the Holocaust which obliterated one third of our people; after the long and arduous struggle for revival; after more than 57 consecutive years of war and terror which did not stop the development of the State of

Israel; after all this – our heart's desire was and remains to achieve peace with our neighbors. Our desire for peace is strong enough to ensure that we will achieve it, only if our neighbors are genuine partners in this longed-for goal. If we succeed in working together, we can transform our plot of land, which is dear to both peoples, from a land of contention to a land of peace – for our children and grandchildren.

In a few days time on the Hebrew calendar, the New Year will begin, the $5,766^{th}$ year since the Creation. According to Jewish belief, the fates of people and nations are determined at the New Year by the Creator – to be spared or to be doomed. May the Holy One, blessed be He, determine that this year, our fate and the fate of our neighbors is peace, mutual respect and good neighborly relations.

From this distinguished podium, on behalf of the people of Israel, I wish all the people of the world a happy New Year.

Shana Tova!

Prime Minister's Office
Communications Department

משרד ראש הממשלה
אגף התקשורת

10

Address by Prime Minister Ariel Sharon 10th Commemoration of the Assassination of Yitzhak Rabin - The Knesset

November 14, 2005
Translation

Rabin Family,
Mr. Speaker,
Distinguished Knesset,

There is no grown man or woman in this country who does not remember where they were or what they did on the night of the murder. We all stood frozen, stunned, at the bitter news - refusing at first to believe that such a crime could take place here.

And just like Job, we too wished that "that night be desolate", but we do not have the right. On the contrary, that night must be remembered. We must remember what hatred, fanaticism and intolerance can breed.

Israeli society, despite the magnificent achievements it has made in its 58 years of existence - is still a society in formation. There are no shortcuts in the maturation process of a society which is, to a large extent, an immigrant society. The Israeli democracy is a genuine source of pride, but still it must confront threats emanating from the ongoing process of integration between cultures, denominations, factions and sectors - on all their diverse traditions.

Amos Oz wrote, "Democracy, of necessity, involves people's right to be different from one another. The difference between people is not a fleeting evil, but a source of blessing - we are different from one another not because some of us have not yet seen the light, but because in this world there are lights and not one light: faiths and convictions, and not one faith or one conviction".

Jewish tradition has always valued diversity. In Succoth a person does not fulfil his/her obligation until all Four Varieties are in his/her hand as a single bundle. In the Four Varieties each one is different – and the commandment is to bind them all together, not despite their diverseness, but because of it. Because of the mutual enrichment which diversity creates and because only in the "togetherness" can there be full representation to all segments of the nation.

Despite the great diversity in Israeli society, it has, in the past year, successfully withstood one of the most important and difficult tests in its history. Various forces tried to question the authority of our elected institutes – the Government and the Knesset – to make decisions and carry them out. These attempts did not succeed.

The apocalyptic prophecies regarding a civil war which would involve casualties – have all been refuted. And disobedience – an affliction which threatened to undermine the foundations of our democracy and endanger our unity – ultimately turned out to be marginal.

However, as in any campaign, yesterday's achievement does not guarantee tomorrow's victory, and the road to a mature society which resolves its internal disputes democratically is still long and challenging.

I often quote a statement made by Yitzhak Rabin in 1993 on the way to reaching this goal, and I quote: "even if we do not see eye to eye, even if there are disagreements – even if there are differences and nuances, it is good and important to argue, but also to grit our teeth, bite our lips and continue together, in order to reach our common goal, when the good of the country takes precedence over any personal or political consideration".

The terrible murder of Yitzhak Rabin is a warning sign to us all, showing what might happen if we prefer that which divides and separates us over that which unites us and brings us together.

Beyond political disagreements, beyond the various viewpoints in Israeli society, beyond the differences of tradition and the variety of opinions – the decisive majority of the people of Israel is united in its love for this land and its loyalty to the State.

Therefore, I am confident that all components of Israeli society will be able to identify the goal, which is common to us all, beyond the sea of disagreements and the mosaic which comprises our society.

Thank you.

Prime Minister's Office
Communications Department

משרד ראש הממשלה
אגף התקשורת

11

Address by Interim Prime Minister Ehud Olmert Opening Ceremony of the Holocaust Martyrs and Heroes Remembrance Day

April 24, 2006

Translation

Honorable President and Mrs. Katzav,
Holocaust survivors and their families,
Distinguished Guests,

A Jew who steps on European soil feels an invisible cloud in the depth of his soul. Under his feet are the traces of a culturally-rich Jewish presence with remarkable heritage, which was wiped out in an instant. Above him are skies tainted by ineradicable smoke. A warning and indictment hangs in the air, with only one word written on it: "remember!"

What did the damned Nazis have with the Jews? Why were they so intent on exterminating our people? Why did they allocate resources, manpower and an intricate organizational system for this purpose, at the expense of the war effort? What was the point of pursuing and persisting with this until the end, even when their defeat was no longer in question? Could the persecuted, tormented nation, crushed under the boots of the oppressor, have stopped the galloping German war train? How many divisions did the Jewish communities in Europe have? How many tanks, fighter-planes, rifles? Poet Uri Zvi Greenberg was right in saying that the Jewish people in Europe had "millions of men, but not one sword"!

It was that we, the Jews, were a horrible threat in the eyes of the Hitlerian regime. Not a military threat, of course, but a moral one. Opposite the lust for blood and satanic racist oppression, opposite the desecration of every humanistic or civilized value, opposite the denial of the image of G-d in man and triumph of good over evil – was the Jewish person, stripped of weapons, holding only the two Tablets of the Covenant and the Bible. "Thou shalt not murder!", he said, "love thy neighbor as thyself", "seek and pursue peace!". He drove the Nazis mad.

This innocent Jew was transformed by the Nazis into a demon, a subhuman monster. They labeled him a reptile, parasite, crawling rat, disease spreader. This pure-hearted Jew, who was armed with nothing but a prayer book, a *talit* and *teffilin*, evoked the murderous fury of the Nazis. He reminded them by his very presence what they sought to forget, make others forget and completely root out of human civilization: the values of justice, equality, grace and faith. The "God's candle human soul", which the Nazis sought to extinguish forever.

As a Jew, I always carry in my heart the seal of pain over the Holocaust of my brothers and sisters. But I am proud that we are the sworn enemy of the Nazi evil; I am proud of the heritage of our forefathers which is the absolute contradiction of the Hitlerian racial and murder doctrine; and I am proud of the founding of the State of Israel – the definitive moral answer to the enemy's scheme.

Anti-Semitism, tyranny, lust for murder and terrorism have not passed forever. Even today, they hang over the head of the free world as a Sword of Damocles. The lesson of World War II is that appeasement, surrender and weakness are a recipe for Holocaust. Only a determined and firm moral stand, only willingness to fight for and protect liberty will guarantee the future of humanity.

Poet Yehuda Amihai, a son of Jerusalem, wrote:

"The forest of remembrance in which we loved was consumed by great fire.

But we remained alive and loving.

In memory of the burned forest and in memory of those who were burned, those remembered by the forest".

The State of Israel carries the memory of the burning, and Yad Vashem is for those who burned. It knows what the hatred of Jews generated in the past, it watches with open eyes the carnival of enmity taking place around it, and it has learned the lesson. The State of Israel has the ability to defend itself, but it calls upon the free world to stand with it in the battle to preserve light and liberty, and protect the values of justice and the image of man.

It calls upon every free and conscientious person to remember, and every peace-seeking nation, never to forget!

Prime Minister's Office
Communications Department

משרד ראש הממשלה
אגף התקשורת

12

Address by Interim Prime Minister Ehud Olmert On Presenting the New Government to the Knesset

May 4, 2006
Translation

Mr. President and Mrs. Katsav,
Speaker of the 17th Knesset, MK Dalia Itzik,
Outgoing Members of the Government,
New Members of the Government,
Members of Knesset,
Distinguished Guests,

Congratulations to you, Madam Speaker, on your election to this prestigious role. This is the first time in the history of the State of Israel that a female member of Knesset is serving as Speaker. You are deserving of this position. For many years, you have served in senior positions in the Knesset and the Government. You are very familiar with the halls and procedures of this institution, the heart of Israeli democracy. Now, you have been given an amazing opportunity to shape its future proceedings, and determine, together with the members of Knesset, the patterns of work, relationships and content which will leave their mark on public life and the system of government of the State of Israel in the coming years. I wish you, on my own behalf and on behalf of the members of Knesset, luck in this important and demanding position.

Members of Knesset,

On April 6, 2006, the President assigned me the task of forming the Government. At the conclusion of the coalition negotiations, conducted with wisdom and responsibility by teams from the various parties, agreements were signed and the new Government's basic guidelines were drafted – they are now before you.

At the beginning of the week, I informed the President that I had succeeded in forming a government. In recognition of this great privilege and heavy responsibility, in modesty and humility, I ask today for the Knesset's vote of confidence in the Government that I am presenting.

In the outgoing Government, it was my privilege to serve as Acting Prime Minister for Prime Minister Ariel Sharon. I stood beside him in times of uncertainty and fateful decisions, and I admired his courage, equanimity and powerful leadership. Even when everything around him was stormy and turbulent, Arik remained in the eye of the storm, quiet and confident, his hand holding the wheel steady and focused. His successful term as Prime Minister will be remembered as a founding chapter in the annals of the State.

Unfortunately, after he led the State of Israel as a loved and admired Prime Minister, and led us to remarkable achievements in a bold and far-sighted policy, Ariel Sharon's health failed. From here, on behalf of the Government of Israel, in the name of the Knesset and the citizens of Israel, I express my hope and prayer that Ariel Sharon will live to see the realization of his political vision.

Yesterday, the State of Israel celebrated its 58th Independence Day. How great is the difference between the situation that the people of Israel were in on May 14, 1948 and our situation today. At the time of the Declaration of the Establishment of the State we stood, only three years after the Holocaust, with our backs to the wall. With meager resources and weaponry, we stood in a desperate military defensive against an invasion, whose declared purpose was the eradication of the newly born state. We were but a step away from extinction. The pages of history of the State of Israel since then are full of heroism, sacrifice, magnificent creation, construction, settlement, massive immigration absorption and a free and enlightened democratic government. The cycle of hostility around us, the war and terrorism, bereavement and pain, did not cease for one minute and did not stop the bursting vitality and the progress and prosperity of the State of Israel. This miracle is unprecedented in the history of nations.

From its birth, the State of Israel advocated two founding bases – the Jewish base and the democratic base: the supreme value of a "Jewish state", at the same time with the uncompromising demand that the democratic state of Israel will provide "complete social and political equality to all its citizens, regardless of religion, race or gender". These two bases embody the core values of the renewed Jewish sovereignty in the land of Israel. If you take one and disconnect if from the state, it is as if you cut off its lifeline.

Therefore, those wishing to look directly into our past, see the reality of our lives and look to the future, must do so with both eyes open – the Jewish eye and the democratic eye. Only then, with both eyes open, do the colors of Israeli society come together into one clear, vivid and meaningful picture.

I, like many others, also dreamed and yearned that we would be able to keep the entire land of Israel, and that the day would never come when we would have to relinquish parts of our land. Only those who have the land of Israel burning in their souls know the pain of relinquishing and parting with the land of our forefathers. I personally continue to advocate the idea of the entire land of Israel as a heart's desire. I believe with all my heart in the people of Israel's eternal historic right to the entire land of Israel. However, dreams and recognition of this right do not constitute a political program. Even if the Jewish eye cries, and even if our hearts are broken, we must preserve the essence. We must preserve a stable and solid Jewish majority in our State.

Therefore, we must focus on the area in which a Jewish majority is secured and ensured. The disengagement from the Gaza Strip and Northern Samaria was an essential first step in this direction, but the main part is still ahead. The continued dispersed settlement throughout Judea and Samaria creates an inseparable mixture of populations which will endanger the existence of the State of Israel as a Jewish state. It is those who believe, as I do, in Jabotinsky's teachings and in full civil equality between Jews and Arabs, who must understand that partition of the land for the purpose of guaranteeing a Jewish majority is the lifeline of Zionism. I know how hard it is, especially for the settlers and those faithful to *Eretz Yisrael*, but I am convinced, with all my heart, that it is necessary and that we must do it with dialogue, internal reconciliation and broad consensus.

This does not mean that the settlement enterprise was entirely in vain. On the contrary. The achievements of the settlement movement in its major centers will forever be an inseparable part of the sovereign State of Israel, with Jerusalem as our united capital. Let us come together around this consensus and turn it into a uniting political and moral fact.

The strength of this nation is in its unity. I will not help those wishing to cause a rift among the sectors of our nation. It is my intention to take all future steps through continuous dialogue with the wonderful settlers in Judea and Samaria. We are brothers and we will remain brothers.

From this podium, I again address the elected President of the Palestinian Authority, Mr. Mahmoud Abbas. The Government of Israel under my leadership prefers negotiations with a Palestinian Authority committed to the principles of the Roadmap, which fights terror, dismantles terrorist organizations, abides by the rules of democracy and upholds, practically and thoroughly, all agreements which have thus far been signed with the State of Israel. Negotiation with such an Authority is the most stable and desired basis for the political process, which can lead to an agreement which will bring peace. This is what we desire.

The guidelines of this Government propose this. The parliamentary majority which will back the Government policy is committed to this process. These conditions cannot be blurred. We will not, under any circumstances, relinquish these demands as a basis for negotiation.

The Palestinian Authority must make fundamental changes in its patterns of behavior, its reactions and its commitments to the principles which are the basis for any future negotiations.

A Palestinian Government led by terrorist factions will not be a partner for negotiation, and we will not have any practical or day-to-day relations.

The State of Israel is prepared to wait for this necessary change in the Palestinian Authority. We will closely follow the conduct of the Authority. We will continue to strike at terror and terrorists. We will not hesitate to reach terrorists, their dispatchers and operators anywhere – I repeat – anywhere, but we will give the Authority an opportunity to prove that it is aware of its responsibilities and willing to change.

That said, we will not wait forever. The State of Israel does not want, nor can it suspend the fateful decisions regarding its future – until the Palestinian Authority succeeds in implementing the commitments it undertook in the past. If we reach the conclusion that the Authority is dawdling and is not planning to engage in serious, substantial and fair negotiation – we will act in other ways.

We will also act without an agreement with the Palestinians to create an understanding which will, first and foremost, be founded on a correct definition of the desired borders for the State of Israel.

These borders must be defensible, and ensure a solid Jewish majority. The Security Fence will be adjusted to the borders formulated east and west. The operational range of the security forces will not be limited, and will be in accordance with the security reality with which we have to deal.

The State of Israel will invest its resources in areas which will be an organic part of it. The borders of Israel, which will be defined in the coming years will be significantly different from the areas controlled by the State of Israel today.

This is the Government's plan, it is the basis for its existence, it is the commitment made to the Israeli electorate whose trust we asked for – and received.

The agreement to which we aspire to shape the Middle East is based on consensus, broad consensus first and foremost within ourselves, and thereafter with our friends around the world.

No political process, certainly not one as fundamentally decisive and comprehensive as the one for which we are preparing, can be realized without the understanding of many officials in the international community. We have no intention of acting alone. We will consult, discuss, talk, and I am certain that we will reach understandings which will create a broad base of international backing for these steps, first and foremost with our ally and close friend, the United States led by President George Bush, and also with our friends in Europe.

Israel strives to improve the understandings and agreements with the countries of Europe. Today's European leaders better understand the complexity of the situation in the Middle East. They understand that there are no simple solutions, certainly given the upswing in fundamentalist religious fanaticism in various countries in the Middle East, and the ascendancy of the pro-Iranian Hamas to the Palestinian Authority. We will deepen dialogue with Europe and strive to include its leaders in the dialogue process with the United States.

I aspire to deepen the ties with Arab countries. Egypt and Jordan, countries with which we have peaceful relations, have leaders who are inspirational. President Mubarak and King Abdullah the Second are welcome, credible and responsible partners – for those goals which I defined. I will do all that I can so that our relations with Egypt and the Jordanian Kingdom will continue to strengthen, and serve as a basis for diplomatic and open relations with additional Arab countries.

The threat emanating from Iran is casting a heavy pall over the entire region and is endangering world peace. The pursuit by this rogue and terror-sponsoring regime of nuclear weapons is currently the most dangerous global development, and the international community must do its utmost to stop it. The statements by the President of Iran should not be taken lightly - he means what he says. The State of Israel, which is targeted for destruction by the evil leaders of Tehran, is not helpless. However, only a decisive and uncompromising international stand against Iran's goals can eliminate this threat to world peace.

Members of Knesset,

The domestic arena in Israel necessitates in-depth transformation. The State of Israel must place at the top of its agenda the good of the citizen - the newborn baby, the pupil, the soldier, the student, the working man and the elderly. The citizens' right to live in dignity, to receive better service from the State institutions and to enjoy economic well-being by reaping the fruits of their labor, should always be borne in mind.

Following the Declaration of the Establishment of the State, Menachem Begin said: "In our nation, justice will be the supreme ruler, the ruler of all rulers. There will be no tyranny, the public servants will serve society and not dominate it. There will be no parasitism. There will be no exploitation. No one in our homes - be it a citizen or a gentile - will be hungry or homeless or unclothed or deprived of basic education. 'And remember that thou was a servant in the land of Egypt'. This supreme decree will determine our approach towards our neighbor. "And thou shalt pursue justice" - this supreme decree will guide the relations between our people".

This concept will guide us in our attitude towards every citizen, either Jewish or non-Jewish. The rights of the minority are craving to be fulfilled, and we will act vigorously to fulfill them.

The gaps within Israeli society are unacceptable. The continued trend of widening gaps is a sure recipe for loss of social solidarity. The State of Israel will lose its moral standing if it evades its responsibility towards the weaker populations - the elderly, the pensioners, the Holocaust survivors, the disabled, the ailing, the children at risk, battered women and those targeted for illegal trade - all those needing protection and assistance, including the children of foreign workers who grow up among us and love our country, and wish to be part of it. It is not only our duty towards them. It is first and foremost our duty towards our moral standards. The Government will act tirelessly to reduce social and economic gaps. We will formulate a detailed plan to combat social hardship, act to improve the health system and particularly the health basket components. We will continue adhering to the correct economic policy, with the aim of diminishing unemployment and creating a climate which will enable more members of Israeli society to join the labor market and earn a decent living.

In recent years, harsh violence has become part of our daily routine – stabbings in places of recreation, hooliganism on Israel's roads and city streets, rapes, robbery and murders. Israeli society must defend itself. We must place the personal safety of the citizens of Israel at the top of our agenda. The Government will act tirelessly to uproot violence. We will combat crime and violence – which constitute domestic terrorism – with the same determination with which we fight terrorism from the outside. The Government will uphold the rule of law, and act to eradicate corruption from all areas of our lives, including corruption in government authorities and public apparatuses, and will protect, with all its might, those involved in enforcing the law, first and foremost, the courts, and especially the Supreme Court of the State of Israel.

Members of Knesset,

Road accidents are a national calamity. The Government will immediately begin implementing the national program to combat road accidents. We will make certain that the roads are a safe place for the citizens of Israel.

The Government will act to improve the education system, from nursery school to higher education. The education system must provide knowledge and skills which are instrumental to functioning in a modern world: analytical skills, creativity and teaching of the values of the State of Israel as a Jewish and democratic state. We will also act to deepen and bolster Jewish education in State schools. We cannot speak of a Jewish state without having its content known to each and every student. In conjunction with formal education, we will strive to enhance informal education, primarily the Zionist youth movements which must regain their natural place as pioneers leading Israeli youth.

Over the last 15 years, the State of Israel has experienced a tremendous wave of immigration from countries belonging to the former Soviet Union. This immigration was a great blessing to the State of Israel. The immigrants from the former Soviet Union are now an essential component of the total strength of Israeli society. Their contribution is dramatic – culturally, academically, industrially, in technological innovation, security, medicine and education. We are proud of the immigrants, and embrace them to our hearts with love and gratitude. Continued immigration is an important element of the growth and prosperity of the Israeli economy and society and the consolidation of our national security. We will act to strengthen our bond with our Jewish brothers in the Diaspora, particularly with the younger generation.

Jerusalem as the capital of Israel will "be elevated above the chief joy" of the Government. We will work to transform Jerusalem into the political, cultural and business center of the State of Israel and the entire Jewish people.

The Government will act to develop the Negev and the Galilee and consider them as areas of national priority. The national plan to develop the Negev and the future plan to develop the Galilee will create a real revolution in these areas. It is a huge challenge which the Government takes upon itself, with a sense of mission.

The Government will continue to uphold the principles which guided its economic policy over the last few years, and will especially preserve fiscal discipline, maintain deficit growth of no more than 3%, and an overall spending ceiling yet be determined, which will, in any event, not deviate from the growth rate of the population of the State of Israel. Responsible economic management, integrating into the international economy, encouraging foreign and local investors, and changing social priorities within the framework of the total national expenditure - are the basis for the economic policy which will continue in the future.

Members of Knesset,

It is my pleasure to present the Government, which is, however, not final. I intend to expand it, and include additional partners in the coming days. I believe I can complete the negotiations, and reach an agreement with United Torah Judaism and Meretz. I wanted, and still want, the Yisrael Beitenu Party to join. Thus far, this has not happened.

These are the names of the Government members and their positions:

Ehud Olmert - Prime Minister and Minister of Welfare

Shimon Peres - Vice Prime Minister and Minister for the Development of the Negev and the Galilee, Responsible for Regional Economic Development

Tzipi Livni – Acting Prime Minister and Minister of Foreign Affairs

Amir Peretz – Deputy Prime Minister and Minister of Defense

Eli Yishai – Deputy Prime Minister and Minister of Industry, Trade and Labor
Shaul Mofaz – Deputy Prime Minister and Minister of Transportation and Road Safety

Yaakov Edri – Minister (Liaison between the Government and the Knesset)

Ariel Atias – Minister of Communications

Rafi Eitan – Minister Responsible for Pensioners

Zeev Boim – Minister of Immigrant Absorption

Binyamin Ben-Eliezer – Minister of National Infrastructures

Yaakov Ben-Yizri– Minister of Health

Roni Bar-On – Minister of the Interior

Avi Dichter – Minister of Internal Security

Avraham Hirschson – Minister of Finance

Yitzhak Herzog – Minister of Tourism

Eitan Cabel – Minister (Responsible for the Israel Broadcasting Authority)

Yitzhak Cohen – Minister (Responsible for Religious Councils)

Meshulam Nahari – Minister

Gideon Ezra – Minister of the Environment

Ofir Pines-Paz – Minister of Science and Technology

Haim Ramon – Minister of Justice

Meir Sheetrit – Minister of Construction & Housing (Responsible for the Israel Lands Authority)

Shalom Simhon - Minister of Agriculture and Rural Development

Yuli Tamir - Minister of Education, Culture & Sport
I ask for the Knesset's vote of confidence in me and my Government.

And now, Madam Speaker, allow me a few personal words. It is customary to say that the responsibility entailed in filling the role of Prime Minister in a state such as ours is almost extraordinary when compared to a similar role in any other country in the world. I am aware of the weight of responsibility that I shoulder, if you place your trust in the Government, and the immense burden involved.

I will do my utmost to be worthy of this trust. I will mobilize all my inner strength for it, apply all the values I learned at home from my parents, Bella and Mordechai Olmert, who taught me and my siblings that there is nothing more important than the welfare, wholeness and prosperity of our small, tormented, brave and talented country.

For thousands of years, the life of the Jewish people has been an unending struggle for its right to exist. Exactly 58 years ago, we realized the generations-long dream of our people, here in this beautiful land, which is unlike any other. We established the State of Israel, and earned the privilege of sovereignty over our lives in our land.

Now, the responsibility to ensure its future has been bestowed on us. I wish my colleagues in the Government which I head and myself that we will be deserving of this great privilege granted us, that we will be wise, responsible and brave enough to know how make it secure, and protect it from those who wish it harm, that we will know how to maintain proper dimensions and necessary balances to strengthen the hope which beats in so many hearts, and to bring joy, peace and security to our country and its citizens.

Thank you, Madam Speaker.

Prime Minister's Office
Communications Department

משרד ראש הממשלה
אגף התקשורת

13

Address by Prime Minister Ehud Olmert to Joint meeting of US Congress

May 24, 2006

Mr. Speaker,
Mr. Vice President,
Distinguished Members of the US Congress,
Ladies and Gentlemen,

On behalf of the people and the State of Israel, I wish to express my profound gratitude to you for the privilege of addressing this Joint Meeting of the US Congress. This building, this chamber, and all of you stand as a testament to the enduring principles of liberty and democracy.

More than 30 years ago, I came to Washington as a young legislator, thanks to a program sponsored by the State Department. I had a chance to tour this building, and I saw then what I believe today – that this institution, the United States Congress, is the greatest deliberative body in the world. I did not imagine then, that a day would actually come, when I would have the honor of addressing this forum as the Prime Minister of my nation, the State of Israel. Thank you.

The United States is a superpower whose influence reaches across oceans and beyond borders. Your continued support, which, I am happy to say, transcends partisan affiliations, is of paramount importance to us. We revere the principles and values represented by your great country, and are grateful for the unwavering support and friendship we have received from the US Congress, from President George W. Bush and from the American people.

Abraham Lincoln once said, "I am a success today because I had a friend who believed in me, and I didn't have the heart to let him down."

Israel is grateful that America believes in us. Let me assure you that we will NOT let you down.

The similarities in our economic, social and cultural identities are obvious, but there's something much deeper and everlasting. The unbreakable ties between our two nations extend far beyond mutual interests. They are based on our shared goals and values stemming from the very essence of our mutual foundations.

This coming Monday, the 29th of May, you commemorate Memorial Day for America's fallen. The graves of brave American soldiers are scattered throughout the world: in Asia and in the Pacific, throughout Europe and Africa, in Iraq and throughout the Middle East. The pain of the families never heals, and the void they leave is never filled.

It is impossible to think of a world in which America was not there, in the honorable service of humanity. On Monday, when the Stars and the Stripes are lowered to half-mast, we, the people of Israel, will bow our heads for you.

Our two great nations share a profound belief in the importance of freedom and a common pioneering spirit deeply rooted in optimism. It was the energetic spirit of our pioneers that enabled our two countries to implement the impossible. To build cities where swamps once existed and to make the desert bloom.

My parents Bella and Mordechai Olmert were lucky... They escaped the persecution in the Ukraine and Russia and found sanctuary in Harbin, China. They immigrated to Israel to fulfill their dream of building a Jewish and democratic state living in peace in the land of our ancestors.

My parents came to the Holy Land following a verse in the Old Testament in the book of second Samuel "I will appoint a place for my people Israel and I will plant them in their land and they will dwell in their own place and be disturbed no more".

Distinguished members of Congress, I come here - to this home of liberty and democracy – to tell you that my parents' dream, our dream, has only been partly fulfilled. We have succeeded in building a Jewish democratic homeland. We have succeeded in creating an oasis of hope and opportunity in a troubled region. But there has not been one year... one week... even one day... of peace in our tortured land.

Our Israeli pioneers suffered, and their struggle was long and hard. Yet even today, almost 60 years after our independence, that struggle still endures. Since the birth of the state of Israel and until this very moment, we have been continually at war and amidst confrontation. The confrontation has become even more violent, the enemy turned even more inhumane due to the scourge of suicide terrorism. But we are not alone. Today, Israel, America, Europe, and democracies across the globe, unfortunately, face this enemy.

Over the past six years more than 20,000 attempted terrorist attacks have been initiated against the people of Israel. Most, thankfully, have been foiled by our security forces. But those which have succeeded have resulted in the deaths of hundreds of innocent civilians... and the injury of thousands – many of them children guilty ONLY of being in what proved to be the wrong place at the wrong time.

These are not statistics.... These are real people with beautiful souls that have left this earth far too soon.

In the decade I served as mayor of my beloved City, Jerusalem, we faced the lion's share of the seemingly endless wave of terrorism.

I remember Galila, a twelve year old Ethiopian immigrant, whose parents worked in the King David Hotel. On one particular morning, her parents, overwhelmed by the fear of her riding a bus in the city of Jerusalem, told her: "Galila, pehaps this morning, just this morning, we will take you in the family car to your school?" And Galila said to her parents: "Oh, come on, don't be silly! I know where to sit in the bus. I will be safe in the bus. Don't worry for me". And it so happened that on that same day a suicide attacker ascended that same bus and chose to sit just next to her.

When I visited her grieving parents, her mother came to me sobbing and said: "You are the mayor. You have so much influence in this city. Will you do us just one last favor: please try to find out something, just one item of remembrance that we will be able to take with us for the rest of our lives, maybe just a shoelace of Galila's..." And I did everything a mayor could do, I summoned the police, I summoned the security forces, I instructed the municipal workers. I told them: "Go look out everywhere you can". And then they came back, and they said to me: "Mr. Mayor, nothing. Nothing. Not even a shoelace."

Among the victims of this brutal and unremitting terror, I am sorry to tell you, are also American citizens. Only last week, Daniel Cantor Wultz, a 16 year old high school student from Weston, Florida, who came to spend the Passover holiday with his parents in Israel, succumbed to his sever injuries, incurred in Israel's most recent suicide attack.

I asked Daniel's parents and sister, Yekutiel, Sheryl and Amanda Wultz, who only finished the traditional period of mourning two days ago, to be with us here today. Daniel was a relative of Congressman Eric Cantor of Virginia, an honorable member of this house. Our thoughts and prayers are with you.

I bring Galila's memory, Daniel's memory, and the loss of so many others, with me to my new post as Prime Minister. I also bring with me the horrific scenes I saw with my own eyes when I visited New York just a few days after the devastating attacks on September 11th. A tragedy that transcends any other terrorist attack that has ever occurred.

As I told my good friend Rudy Giuliani, on that dreadful day, our hearts went out to you. Not only because of the friendship between us, but because, tragically and personally, we both know what it is to confront the evil of terrorism at home.

Our countries do not just share the experience and pain of terrorism. We share the commitment and resolve to confront the brutal terrorists that took these innocent people from us. We share the commitment to extract from our grief a renewed dedication to providing our people with a better future.

Let me state this as clearly as I can: we will NOT yield to terror... we will NOT surrender to terror..... and we WILL WIN the war on terror and restore peace to our societies.

The Palestinian Authority is ruled by Hamas - an organization committed to vehement anti-Semitism, the glorification of terror and the total destruction of Israel. As long as these are their guiding principles, they can never be a partner.

Therefore, while Israel works to ensure that the humanitarian needs of the Palestinian population are met, we can never capitulate to terrorists or terrorism. I pay tribute to the firmness and the clarity with which the President and this Congress uphold this crucial principle which we both firmly share.

Israel commends this Congress for initiating the Palestinian Anti-Terrorism Act which sends a firm clear message that the United States of America will not tolerate terrorism in any form.

Like America, Israel seeks to rid itself of the horrors of terrorism. Israel yearns for peace and security. Israel is determined to take responsibility for its own future and take concrete steps to turn its dreams into reality. The painful but necessary process of Disengagement from the Gaza Strip and Northern Samaria was an essential step.

At this moment, my thoughts turn especially to the great leader, who, in normal circumstances, should have stood here. Ariel Sharon, the legendary statesman and visionary, my friend and colleague, could not be here with us but I am emboldened by the promise of continuing his mission. I pray, as I am sure you all do too, for his recovery.

Ariel Sharon is a man of few words and great principles. His vision and dream of peace and security transcended time, philosophy and politics. Israel must still meet the momentous challenge of guaranteeing the future of Israel as a democratic state with a Jewish majority, within permanent and defensible borders and a united Jerusalem as its capital – that is open and accessible for the worship of all religions.

This was the dream to which Ariel Sharon was loyally committed. This was the mission he began to fulfill. It is the goal and the purpose of the Kadima party that he founded and to which I was the first to join. And it is this legacy of liberty, identity and security that I embrace. It is what I am working towards. It is what I am so passionately hoping for.

Although our government has changed, Israel's goal remains the same. As Prime Minister Sharon clearly stated: "The Palestinians will forever be our neighbors. They are an inseparable part of this land, as are we. Israel has no desire to rule over them, nor to oppress them. They too have a right for freedom and national aspirations."

With the vision of Ariel Sharon guiding my actions, from this podium today, I extend my hand in peace to Mahmoud Abbas, elected President of the Palestinian Authority. On behalf of the State of Israel, we are willing to negotiate with a Palestinian Authority. This authority must renounce terrorism, dismantle the terrorist infrastructure, accept previous agreements and commitments, and recognize the right of Israel to exist.

Let us be clear: peace, without security, will bring neither peace nor security.

We will not, we cannot, compromise on these basic tests of partnership.

With a genuine Palestinian partner for peace, I believe we can reach an agreement on all the issues that divide us. Our past experience shows us it is possible to bridge the differences between our two peoples. I believe this – I KNOW THIS - because we have done it before, in our peace treaties with Egypt and with Jordan. These treaties involved painful and difficult compromises. It required Israel to take real risks.

But if there is to be a just, fair and lasting peace, we need a partner who rejects violence and who values life more than death. We need a partner that affirms in action, not just in words, the rejection, prevention and elimination of terror.

Peace with Egypt became possible only after President Anwar Sadat came to our Knesset and declared: "No more war, no more bloodshed." And peace with Jordan became possible only after the late King Hussein, here in Washington, declared the end of the state of belligerency, signed a peace treaty with us, and wholeheartedly acknowledged Israel's right to exist.

The lesson for the Palestinian people is clear. In a few years they could be living in a Palestinian state, side by side in peace and security with Israel. A Palestinian State which Israel and the international community would help thrive.

But no one can make this happen for them if they refuse to make it happen for themselves.

For thousands of years, we Jews have been nourished and sustained by a yearning for our historic land. I, like many others, was raised with a deep conviction that the day would never come when we would have to relinquish parts of the land of our forefathers. I believed, and to this day still believe, in our people's eternal and historic right to this entire land.

But I also believe that dreams alone will not quiet the guns that have fired unceasingly for nearly a hundred years. Dreams alone will not enable us to preserve a secure democratic Jewish state.

Jews all around the world read in this week's Torah portion: "And you will dwell in your land safely and I will give you peace in the land, and there shall be no cause for fear neither shall the sword cross through the Promised Land".

Painfully, we the people of Israel have learned to change our perspective. We have to compromise in the name of peace, to give up parts of our promised land in which every hill and every valley is saturated with Jewish history and in which our heroes are buried. We have to relinquish part of our dream to leave room for the dream of others, so that all of us can enjoy a better future. For this painful but necessary task my government was elected. And to this I am fully committed.

We hope and pray that our Palestinian neighbors will also awaken. We hope they will make the crucial distinction between implementing visions that can inspire us to build a better reality, and mirages that will only lead us further into the darkness. We hope and pray for this, because no peace is more stable than one reached out of mutual understanding not just for the past but for the future.

We owe a quiet and normal life to ourselves, our children and our grandchildren. After defending ourselves for almost 60 years against attacks, all our children should be allowed to live free of fear and terror.

And so I ask of the Palestinians: How can a child growing up in a Culture of Hate dream of the possibility of peace? It is so important that all schools and all educational institutions in the region teach our children to be hate-free.

The key to a true lasting peace in the Middle East is in the education of the next generation.

So let us today call out to all peoples of the Middle East: replace the Culture of Hate with an outlook of hope.

It is three years since the Road Map for Peace was presented. The Road Map was and remains the right plan. A Palestinian leadership that fulfils its commitments and obligations will find us a willing partner in peace. But if they refuse, we will not give a terrorist regime a veto over progress, or allow it to take hope hostage.

We cannot wait for the Palestinians forever. Our deepest wish is to build a better future for our region, hand in hand with a Palestinian partner, but if not, we will move forward, but not alone.

We could never have implemented the Disengagement plan without your firm support. The Disengagement could never have happened without the commitments set out by President Bush in his letter of April 14, 2004, endorsed by both houses of Congress in unprecedented majorities. In the name of the People of Israel, I thank President Bush for his commitment and for his support and friendship.

The next step is even more vital to our future and to the prospects of finally bringing peace to the Middle East. Success will only be possible with America as an active participant, leading the support of our friends in Europe and across the world.

Should we realize that the bilateral track with the Palestinians is of no consequence, should the Palestinians ignore our outstretched hand for peace, Israel will seek other alternatives to promote our future and the prospects of hope in the Middle East. At that juncture, the time for realignment will occur.

Realignment would be a process to allow Israel to build its future without being held hostage to Palestinian terrorist activities. Realignment would significantly reduce the friction between Israelis and Palestinians and prevent much of the conflict between our two battered nations.

The goal is to break the chains that have tangled our two peoples in unrelenting violence for far too many generations. With our futures unbound peace and stability might finally find its way to the doorsteps of this troubled region.

Mr. Speaker,
Mr. Vice President,

Allow me to turn to another dark and gathering storm casting its shadow over the world....

Every generation is confronted with a moment of truth and trial. From the savagery of slavery, to the horrors of World War Two, to the gulags of the Communist Bloc. That which is right and good in this world has always been at war with the horrific evil permitted by human indifference.

Iran, the world's leading sponsor of terror, and a notorious violator of fundamental human rights, stands on the verge of acquiring nuclear weapons. With these weapons, the security of the entire world is put in jeopardy.

We deeply appreciate America's leadership on this issue and the strong bipartisan conviction that a nuclear-armed Iran is an intolerable threat to the peace and security of the world. It cannot be permitted to materialize. This Congress has proven its conviction by initiating the Iran Freedom and Support Act. We applaud these efforts.

A nuclear Iran means a terrorist state could achieve the primary mission for which terrorists live and die: the mass destruction of innocent human life. This challenge, which I believe is The Test of Our Time, is one the West cannot afford to fail.

The radical Iranian regime has declared the United States its enemy. Their President believes it is his religious duty and his destiny to lead his country in a violent conflict against the infidels. With pride he denies the Jewish Holocaust and speaks brazenly, calling to wipe Israel off the map.

For us, this is an existential threat. A threat to which we cannot consent. But it is not Israel's threat alone. It is a threat to all those committed to stability in the Middle East and the well being of the world at large.

Mr. Speaker,
Mr. Vice President,

Our moment is NOW. History will judge our generation by the actions we take NOW...by our willingness to stand up for peace and security and freedom, and by our courage to do what is right.

The international community will be measured not by its intentions but by its results. The international community will be judged by its ability to convince nations and peoples to turn their backs on hatred and zealotry.

If we don't take Iran's bellicose rhetoric seriously now, we will be forced to take its nuclear aggression seriously later.

Mr. Speaker,
Mr. Vice President,

The true Israel is not one you can understand through the tragic experiences of the complex geopolitical realities. Israel has impressive credentials in the realms of science, technology, high-tech and the arts and many Israelis are Nobel Prizes laureates in various fields.

A land with limited resources, eager to facilitate cooperation with the United States, Israel devotes its best and brightest scientists to Research and Development for new generations of safe, reliable, efficient and environmentally friendly sources of energy. Both our countries share a desire for energy security and prevention of global warming. Therefore, through the United States – Israel energy cooperation act and other joint frameworks, in collaboration with our US counterparts, Israel will increase its efforts to find advanced scientific and technological solutions, designed to develop new energy sources and encourage conservation.

Just one example of Israel's remarkable achievements is the recent 4 billion dollar purchase by an American company of Israel's industrial giant *Iscar*. This is an important endorsement of the Israeli economy, which has more companies listed on NASDAQ than any country other than the United States and Canada. It is also a vote of confidence in Israel's strategic initiative to enhance the economic and social development of our Negev and Galilee regions.

But above all, it is recognition that what unites us, Israel and America, is a commitment to tap the greatest resource of all – the human mind and the human spirit.

Ladies and Gentlemen,

We believe in the moral principles shared by our two nations and they guide our political decisions.

We believe that life is sacred and fanaticism is not.

We believe that every democracy has the right and the duty to defend its citizens and its values against all enemies.

We believe that terrorism not only leads to war but that terrorism is war. A war that must be won every day. A war in which all men and women of goodwill must be allies.

We believe that peace amongst nations remains not just the noblest ideal but a genuine reality.

We believe that peace, based on mutual respect, must be and is attainable in the near future.

We, as Jews and citizens of Israel, believe that our Palestinian neighbors want to live in peace. We believe that they have the desire, and hopefully the courage, to reject violence and hatred as means to attain national independence.

The Bible tells us that as Joshua stood on the verge of the Promised Land, he was given one exhortation: 'Chazak Ve'ematz' 'Be strong and of good courage".

Strength, without courage, will lead only to brutality. Courage, without strength, will lead only to futility. Only genuine courage and commitment to our values, backed by the will and the power to defend them, will lead us forward in the service of humanity.

To the Congress of the United States and to the great people of America, on behalf of the people of Israel I want to say 'Chazak Ve'ematz' be strong and of good courage, and we, and all peoples who cherish freedom, will be with you.

God bless you and God bless America
Thank you.

Index

The names Ariel and Arik Sharon do not figure in this index, for obvious reasons. Names of institutions and organizations have been italicized.

A

B

C

D

F

G

H

I

J

K